RENEWALS 458-4574

DATE DUE

GAYLORD			PRINTED IN U.S.A.

Writing History in Twentieth-Century Russia

A View from Within

Alter L. Litvin
Professor of History and Historiography
Kazan' State University

Translated and Edited by

John L. H. Keep
Professor Emeritus
University of Toronto

First published 2001 by
PALGRAVE
Houndmills, Basingstoke, Hampshire RG21 6XS and
175 Fifth Avenue, New York, N. Y. 10010
Companies and representatives throughout the world

PALGRAVE is the new global academic imprint of
St. Martin's Press LLC Scholarly and Reference Division and
Palgrave Publishers Ltd (formerly Macmillan Press Ltd).

ISBN 0–333–76487–0

This book is printed on paper suitable for recycling and made from fully managed and sustained forest sources.

A catalogue record for this book is available from the British Library.

Library of Congress Cataloging-in-Publication Data
Litvin, A. L. (Alter L'vovich)
     Writing history in twentieth-century Russia : a view from
     within / Alter L. Litvin ;
   translated and edited by John L. H. Keep.
        p. cm.
     Includes bibliographical references and index.
     ISBN 0–333–76487–0
     1. Historiography—Soviet Union. I. Title.

DK38 .L55 2001
907'.2047—dc21

2001034806

10   9   8   7   6   5   4   3   2   1
10   09   08   07   06   05   04   03   02   01

Printed and bound in Great Britain by
Antony Rowe Ltd, Chippenham, Wiltshire

Contents

Preface

I am happy to have the opportunity to present to English-speaking readers these reflections on historical thought and writing in Russia over the past hundred years or so. I hope they may be of interest to the general reader as well as to specialists. Partly for reasons of space, I have confined myself to material dealing with the twentieth century and Russian problems. This does not mean that the work of my colleagues who write on remoter epochs, or on other countries, is unworthy of interest, but it would take several monographs to do justice to their output. As it is, in this slim volume the treatment of issues has been rather selective. I have not had much to say about socio-economic or cultural questions, whose importance is likewise undeniable.

This political emphasis is also due to the heavy legacy of the Soviet past, which to a large extent still shapes the way people in Russia think and act today, as I hope to make plain. This means that I have paid a good deal of attention to some of the more violent episodes in Russia's twentieth-century experience. Some Western readers may be shocked by this, but I venture to hope that they, too, may find the shock a salutary one. After all, there is no advantage to be gained by closing our eyes to unsavoury "negative phenomena" where they are of historical significance. Would we write the history of Germany between 1933 and 1945 without mentioning the Holocaust?

I have lectured on Russian historiography at Kazan' State University and other institutions for some thirty years, and have made use of my teaching materials here; where it seemed appropriate, I have also drawn on my own life experience outside the university walls, so that this is to some degree a personal account of the historiographical scene, as the book's subtitle suggests. I trust this approach will not be thought presumptuous; after all, one man's fate may encapsulate that of a whole cohort of his peers, and if some of my colleagues feel tempted to offer their own appreciations of the topic, I would be the first to welcome this.

It has not been easy for me to write this book in Kazan'. Although the Tatarstan capital is a large city with a rich historical heritage and cultural life, local libraries have large gaps, especially in regard to works published abroad. Fortunately I have been able to obtain some titles I needed elsewhere, or as gifts from colleagues and friends abroad. John Keep helped in many ways, by adding some references, compiling the bibliography and index, and streamlining my text to make it more readable. Our partnership has been smooth and mutually enriching. The idea for this volume was partly his, but the responsibility for the opinions expressed is mine alone.

By Western standards the situation of historians in twentieth-century Russia has been rather odd – unenviably so. They have lived through turbulent times. The form of state changed rapidly in 1917, from monarchical absolutism through democracy of a kind to Bolshevik dictatorship; Soviet rule lasted for over seventy years, passing through several different phases but retaining an underlying continuity; then in 1991 the USSR collapsed, giving way to a parliamentary republic with a strong presidential power. People of a single generation might have found themselves singing five different national anthems: *God Save the Tsar* (to 1917), *La Marseillaise* (1917), *The Internationale* (1918–44), *Union Unbreakable . . .* (1944–91), and since 1993 a "song without words" set to music by Mikhail Glinka. In late December 2000 President Putin confirmed as Russia's state symbols the tricolour flag, the coat-of-arms with the double-headed eagle, and . . . the old Soviet anthem with a text revised by the 87-year-old Sergei Mikhalkov, who had first composed it in 1944 (and updated it in the 1970s). The public reaction varied. Many people were afraid that the old symbols of tsarist and Soviet imperialism might suggest that the country was moving back to its recent totalitarian past. But I hope this will not happen and that in time Russia will adopt new state symbols and a more appropriate national anthem.

Among historians there were always a fair number who placed their pens at the service of the existing order. Paradoxically, they were often among the first to be subjected to repressive measures, particularly in Soviet times. Others tried to adapt but failed; and a few stoutly refused to conform to the political leaders' requirements, remaining true to the highest standards of their profession.

I must admit that for a long time I was not in the latter category. I was born under Stalin and from my boyhood onward bore a dual stigma: my father was categorized as an "enemy of the people" and our family is Jewish. This meant that my chances of a career were limited and I could not choose an area of specialization freely. In 1950 I graduated from a school for working youth in Kazan' with a silver medal and applied for admission to the Physics faculty of Kazan' State University. This academic discipline was fashionable at the time. But my application was turned down on the grounds that admission was restricted to politically "loyal" students. It was suggested that I try the Historical–philological faculty instead, which I did. I had to earn my living as a school teacher and assistant in a local museum, and when I took my examination for the candidate's degree I did not have the benefit of having gone through seminar training (*aspirantura*). In my first scholarly writings I conformed to the demands made upon me. Several times I was penalized by having articles censored, but luckily enough was not seriously victimized. Like many of my colleagues, I wanted to survive, but not at any price – a viewpoint I came round to under my own steam, so to speak.

We historians' understanding of our craft did not undergo radical changes until Gorbachev's policies of *perestroika* and *glasnost'* (openness in lieu of secrecy), which led in 1991 to the collapse of the CPSU with its crushing ideological monopoly. Professional historians responded positively, if with some delay, to these changes. Those nostalgic for the Communist past turned to other means of earning a living or else sought ways of making themselves useful to the new (or not-so-new) authorities. But the main thing was that after 1991 scholars were no longer afraid. They saw that the functionaries who had once exerted authoritative guidance over them were "emperors who had no clothes", and they felt ashamed of their former subservience.

At the present time Russian historians are gradually emerging from the lengthy crisis brought about by the politicization of their discipline. Many of them feel, as I do, that it is important to publish new documentation and to open the archives to researchers. The debate ought not to be one between historians but rather between the sources they use, once these have been authenticated as genuine and reliable.

This means that there is plenty of work to be done. There are 10.6 million files in the secret archives of the former KGB alone![1] Masses of papers have yet to be examined properly in the archives of the various ministries, notably those of Foreign and Internal Affairs. Unless these treasure-troves of knowledge are explored thoroughly it is hard to see what future the writing of history can have in our country.

Historians can never claim to have arrived at the final answer to any question. Only totalitarian rulers like Stalin or Hitler claimed that they knew what was right for their peoples and that their power was firmly based for eternity – and we know what happened to them! On the eve of the new millennium Russian pollsters asked who had been the greatest figure of the twentieth century. Well-informed respondents put forward the names of Lenin, Stalin – and A.D. Sakharov.

Political control of scholarship is disastrous. It should not be allowed to happen again. This book attempts to draw some lessons from Russia's past and to make it more comprehensible. If it succeeds in doing so, even if only slightly, I shall feel that I did not labour in vain.

Acknowledgements

The author and translator gratefully acknowledge the invaluable help they have received from Mr T.M. Farmiloe (Macmillan, now Palgrave); Professor Alexander Mazo (Kazan'); Dr Alfred Steinegger (Venthône); Mr Christophe von Werdt, Ms Irmela Schweizer and others at the Schweizerische Osteuropa-Bibliothek, Bern, which provided an ideal working environment for the preparation of this translation.

Part I
Russia's Historical Profession

1
Did the Scholarly Tradition Survive?

Before and after the October revolution

What do we mean by a historical tradition? As a rule this implies that the work of a great teacher is carried on by his students, who use the knowledge acquired to score new successes. During their research they may discover truths which contradict those they have been taught, yet there is still an element of continuity in the way the subject is studied.

At the dawn of the twentieth century the best-known historical school in Russia was that of Vasilii Osipovich Kliuchevsky (1841–1911), who spent most of his career in Moscow. Of his most prominent students many were destined to encounter hardships. Some had to emigrate, as did G.V. Vernadsky, M.M. Karpovich, A.A. Kizevetter and P.N. Miliukov. Those who remained in Soviet Russia fell victim to repressive measures: arrest, exile and forced labour camps. This was the fate of Iu.V. Got'e, M.K. Liubavsky, V.I. Picheta and N.A. Rozhkov, for example. The works of Kliuchevsky and his followers, as well as those of their colleagues in St Petersburg (A.S. Lappo-Danilevsky, S.F. Platonov) and in the provinces are testimony to the rapid and fruitful way the discipline developed in tsarist Russia. That was not, however, what was said about it in the Soviet era. Right up to the late 1980s Soviet historians took the line that Marxism-Leninism was the pinnacle of social thought, and since pre-revolutionary scholars had not attained that level their work was tragically deficient.[1] Before 1917, they claimed, historiography had been in a state of crisis; indeed that view may still sometimes be heard today.[2]

However, the term "crisis" implies that a certain platform has been reached in the development of a scholarly discipline which may or may not lead to a higher stage. This is what happened in the 1920s among non-Marxist historians in Russia. Their colleagues outside the country also had an abiding respect for the work of pre-revolutionary scholars.[3] They saw a crisis as occurring not before 1917 but afterwards, when the Bolshevik Party leaders interfered so crassly in the discipline.[4] Today, in post-Soviet Russia, a discussion is in progress as to when and why there was a crisis in Russian historiography, but most contemporary scholars tend to the view that it was the result of the Bolsheviks' seizure of power and the subsequent creation of a totalitarian state. They see the crisis as a Soviet, and to some extent world-wide, phenomenon. Thus in 1991 A.Ya. Gurevich argued that historians had to adjust their methodological and gnosiological principles as a result of changed political circumstances; two years later, at an international colloquium in St Petersburg on the 1917 revolution, both L. Haimson and P.V. Volobuev said that contemporary historiography was in crisis, whereas B.V. Anan'ich held that this was so only in regard to pro-Communist historians and ideologues.[5]

Soviet historians are not of one mind in evaluating the work of Kliuchevsky and his students. They ignored or dismissed the emigrés, but in that respect the situation is very different today. A number of studies have appeared on the pre-revolutionary historians, the traditions they upheld, and their international connections.[6] Scholarly exchanges, which were impossible so long as the "iron curtain" existed, are now seen as something normal and essential for the study of history, as of other disciplines, since scholarship cannot be carried on by a single country in isolation.

Kliuchevsky's teacher was S.M. Solov'ev (1820–79). From his time onwards Russian historians habitually laid emphasis on geographic, demographic and ethnic factors in the country's social development. They were much concerned with Russia's relationship with Europe over the centuries, the reasons for its socio-economic lag behind the West, the great role played by the state due to incessant warfare and the colonization of new lands, the prevalence of serfdom, and the people's subjugation to authority – to mention only the principal questions.[7] Here we may simply note their professionalism as regards historical method and the high moral standards that governed their personal relations.

A splendid scholar and teacher, Kliuchevsky demanded a lot of his students. In 1892 Miliukov, the first to graduate under his supervision, defended his M.A. thesis on the Russian economy under Peter the Great, later published as a hefty volume. Two other members of the university's examining board, P.G. Vinogradov and V.I. Ger'e, recommended that Miliukov be granted a doctorate straight away. The idea won the support of several colleagues but, as Miliukov recalled later, "Kliuchevsky protested and . . . when his colleagues told him that it was an excellent book, replied: 'then let him write another one; the discipline will only gain thereby.'"[8] Miliukov took lifelong offence. Although he later wrote several other works, he never sat for a Ph.D. degree; yet despite this he always spoke with the utmost respect of his teacher.[9] What needs stressing here is that the coolness between the two men, and their scholarly differences, did not lead to hostility. Kliuchevsky and Miliukov continued to correspond with one another; in 1892 the former intervened to get him the Solov'ev Prize and later, when Miliukov was arrested for his political activities, wrote two letters to the Minister of Interior pleading for his lot to be alleviated.[10] Unfortunately this tradition of decency was not always upheld by historians in the Soviet era. The members of Kliuchevsky's school included men of various political convictions: Miliukov and Kizevetter were liberals, Liubavsky a conservative, Rozhkov a Marxist.[11] All that mattered to Kliuchevsky was that a scholar should seek the truth, whereas in Soviet times unanimity of view prevailed; discussion was permitted only on points of detail, but on questions of principle one had to toe the wavering "Party line".

Nor did official Soviet historians find Kliuchevsky's scholarly outlook acceptable, for in his view the state ought to express the interests of the entire nation; the process of historical development, he held, had been based on co-operation between the various social classes; and Russia's history was bound up with that of mankind as a whole. None of these notions was compatible with Bolshevik teaching, which maintained that the Soviet state was a dictatorship of the proletariat; that the motive force of history was inexorable class struggle; and that the ruling Party was leading the country along a different path from that taken by the rest of the world. Whereas the appearance of Kliuchevsky's lectures, published between 1904 and 1910 as *A Course of Russian History*, had been a major event in pre-revolutionary Russian intellectual life, Soviet historians such as M.V. Nechkina or N.L. Rubinshtein relegated their great forerunner to the ranks of "bourgeois" scholars. That is probably why, in the late 1940s, an honest young historian, A.A. Zimin, was not allowed to choose Kliuchevsky's writings as a topic for his doctoral thesis.[12]

Of course one should study the way historiography was politicized in the USSR and brought under the control of the ruling Party's leading bodies, indeed for a time by its Leader in person. In *1984* George Orwell, as is well known, wrote of the way people's memory could be manipulated in order to serve state interests: "who controls the past controls the future: who controls the present controls the past."[13] The Bolsheviks proceeded from the principle that the only scientific methodology was the Marxist one. For decades historians, and history too, were judged from a class viewpoint: "reactionary", "petty bourgeois," "progressive" and so on. No one stopped to ask why Platonov, Miliukov or other scholars who had been the pride of the profession before 1917 should now be considered reactionary. Perhaps A.V. Lunacharsky put it best when he wrote, following Lenin: "everything that helps the proletariat is good; whatever harms it is bad."[14]

The throttling of "reactionary" historical scholarship – including works written by non-Bolshevik or dissident Marxist Social Democrats like Rozhkov or D.B. Riazanov – and the departure from the profession's best traditions was carried out initially by destroying the old scientific centres, squeezing out the people who worked in them, suspending state support for any research that did not serve to bolster the new official *Weltanschauung*, and setting up new Communist institutions of learning. The atmosphere at the time can be illustrated by the situation of V.V. Adoratsky (1878–1945), a trained jurist who had joined the Bolsheviks in 1904. Lenin trusted him and in 1919 suggested that he should write a brief account of the October revolution. Early the next year he wrote to ask why nothing had appeared so far. Adoratsky replied that in Kazan', where he was then living, it was cold and he had nothing to eat. Lenin asked the local authorities to allot him supplies of food, firewood and so on.[15] Or take the case of Rozhkov (1868–1927), a professional historian of the Kliuchevsky school, an ex-Menshevik who was arrested several times in 1921–2. Lenin suggested that he should be sent either abroad or else to Pskov and held there "under close surveillance, because this fellow is our enemy and will probably remain one for the rest of his life."[16]

Among the new institutions set up at this time were the Socialist Academy (1918), the Institute of Party History (*Istpart*, 1920), the Marx and Engels Institute (1920), the Lenin Institute (1923), and the Institute of Red Professors (IKP, 1921). There were also so-called "Communist universities", an institute for trade-union history (*Istprof*, 1922), and from 1925 the Society of Marxist Historians (OIM). The previous year, social scientists from all disciplines were brought together in an association known for short as RANION. All these bodies had the right to put out their own publications. Especially in RANION, most researchers were specialists who had been trained under the old regime. The historians among them had to change their fields and study the revolutionary movement or socio-economic problems. Graduate students had to take examinations in Marxism held by professors who were Party members. The people who headed all these institutions were functionaries without special historical training such as M.S. Ol'minsky (Istpart), L.B. Kamenev (Lenin Institute), or Yu.K. Milonov (Istprof). The biggest role was played by M.N. Pokrovsky (1868–1932), who held no less than 19 posts![17]

The Socialist Academy, opened in style on 1 October 1918, had four departments, one of which was for social history. More members of staff were readers (*dotsenty*) than professors; Bukharin, Lunacharsky and Riazanov, who also taught there, had not completed their higher education. The job of each section was to train Marxist cadres and to ensure that all research was carried out in the proper Marxist spirit.

Pokrovsky soon decided that the academy's name made it look

like a Socialist-Revolutionary (SR) institution rather than a Bolshevik one,[18] and so in 1924 it took the name "Communist". The institution lasted until 1936 when, according to one of its graduates who defected, "a word from the two NKVD secret agents on the 'philosophical front', [M.B.] Mitin and [P.F.] Yudin, was enough to put the whole Communist Academy into its cellars".[19] During the 1920s it had been the Party Central Committee's "theoretical laboratory", the chief authority in all the social sciences. Its statute defined its function as "to elaborate questions of Marxism-Leninism, to struggle against bourgeois and petty-bourgeois distortions of Marxism, [and] to fight for strict application of dialectical materialism . . ."[20]

Much the same task fell to the Institute of Red Professors. According to Pokrovsky, the original idea for the IKP came from Lenin, who told him: "all social science teachers should be set the task of studying the fundamentals of Marxism in the shortest possible time, so that in future their teaching will be wholly in accordance with Marxist programmes."[21] Admission of students followed the same principles. Proletarian origin took precedence over historical qualifications. As a result the graduates were political activists lacking any real competence in history. Their teaching was coloured by a dogmatic, obscurantist outlook and an immoral readiness to inform on others. Between 1924 and 1929, 236 students completed the course, of whom 60 were historians. When the IKP was closed down, by a decree of 7 January 1938, 20 of its 38 teachers had been repressed.[22] Another body worth noting was the Party History Institute. Set up in 1930 under the auspices of the Lenin Institute (IMEL), it was a rival to the earlier Istpart, which was evidently suspected of "liberal" inclinations. Its two hundred students were supposed to combine teaching and research with "practical Party work".[23] From this stable came P.N. Ponomarev who, under Khrushchev, was Central Committee (CC) secretary with responsibilities in the ideological domain and in this capacity "supervisor" of successive Party histories which were obligatory reading in places of learning throughout the land.

Party historians formed a special group whom one can scarcely place within the historical profession. They took their cue from Lenin's works, which were published in enormous print runs:

over six million copies in all languages to December 1923 alone.[24] The five editions of his *Completed Works* which appeared later were by no means complete. At the present time, more than three thousand unpublished documents by Lenin's hand or with his signature are still in his personal archival *fond* (RTsKhIDNI, f. 2); long kept secret, since 1991 they have been used *inter alia* by D.A. Volkogonov and R. Pipes. They often end with directions that people ought to be shot or otherwise penalized.

Other Soviet leaders were likewise honoured with massive editions of their collected works in the regime's early years: Trotsky's in twelve volumes, Zinov'ev's in sixteen, and Kamenev's in twelve. It was not long before they were all suppressed and replaced by collections of Stalin's writings. This practice continued into the post-Stalin era, when the demand for such works was much reduced, so that in 1986 no less than 779,000 copies of 166 books or pamphlets by Brezhnev and other Party functionaries which had piled up in storage had to be withdrawn and were presumably pulped.[25]

Access to and publication of historical documents was a monopoly of the Party-state during the Soviet era. In 1925 the CC ordered that all work on Lenin was to be handled exclusively by the Lenin Institute. One year later Molotov, a CC secretary, and another official laid it down that the papers of the tsarist gendarmerie should be seen only by staff of Istpart, the OGPU (secret police) and the Supreme Court, and then it was the turn of the RSFSR government to regulate access to archival repositories.

Soviet censorship is a subject in its own right.[26] Nothing could be published without the sanction of the appropriate bodies, which at the local level at least were often staffed by ignorant officials prone to behave in an arbitrary way. My own experience may be relevant here. In 1975 I wrote an article on the Soviet historian S.A. Piontkovsky (1891–1937), a Stalin purge victim. No sooner had I corrected the proofs than I was summoned to the local censorship bureau (*obllit*, a subordinate agency of Glavlit). There I was told that, as a Jew, I was forbidden to make propaganda for the views of someone who "had been a Jew and a Menshevik since 1905" and that I had been reported to the local Party committee (*obkom*). I tried to justify myself by showing the officials excerpts from the register of Piontkovsky's birth and baptism, which showed that he had been christened and was aged only fourteen in 1905. But these arguments had no effect and I was threatened with loss of my job (as a teacher at the Kazan' State Pedagogical Institute) for "spreading Menshevism". In haste I submitted the article for expert assessment by the most authoritative agency for ideological matters, the CC's Institute of Marxism-Leninism. Its report, written by two staff members, P.A. Golub and L.M. Spirin, and verified by a deputy director of IMEL, concluded that my article was "methodologically sound" and [written] from the position of contemporary "Soviet historiography". With this safe-conduct in hand I went back to the local obkom's scientific department – nevertheless the article was not published. Ten years later, in 1986, I was asked to write another piece on Piontkovsky. The anonymous reviewer turned it down because in the early 1920s this historian had written favourably about Trotsky and Bukharin, who were not rehabilitated until 1988. My article only came out in 1990, and even so was couched in the most moderate terms, for by now I had grown sick of challenging fate.

Stalin and the historians

Coming back to the situation in the 1920s, both Istpart and the Lenin Institute were departments of the CC, and so it was this body (or its General Secretary, J.V. Stalin) which appointed historians to their posts or decided on journals' print runs and the like. Emigré publications were no longer accessible after 1927, when it was ruled that copies of these should be held in one of the central archives (TsGAOR). At this time Stalin took measures to ensure that published collections of documents should contain no reference to prominent Bolsheviks who had become "oppositionists". Accordingly a special commission was set up to vet publication of the minutes of the Petrograd military-revolutionary committee in 1917, and Stalin's confidant I.P. Tovstukha was instructed to decide where the originals should be kept.

Also in 1928 (May), the CC decided to merge the Lenin Institute with Istpart, and in March of the following year RANION's Institute of History was fused with a corresponding body in the Communist Academy. Pokrovsky justified the latter measure by referring to "the problem of changing generations among historians. When we saw that they were starting to train graduates according to a formula dating from 1910, . . . we solved the matter by shifting RANION's Institute of History into the Communist Academy system to give it a Marxist setting . . . and to remove those elements which are of absolutely no use in Soviet conditions."[27]

These organizational changes affected the way historians were trained. In universities the time-tested historical-philological faculties were replaced by social-science ones (FONs), in which the teaching programme was clearly geared to propaganda and enforcing Marxist methodology. In the later 1930s, however, when Stalin's "general line" had triumphed, in several universities historical-philological faculties were restored (for example, in Moscow in 1934 and in Kazan' in 1939).

A totalitarian state cannot exist unless its archive repositories are closed to researchers.[28] Already on 1 June 1918 Lenin signed a decree putting all the country's archives under state control, but until the early 1930s they were administered federally. In 1938 the NKVD took over their management, by which time their holdings had become inaccessible to historians and there was massive falsification of documents. Many priceless papers were burned when their owners were arrested and purged, or else destroyed by the ton in the course of so-called "waste-paper campaigns".[29] Closure of the archives meant among other things that people charged with political offences in the 1930s could not prove their innocence when, for example, they were falsely said to have been Okhrana agents before the revolution.[30] Two secret police officials who gave evidence against Bukharin at his show trial in 1938 claimed falsely that, at his direction, they had destroyed several sheets of the minutes of meetings of the Party's Moscow bureau in 1918 which threw discredit on the Left Communists (of whom Bukharin had been one); actually these minutes have survived untampered in RTsKhIDNI (f. 60, op. 1, d. 21). This latter archive contains documents of the Bolsheviks and other Russian political parties, as well as the personal *fondy* of many of the country's leaders.[31]

In the Stalin era the Party-state's total control of archives, journals, publishing houses, historians' appointments and so on meant that scholarship was entirely subordinate to its whims and dictates: history was the handmaiden of ideology and politics. The Leader and his intimates could manipulate the historical record as it suited them in their struggle to gain and maintain power.

In 1931 Stalin wrote a celebrated letter to the editors of the journal *Proletarskaia revoliutsiia*. One of Pokrovsky's star pupils, A.M. Pankratova, sent him the text, adding that it was a political landmark, "especially in the realization of the principle of Party-mindedness (*partiinost'*) in historical scholarship". She went on: "now the entire historical community is being 'straightened out'".[32] Stalin's reasons for sending the letter are still somewhat obscure. Why did he pick on the articles by A.G. Slutsky and V.O. Volosevich, on obscure points in Bolshevik history, as his main target? The draft of his letter bears corrections in his own handwriting.[33] But there is no doubting the missive's enormous consequences for Soviet historiography. For in it Stalin proclaimed himself the sole interpreter of Marxism-Leninism and demonstrated his gift for replacing scholarly argument by charges of political unreliability. His letter was taken as a directive to unearth "Trotskyist falsifiers", "counter-revolutionary saboteurs" and the like. His thesis that one should not believe the findings of "archive rats" but rather take one's cue from the deeds of the Party and its leaders, coupled with the ongoing campaign against "bourgeois" historiography and the arrest of historians, even those once close to the Party like Riazanov,[34] meant a complete departure from the traditions of pre-revolutionary scholarship. Henceforth the events of the past could be treated solely in accordance with the current interests of the regime. All the historical periodicals praised Stalin's letter in extravagant terms. Meetings were held in various institutes at which speakers inveighed against "rotten liberalism" and "conciliationism" (the sins of which the errant Slutsky and his comrade were supposedly guilty). In future, journals were expected to be "organs of militant Bolshevism on the historical front".[35] The editor of *Bor'ba klassov* ("Class Struggle"), I.A. Teodorovich, was condemned as a "rightist", and *Katorga i ssylka* ("Forced Labour and Exile"), a periodical devoted to the sufferings of Old Bolsheviks and other revolutionaries under tsarism, was closed down because its subject matter was no longer deemed relevant. The archives show that Stalin's letter was discussed by historians *before* it appeared, and that members of the profession actually backed the new line; they were more than just its victims.[36]

In his hitherto unpublished diary Piontkovsky noted (3 February 1932) that as a result of the letter "dozens of university teachers were sacked and expelled from the Party for some kind of mistake committed five years ago – thrown out and reduced even to attempting suicide and going mad". Even E.M. Yaroslavsky, he went on, gave the impression of labouring under a psychic trauma, for having led the fight against Trotsky he was now publicly proclaimed to be a secret Trotsky supporter. "I found him in an empty office in the Central Control Commission, holding his head in his hands and looking wildly out of the window." He could not explain what was going on, only that Stalin was dissatisfied with him.[37]

At the time Stalin was sending out even more menacing signals: the obviously staged trials of the so-called Industrial and Toiling Peasant parties and of the Mensheviks' Union Bureau. In 1931 alone, the OGPU's Special Board took extra-judicial action against nearly 2500 individuals in state employment, including 85 professors, 1152 engineers and technicians, 249 economists, 310 agronomists, 22 veterinarians, and 666 others – that is to say, over 4 per cent of all the old-regime specialists in the country.[38] N.V. Krylenko, the Procurator General, proudly gave figures for the number of "White Guardists" and "wreckers" arrested and proclaimed: "we shall not lay down the weapon of terror."[39]

Among historians the process of subordination to the state gathered force. A directive of 15 May 1934 laid down that school history textbooks should be uniform all over the country, and the journal *History in Secondary Schools* acquired the function of central directing organ. The Society of Old Bolsheviks was dissolved (1935). Next year it was the turn of the Communist Academy's Institute of History, which merged with another body to form the nucleus of the Institute of History of the USSR Academy of Sciences.

In March 1937 – the year the Great Terror began – *Pravda* came out with a denunciation of "idiotic carelessness" in the journal *Istorik-marksist* ("Marxist Historian"). The new institute's deputy director, N.N. Vanag, and the dean of Moscow University's history faculty, G.S. Fridliand, were but two of several scholars referred to by the ominous term "enemy of the people". Up until the end of that year, many historians who had previously been arrested and released were still allowed to work in the IKP, but on 31 October one of the professors there, A.V. Shestakov, delivered a lecture, "Methods of Wrecking on the Historical Front". His message was that Pokrovsky should be criticized and certain (named) colleagues annihilated as "enemies of the people".[40]

At this time preparations were already in hand to publish the *Short Course* of Party history, "the bible of the Stalin era". The dictator, who wrote part of it himself, was assisted by Yaroslavsky, V.G. Knorin and P.N. Pospelov. A hagiographical life of Stalin came out under the editorship of G.F. Aleksandrov, M. Galaktionov, V. Kruzhkov, Mitin, M. Mochalov and Pospelov – a cohort of historians ready to write whatever appealed to the Leader's primitive taste and to shower imprecations on their colleagues who had been sent to the executioners' cellars.

We should remember that history is always a matter of individuals. In historiography too it is they who sustain and develop scholarly traditions. Natural causes may have been partly responsible for lowering the moral tone in the profession, for by the mid-1930s the most prominent of Kliuchevsky's pupils had passed away: Rozhkov in 1927, M.M. Bogoslovsky in 1929, Kizevetter in 1933, Liubavsky in 1936. To be sure, there were still Got'e, Picheta and E.V. Tarle, but they had returned from exile as broken men. Among other historians with a pre-revolutionary background were Grekov, S.B. Veselovsky and M.N. Tikhomirov. Some of them were more scared of the terror than others, but all lived in a state of fear.

How much did these events owe to the late Pokrovsky's example? To protect his conception of history and his power base, this scholar-cum-bureaucrat had intrigued against and fiercely attacked his scholarly rivals. Lauded in his lifetime, he was excoriated soon after his death in 1932. His career shows the fatal consequences of linking history to political struggle. In his last years, stricken with cancer, he made a titanic effort to demonstrate his devotion to Stalin and the regime. Writing to K.B. Radek early in 1931, he suggested forming a "Marxist fraction" in the editorial board of the *Great Soviet Encyclopedia*, which should exercise "a dictatorship over all the social sciences".[41] By this time he was less concerned with scholarship than with "exposing" the errors of others. In 1931 he and his colleagues wrote several books on this theme, as well as letters to the CC Secretariat that amounted to denunciations.[42] Characteristically, when the exiled Tarle wrote to him from Alma-Ata asking for help, Pokrovsky cynically replied that exile was a mild penalty and one could also do research in Solovki (the principal forced-labour camp complex up to this time), even if it was difficult to publish there. On 28 January 1932 he reported to the OGPU that he was getting letters from exiled historians such as Tarle, A.I. Yakovlev and Picheta, "which I am sending on to you as I don't need them and they may be of interest to the OGPU".[43] Already in 1927 he had written an article in *Pravda* to mark the tenth anniversary of the foundation of the Cheka in which he defended its terroristic procedures, adding that not a single Bolshevik would refuse a summons to work for the secret police. These screeds scarcely did him credit. Unfortunately Yaroslavsky, his chief opponent, was no better in this respect.

On 1 December 1931 the ailing Pokrovsky gave his final speech to a meeting at the IKP, which was celebrating ten years of existence. After praising Stalin and the "general line", he acknowledged that he himself had sinned through excessive "academicism". It was unfitting for a Bolshevik, he averred, to show respect for learned authorities; this meant that one attributed to science an objective character, whereas "Bolshevik science should be Bolshevik."[44] Similar "confessions" were made at this time by I.I. Mints (in a letter to the OIM of 21 November 1931) and Piontkovsky. M.L. Lur'e suggested to Stalin that historical documents should no longer be considered a primary source, but rather one should go by what had resulted in practice from these documents.[45] All this shows that Soviet historians had lost their bearings and were ready to do whatever they were told.

After Stalin's death Pokrovsky was partially rehabilitated, but only as a revolutionary and scholar; his idea that the Bolshevik revolution had not been a "law-governed" event remained taboo. Some writers, in Russia and abroad, emphasized Pokrovsky's political evolution during his lifetime, from liberalism by way of Social Democracy to Stalinism; others examined his disagreeable character, especially his servility towards the ruling clique.[46] Piontkovsky noted in his diary (4 May 1932) that "the historian in him spoiled the politician and the politician in him spoiled the historian, so that at the end of his life he was neither one nor the other." He had been an unreasonably stubborn man (*samodur*), devoid of respect for others, "a satrap". "Having known him for twelve years, I cannot recall a single favourable characteristic."[47] In my view he remains a tragic figure who betrayed the country's historical tradition by devoting his undoubted talents as scholar and administrator to a lost cause, which explains why his life was a failure. The First Five-year Plan era witnessed a deformation of historiography, which became an adjunct of the Stalinist regime. The Academy of Sciences was ruthlessly subordinated to Party controls and, as we have seen, many historians were physically liquidated – no less than 130 in 1929 alone.[48]

Why did Stalin engineer this great change? V.D. Solovei, following such authorities as A. Nekrich and M. Heller, sees the prime reason in the ideological shift from the internationalism of the 1920s, when the Bolsheviks lived in expectation of world revolution, to the drive to build socialism in a single country. In the new conditions it was no longer thought desirable for historians to criticize Russian imperial traditions; instead they should help consolidate the new Soviet empire. The new line found expression in Stalin's well-known dictum early in 1931 that Russia had always been beaten by foreigners because she had lagged behind in her development, and in the May 1934 directive on teaching history in schools, which emphasized pride in one's socialist fatherland. In this way history – and people's memories – were manipulated in order to legitimize the regime.[49]

It was much more than a matter of Stalin trying to use history for his personal purposes, to buttress his own power, as D.A. Volkogonov and M. Reiman argued in 1989–90.[50] After all, the concept of world revolution was not explicitly rejected, but rather this was seen as coming about as a consequence of the establishment of a strong "socialist" state. In Soviet Russia the writing of history was always influenced by "conjunctural" considerations, that is, adapted to even the slightest nuances in the ruling Party's policy; it was, as K. Shteppa puts it, "a microcosm in the macrocosm".[51] The agencies of control underwent some modification over the years but essentially the system remained the same until the early 1990s; even Gorbachev's perestroika did not do much to weaken it, although it was then, in 1987–9, that archive access was liberalized and over 300,000 library books transferred from secret repositories (*spetskhrany*) to the open shelves.[52] For example, as late as 1991 foreign works critical of Gorbachev were still kept under lock and key. In this respect real change came only with Yeltsin, who on 24 August 1991, just after the abortive Moscow coup, issued decrees which *inter alia* placed the KGB and Party archives under the state's central archive agency (or "service" as it was soon to be called).[53] At this point it may be worth explaining what it was like to work in a secret repository, whether in a library or an archive. The practical difference between them, from the researcher's point of view, was that, from the former, one could take out one's notes whereas in the latter these were censored. One had to apply for permission to work there to the "special department" (*spetschast'*) of the institution where one was employed, which, if one was lucky, issued an authorization called "form no. 2". One was not allowed to see the archive registers (*opisi*) and, when it came to publication, could not give detailed references to the *fond*, register, file and folio numbers, in the normal way, but could only mention the name of the archive and the collection.

The authorities had various methods at their disposal to keep historians in line, ranging from simple reprimands and "confessional" gatherings to dismissal, arrest, exile and physical "liquidation". The fabricated charges levelled against them were absurd: for example, planning "terrorist acts" against Party leaders. Among the first to be arrested, early in 1935, was V.I. Nevsky, director of the Lenin Library, and three of his associates in a study group on working-class history in the Communist Academy. Next year the prominent victims included Fridliand and S.G. Tomsinsky, director of the archaeographical institute in the Academy of Sciences. In 1937 it was the turn of Dubrovsky, dean of history in Leningrad, Knorin of the IKP, the Moscow historian P.O. Gorin and many others – not to mention those "taken" in the provinces. On 31 March of that year N.M. Lukin, director of the USSR Academy's Institute of History, stated at a Party meeting

that his institute was ahead of all others in the academy as regards exposure of "enemies of the people". Lukin was also
editor-in-chief of *Istorik-marksist*. In May, after criticism in *Pravda*,
he admitted that the journal had committed errors, and three of
his eight colleagues on the editorial board were labelled her-
etics. Even worse was the behaviour of V.V. Maksakov, deputy
editor of *Krasnyi arkhiv*, who acknowledged that he had been
wrong to publish two documentary contributions (on "Bloody
Sunday" in 1905 and the investigation into the Pugachev revolt)
because these had been introduced by Piontkovsky, who in the
meantime had been shot.[54] Finally, the NKVD fabricated evidence
of alleged espionage in the Central Archive Administration, where
many of the staff were put to death in 1938. As for Lukin, he
was arrested in August 1938 for being indirectly related to Bukharin,
and died of heart failure in a concentration camp in June 1940.
The Great Terror's victims among the historians were less likely
to be men trained before the revolution than Bolsheviks who
had tried to preserve a modicum of professionalism.

Courage and compromise

Since 1991 I have had an opportunity, as a member of the Tatarstan
Republic legislature's rehabilitation commission, to go through
many investigation records of the 1930s, including those of such
historians as Platonov, Vanag, Lukin, Nevsky, Piontkovsky, Riazanov,
V.M. Steklov and others.[55] It is quite clear that the accused were
compelled by blackmail and physical pressure to put their signature to evidence that had been falsified about their supposed
subversive intentions. Their interrogators paid scarcely any heed
to their actual views on history or anything else. The historians
who were purged were not chosen because of anything they had
done but because the dictator and his acolytes were afraid of
what they might do out of adherence to the traditions of their
profession, and these traditions had to be crushed, cost what it
may. Despite enormous pressure, in the 1920s these traditions
did manage to survive in the works of Platonov, Liubavsky,
Presniakov, and others who had stayed in the country rather
than emigrate. It was impossible for the Party to impose uniformity of thought. Kliuchevsky's student Got'e, A.A. Novosel'sky

(d. 1967), S.B. Veselovsky (d. 1952) and M.N. Tikhomirov (d. 1965) were also among those who kept the heritage of their pre-revolutionary teachers alive. Novosel'sky published two important works on seventeenth-century Muscovy in 1929 and 1948; Veselovsky's articles on the same era came out in 1969; and Tikhomirov achieved renown for his work on medieval Russian towns (1956).[56] It is of course true that they were compelled by circumstances to devote themselves to relatively remote periods of Russian history, since it was not politically possible for them to write on themes of more immediate relevance to the present day. Accordingly the best work on the late tsarist and Soviet periods has been done in the West since the Second World War. Only now are scholars in post-Soviet Russia catching up, notably with studies of Stalin's repressive policies and other "blank spots" in the record.

It is an exaggeration to say that scholarship was expelled from Russian historiography from the 1920s onward.[57] For as in other disciplines a lot depends on the creative powers of the individual researcher, whose voice is often a dissonant one in the general chorus. Just because all the others are singing louder doesn't mean that they are right! We have seen that the Soviet leaders tried to silence all professional scholarship in the humanities and social sciences, but how far did they succeed? Even if there was only one scholar who kept to pre-revolutionary standards, their victory was less than complete.

In 1994 an international scholarly conference was held at Moscow University to mark the ninetieth birthday of P.A. Zaionchkovsky (1904–1983). A pupil of Yu. V. Got'e, he taught many historians who later attained renown: N.P. Yeroshkin, B.S. Itenberg and A.A.Tvardovskaia among Soviet scholars and Terence Emmons, Richard Wortman and Dietrich Beyrau among foreign ones. A student of his, L.G. Zakharova, later wrote that Zaionchkovsky's historical school was marked by respect for the facts and knowledge of the sources; "free from any deliberate ideological tendentiousness", it had "united modern Russian historiography with the best traditions of pre-revolutionary Russian scholarship and that of other countries". Emmons also noted this continuity with the work done before 1917 and called Zaionchkovsky's school "a unique phenomenon in Soviet historical writing".[58]

Historiography was even more permeated by ideology than other disciplines under Stalin (and later) – it used to be said that history was not a science but politics retrojected into the past – and it was a dangerous profession to pursue since the Party line was often unpredictable. Those who were brought up on Shestakov's and Pankratova's textbooks (for elementary and secondary schools respectively) believed what they were taught. Likewise many who were to become dissidents have acknowledged that at first they were loyal to the regime and "took the noose round their necks . . . for emancipation, as something historically inevitable"; the turning-point for them was their "decision to face up to their doubts instead of running away from them".[59] A personal reminiscence: I first went to school in Kazan' in 1939, used the same history textbooks and believed what was in them even after my father was arrested and I found myself categorized as "a son of an enemy of the people". In 1948 I had to leave school and go to work in a garage, studying in the evenings. Of course I didn't understand why my father, who worked at a furrier's, had been arrested, or why our family was so badly off: I just adapted and survived. At school I got into trouble for writing an essay in which Stalin's name was hyphenated and appeared on two lines. A similar fault was committed by the editor of our local paper; he was arrested along with the proof-reader, for leaders' names did not obey the rules of grammar!

In 1931–41 Moscow's Institute of History, Philosophy and Literature, known as MIFLI, was the sole college in the country where history was taught in such a way as to maintain a thread of continuity with the pre-1917 era, because Got'e, R.Yu. Vipper and E.A. Kosminsky were members of the staff.[60] Probably, this "thread" led some students who went on to become historians (M. Heller, who later emigrated, was among them) to harbour doubts and even to ventilate them despite the risks involved. But these doubters, it must be remembered, were as a rule Party members who defended their views by invoking the same authorities – Lenin, Stalin, Party decisions – as did the functionaries who criticized their unorthodoxy.

One of the first to show some spirit was Pankratova, a leading expert on the history of the Russian labour movement,[61] who in 1941 was evacuated to Alma-Ata along with several of her colleagues in the Institute of History. Over the next three years she sent a number of letters to the Party CC requesting its aid in solving certain historical problems: how to characterize correctly peasant revolts and national movements, notably in connection with the formula that tsarist colonial expansion in Central Asia had been a "lesser evil" than foreign (British) rule; this notion was in vogue among nationally-minded Russian Communist writers. Her letters led to the convocation in May–June 1944 of a conference in Moscow under the patronage of three CC secretaries (A.A. Andreev, G.M. Malenkov, A.S. Shcherbakov). This showed that even under Stalin different approaches to such questions were possible and also that the general level of historical knowledge was low. Another consequence was that Pankratova herself came under fire.[62] Although her report was wholly orthodox and she regarded the CC as the sole authoritative interpreter of what was ideologically correct, the reaction among Secretariat officials was hostile, for they saw her as infringing their prerogative to pose questions and answer them. Any initiative from below was suspect, and so Pankratova was charged with "anti-Party conduct" and lost her job as deputy director of her institute. This did not stop her seeking historical truth, for she was a courageous woman. In 1944, at the height of the wave of deportations eastward of the "punished peoples" of the North Caucasus and Crimea, she wrote that Russian colonization had not always been a progressive phenomenon. Later, in 1952, when state-sponsored anti-Semitism was at its peak, she agreed to be official "opponent" at the defence of a thesis by a Jew (and war invalid), G.N. Vul'fson of Kazan' State University, and when warned that the candidate was politically unreliable, demanded to know what grounds there were for the allegation. There were none – and Vul'fson passed!

Two months after Stalin's death in March 1953, at the beginning of the "thaw", Pankratova was appointed editor-in-chief of the principal historical journal, *Voprosy istorii* (successor to *Bor'ba klassov*). Khrushchev's "secret speech" at the Twentieth Party congress, in which he denounced some of Stalin's crimes, gave an enormous fillip to critical thinking. E.N. Burdzhalov published an article in the journal (no. 4, 1956) recalling that in March 1917 Stalin had been at odds with Lenin over Bolshevik strategy toward the Provisional government. He had agreed with the "soft" Party leader Kamenev (and the Mensheviks!) that it should be tentatively supported rather than opposed as Lenin wanted. This fact was not new, but had been forgotten since the 1920s and so Burdzhalov came in for sharp criticism from two CC organs, *Kommunist* and *Partiinaia zhizn'* – the first such overt polemic for many years. Pankratova was summoned to the Secretariat to explain herself. The functionaries there were particularly embarrassed by Burdzhalov's ability to marshal scholarly evidence in support of his argument. Pankratova defended herself skilfully, but the Party was no more willing than before to countenance freedom of speech and in 1957 the journal's editorial board was purged. Pankratova, sick and tired of persecution, died in May of that year.[63] The politicians had won. The new editors, S.F. Naida and later V.G. Trukhanovsky, were not inclined to take any risks. Burdzhalov, whom I met in the early 1970s, never changed his opinion that in 1956 he had been right to challenge the Stalin cult.

During the Khrushchev era the general intellectual climate remained oppressive. Officially Soviet history was now divided into good years under Lenin and not-so-good ones under Stalin (at any rate from the mid-1930s onward, for nothing could be said about Trotsky or collectivization, for example!) The "cult", the euphemism used for all "negative" phenomena such as the Terror, camps and so on, was said to have hindered the construction of socialism but not prevented its triumph. Archive access was eased and a little more contact allowed with colleagues abroad, but the USSR remained a closed society: suffice it to say that the text of the "secret speech" was not published until 1989![64]

The historians of the 1960s–1980s may be divided into four groups: dissidents, Bolshevik conservatives, devotees of regional or local history (the great majority, who pursued narrow topics to keep out of trouble), and those who placed genuine scholarship above political conformism. The last mentioned were in the stream of Russia's historical tradition; their names and works are fairly familiar, as are the polemics they engendered. But let us begin with a glance at the first groups.

Between 1965 and 1970, according to the KGB, the dissidents produced about 400 works on historical, economic, political or philosophical themes. In the aftermath of de-stalinization, groups were formed of students who re-read Marx and Lenin critically and contemplated reforms. Among them were the circles of the Leningrad mathematician R. Pimenov and of L. Krasnopevtsev in Moscow. But the dissident movement did not take off until after the Siniavsky–Daniel trial of 1966 and more will be said of it later.

The conservatives included establishment figures like S.P. Trapeznikov and E.M. Zhukov, who held jobs in the CC and the Academy of Sciences respectively, as well as the bulk of Party historians. They did all they could to contain criticism of Stalin and stood for "the purity of Marxism–Leninism" or, after Khrushchev's fall, for "the struggle against subjectivism and voluntarism". In Kazan', which had 14 institutions of learning, there were at least 140 of them. They set great store by official anniversaries, organized the publication of collective works, and supervised the censorship of publications. As an instance of the latter type of control I might mention an episode that occurred in 1985. L.M. Spirin and I had submitted for publication a book on the Russian civil war. We were summoned by the censor (in the Leningrad *obllit*), who told us that he had counted sixty-four references to Stalin, all of them negative. I asked him what the right number ought to be so that the book might be published. He referred us to K.V. Gusev of IMEL, who suggested a cut of one-third and gave his imprimatur; as a result the volume duly appeared.

One of the leading independent-minded scholars was A.A. Zimin (1920–1980). In the late 1940s he was a victim of what might be called "moral-professional repression": as we know, he wanted to write his thesis on Kliuchevsky and publish his papers, but A.L. Sidorov warned him off the topic. He had to change his field, but later did manage to write several articles on the master and help publish his collected works (although in an incomplete edition).[65] In 1963 Zimin wrote a monograph on the medieval epic *The Lay of Igor's Host* in which, on the basis of scrupulous historical and philological analysis, he came to the conclusion that it had been compiled in the eighteenth century rather than the twelfth. His work – or rather its basic propositions, which were duplicated in a hundred copies marked for official use, that is, kept secret from the general public – was formally discussed in the Academy of Sciences History Division in May 1964. Zimin was accused of inadequate patriotism and had to abandon his academic career. For putting professional scholarship ahead of political considerations he was subjected to what were called "organizational conclusions" (*orgvyvody*), which meant *inter alia* that most of his writings were not published until the 1990s. Even so not all of his study of *Igor's Lay* has appeared even now, although we do at least have an excerpt from his memoirs in which he discusses his students.[66] Perhaps the foremost of these scholars is my friend S.M. Kashtanov, through whom I got to know Zimin personally. This talented historian was a fine human being who could not but challenge the authorities since he cherished truth above all other values.

The next leading scholar to suffer persecution was A.M. Nekrich, a war veteran who in a book that came out in 1965[67] showed that Stalin's leadership on the eve of the Soviet-German war had been highly deficient. This implied that later leaders could err likewise, and so was deemed subversive. A formal discussion was held of the volume in IMEL in February 1966. (A record of this trial – which is what it amounted to – was published abroad, in France and Italy.) Nekrich was summoned to the CC, where an "instructor" asked him: "what do you think is more important, political expediency or historical truth?" He replied: "historical truth" – and promptly lost his job; later he was obliged to emigrate.[68]

Another important episode was the closure in 1968–70 of M.Ya. Gefter's seminar on historical methodology, which sought to situate Marxist thought in the context of other social theories.[69] In 1970, K.N. Tarnovsky conducted a brilliant defence of his thesis on Russian socio-economic history prior to 1917, only to have his work rejected by the attestation commission (VAK), so that he had to submit another dissertation on a politically more acceptable topic. Among the other historians who suffered at this time were V.P. Danilov, whose book on collectivization was suppressed, and P.V. Volobuev. The latter, director of the Institute of History from 1969 to 1974, was sacked in 1974 by a resolution of the CC and given another job teaching history of science; Gefter, too, had to move elsewhere. There was an element of witch-hunting about all this, but at the time it was no laughing matter for those concerned, even if none of the errant historians was arrested.

Volobuev and Tarnovsky were both associated with the "New Directions" movement, which argued that there had been many facets to Russia's economy before the revolution, so that it was arguable whether, as had long been asserted, the October overturn was a "law-governed", that is, predetermined, phenomenon; in fact, they implied, other avenues of development had been possible.[70] On one occasion when the ideas of this group were being discussed, the arch-Stalinist Pospelov appeared and angrily set forth his political credo: "we don't need specialists, what we want are Leninists".

The authorities treated the independent expression of opinions by historians as a politically-inspired *fronde*. Volobuev, Tarnovsky and Danilov had all at one time been on the staff of the Party CC but for various reasons had left it to become professional historians. They remained Marxists and even Leninists, but wanted to base their analysis on the sources instead of mechanically repeating Party dogma. They did not let themselves be intimidated by the usual repressive measures, for the thaw of the 1950s had left its mark. Zimin won the backing of the literary scholar Academician V.V. Vinogradov and a group of historians came out in support of Volobuev and his colleagues.[71] This showed that Soviet society was no longer what it had been.

Much can now be learned about historians' relationship to the state from recently published diaries and memoirs.[72] Their diaries show that they led double lives, saying what was expected of them in public while in private making observations of a very different character that reflected what they sincerely felt about what was going on. S.S. Dmitriev (1906–91) is a case in point. He was a professor in Moscow University's history faculty and often gave lectures to students at the Central School of the Komsomol. His diary, which covers the period 1949 to 1991, shows that he was opposed to the "anti-cosmopolitan campaign" of 1949 and sympathized with Boris Pasternak when the writer was scurrilously attacked over *Dr. Zhivago*. In 1955 he noted, after viewing on television the October Revolution anniversary parade in Moscow, that Kaganovich looked "old and feeble;

he speaks badly, whispering and swallowing words, and gesticulating in a cheap manner . . . the whole presidium of the meeting are a boring grey bunch . . . One has the feeling that the revolution is long past; all the revolutionaries have been done away with, so that we are ruled by bureaucrats and nonentities."[73] Yet he did not allow any hint of his critical views to emerge in his publications or lectures. Outwardly he seemed to be completely loyal and his double-thinking apparently passed undetected.

S.B. Veselovsky comes over from his diary as a more principled character. His books on the "feudal" period were so scholarly and unpolitical that officials wondered whether he was really a "Soviet person".[74] His historical views took shape under the influence of Kliuchevsky, N.P. Pavlov-Sil'vansky and A.Ye. Presniakov. Like Zimin and Zaionchkovsky, he chose to write on the pre-revolutionary era. Matters were different with those who dealt with the Soviet period.

The term "historical school" was not used much then, because officially scholars were classified according to social or political categories ("petty-bourgeois", "conservative" and so on). When pre-revolutionary writers such as N.I. Kareev, Miliukov or Presniakov spoke of the Moscow and St. Petersburg schools, they had in mind not some sort of institute but informal groupings of researchers who were either bound together by their interest in a particular problem or else were disciples of a particular leading scholar. Today we can see that they were also united by their respect for the work being done in the West, especially in Germany and France; they had as a rule studied abroad and were familiar with the methodology applied by their colleagues in these countries.[75]

Soviet historians claimed that they adhered to a single "Marxist-Leninist camp". Most of them indeed did so, adjusting their views to the twists and turns of current policy and following the instructions handed down by successive Party leaders – although there were some exceptions. In the 1920s and early 1930s people spoke of a "Pokrovsky school", but in attaching such a label they were just following pre-revolutionary tradition. Then in the mid-1930s the pejorative term "mini-school" (*shkolka*) entered the political vocabulary with reference to Pokrovsky's followers. Towards the end of the decade, when Pokrovsky's school was liquidated with the active cooperation of some of his students, the whole notion of a "historical school" went out of favour. Yet actually such schools continued to exist in the form of intellectual links between leading scholars, who transmitted ideas and values from one generation to the next. Many of the historians in the so-called "New Directions" movement, such as Volobuev, Gefter and Tarnovsky, were former students of A.L. Sidorov, who had once been a follower of Pokrovsky but had turned against him; as a hard-line Stalinist, he played a key role in the post-war struggle against "cosmopolitanism" but thereafter became the leader of a group of young scholars "who formed the backbone of historical revisionism", as Roger D. Markwick writes. He calls Sidorov "the white raven of his generation".[76]

Both Pokrovsky and Sidorov worked in Moscow and were of a critical frame of mind. First Pokrovsky exposed the shortcomings of "bourgeois" historiography, then Sidorov exposed those of his teacher. Similarly, the "New Directions" movement developed in large measure out of criticism of the inadequacies of Stalin's dogmatic *Short Course*. Its practitioners remained within the bounds of Leninism, holding, for example, to Lenin's notion that Russia's economic structure consisted of several layers at unequal levels of development (the term used was *mnogoukladnost'*: see chapter 3), or that the October revolution had been driven forward by a spontaneous popular dynamic, rather than being the handiwork of the Bolsheviks as the Stalinists insisted.

In Leningrad, as St Petersburg was then called, the study of Soviet history developed on rather different lines from the way it did in Moscow. The "St Petersburg school" was founded by K.A. Bestuzhev-Riumin and S.F. Platonov; the latter held the chair of Russian history at the university in the Imperial capital for many years. The characteristic feature of this school, as Presniakov emphasized, was that its practitioners paid scrupulous attention to their sources and attempted to establish historical facts with the utmost precision, whereas the adherents of the "Moscow school" took a more theoretical approach. Presniakov was a student of Platonov's, as were P.G. Liubomirov, G.V. Vernadsky and Pavlov-Sil'vansky. "The first generations of Kliuchevsky's and Platonov's students cut their teeth on their works", as was said by the diplomatic historian B.A. Romanov (1889–1957), who was taught by Presniakov.[77] A significant number of the older historians who were recently working, or still are, in St Petersburg – such as R.Sh. Ganelin, S.N. Valk (1887– 1975) or V.N. Ginev – were in turn students of Romanov. They continued to practice what they had learned from their teachers as regards the study of sources (*istochnikovedenie*) and had an orientation towards socio-economic problems. This inter-generational continuity is important both in a scholarly context – choice of topics, professional approach – and in a moral sense, for the "children" do not repudiate their "fathers" but are proud of them and try to carry on their legacy.

Both the Moscow and St Petersburg historical schools originated in the nineteenth century and had their evolution brutally cut short in 1929–30 by charges of counter-revolutionary conspiracy, followed by arrests: Platonov, Tarle and Romanov in Leningrad, Gol'e, S.V. Bakhrushin and A.I. Yakovlev in Moscow. Some twenty years later there was another pogrom, particularly severe in Leningrad, in connection with Stalin's drive against "bourgeois objectivism" and "cosmopolitanism". The object of this campaign was to discredit historians and other scholars of Jewish nationality. They were accused of lack of patriotism, minimizing Russia's role in world history and the like. Among their most energetic persecutors were, alas, certain fellow-historians such as M.P. Kim, Sidorov and D.A. Chugaev, along with graduate students at the Party's Social Sciences Academy. In Moscow their targets included I.I. Mints, I.M. Razgon and N.L. Rubinshtein, to name only the most prominent; in Leningrad one should mention O.L. Vainshtein, a medievalist, and S.N. Valk, who did valuable work on sources for the history of the revolutionary movement. This political campaign was conducted in much the same way in institutes of the Academy of Sciences as it was in universities.[78]

Shortly afterwards the "Petersburgers" suffered another blow. Just after Stalin's death, on 20 March 1953, the Leningrad division of the academy's Institute of History (LOII), which had existed since 1936, was abolished and all its staff dismissed. The motive given was that many of its scholars' works were "ideologically sullied" and that the authorities were no longer confident of their political reliability. LOII was re-established early in 1956, but it proved much harder to reassemble competent staff. Even so, B.V. Anan'ich and V.M. Paneiakh, who have made a special study of the St Petersburg school, conclude that the successive pogroms did not succeed in breaking the continuity of relationships. Their finding is important for those who seek a balanced assessment of the conflict between professionalism and ideology among Soviet historians.[79]

To categorize historians according to schools or "directions" during the Soviet era is not a simple matter. Individuals who were accused of deviant behaviour or repressed might suddenly cease to be considered Marxist–Leninists and find themselves categorized as "bourgeois" or "petty-bourgeois". It seems to me best to assume that there was a single Russian historiography whose practitioners sometimes leaned one way and sometimes another. One could of course say that the St Petersburg school was more western in orientation, noting that the Academy of Sciences was still located in that city until 1925, whereas in Moscow, site of the country's first university (1755), historians first tended towards Slavophilism and then, once the Bolsheviks were in power, were likelier to adopt Marxism than their colleagues in the old capital, where many historians in the surviving academic institutions had entered the profession before the revolution. But gradually this distinction lost force. It ceased to be the case that St Petersburg/Leningrad historians preferred to work from primary sources or opt for the pre-modern era. Instead the two schools were drawn together by the new circumstances in which they found themselves under Stalinism. As regards the study of the sources on early Rus' and what Soviet historians called the "feudal" era (roughly, to the mid-nineteenth century) there was not much to choose between the views of Zimin, Kashtanov and Cherepnin in Moscow and Ya.S. Lur'e or Paneiakh in Leningrad; nor was there much difference between the approaches of Volobuev (Moscow) or Anan'ich (Leningrad) as regards the 1917 revolution. The contrast between the two schools was most marked during the first third of the twentieth century. As for other centres of learning in the country, schools made themselves felt mainly in studies of the region where they were located. In the national republics there was naturally a focus on problems of the titular nationality, whose history was now studied, in some cases virtually from scratch.

In May 1999 a conference was organized in Moscow by a recently reconstituted body, the Commission on the History of Historiography, at which several speakers referred to the leading role played by the Moscow and Leningrad schools. Summing up the discussion, A.N. Sakharov suggested that the "state school" of the later nineteenth century had been reborn under the Soviets when the state's interests and official ideology were once again in the forefront of attention; at the present time, he warned, a correlation was again evident between what historians were writing and the political context.[80]

Gorbachev and after

The election of M.S. Gorbachev as Party leader in March 1985 and his policy of perestroika, or "reconstruction", met with different responses from the public. Some people wanted rapid radical moves in the direction of democracy; others dreamed of "socialism with a human face" à la Dubcek; a third group adhered to Stalinist principles. Yet there was a general expectation that changes were imminent, and when *glasnost'* brought a measure of freedom of speech, Russians were for a time intoxicated by their new liberties. From 1987 onward, pressure from below led journalists, and some historians too, to produce articles and books that exposed past and present wrongdoings, and these soon became best-sellers. I remember that when Professor Yu.S. Borisov delivered one of the first public lectures on Stalin at the Historical Archive Institute, police had to be called out to keep order in the crowd. Yu.N. Afanas'ev (of the Historical Archive Institute) came to speak in Kazan' before an audience of two thousand; the hall was filled to capacity. Volobuev and many others who had been denied permission to publish their work were now free to do so. New journals and publishing houses sprang up; translations of Western works critical of Communism appeared and were eagerly read.

Initially historians were also optimistic when perestroika began but soon afterwards disappointment set in. N.A. Troitsky of Saratov, an eighteenth-century expert, writes that liberalization struck him "as the beginning of an upsurge of civic consciousness among Russians"; he reckoned that the days of dictatorship were over and that he would be able to work more productively. But in

1996, five years after the Soviet collapse, he quoted the poet Nekrasov:

> There were times when things were worse
> But never before were they so vile.

He complained of the lack of funding for research and the distortions of history to be found in the new textbooks, where more space might be given to a benign portrait of Tsar Nicholas II than to the war of 1812 or Russian culture in the late nineteenth century. V.V. Shelokhaev thought it unpardonable that under Gorbachev the old myths should have been superseded by new ones, for instance, that the Party was pursuing universal human values.[81] This mood of frustration, understandable in the circumstances, had deep roots.

In 1988 a collection of articles came out with the pretentious title *There Was No Other Way* – although it soon became clear that more alternatives had existed than the contributors thought possible. It was a veritable hymn to perestroika. Gefter (1918–1995), who wrote on political themes as well as history, gave an interview printed under the title "Stalin Died Yesterday". In it he discussed the occasions when opportunities to change things for the better had been missed in the Soviet past, for instance, in 1923–4 when Trotsky's Left Opposition had been defeated, in 1928 when Bukharin's "rightist" alternative to Stalinism had met the same fate, or in 1934 when there had been a kind of neo-NEP prior to Kirov's assassination. But each time Stalin had got his own way. Gefter saw perestroika as the final death of Stalinism.[82] He was mistaken, as were many who confused their hopes with realities.

At that time people who had lived under Stalin were still around, as indeed some of them are even now. Khrushchev, too, had made his career under the dictator and was guilty of sending tens of thousands to the Gulag (or worse) when he was first secretary of the Moscow and then Ukrainian Party organizations. Yet, for various reasons, after he came to power, he authorized the release and rehabilitation of certain groups of prisoners and dissociated the post-Stalin leadership from the former policy of mass repression. Those who came to be known as "the men of the sixties" believed his promises, although the democratization and plenty they expected failed to materialize. Instead the suppression of the 1956 Hungarian revolution, the shootings at Novocherkassk in 1962, and the harassment of intellectuals, aroused much antagonism. The same was true, *mutatis mutandis*, of Gorbachev's reform era: the regime did not break entirely with Stalinism.

Certainly, the historians who from 1987 onward came out with criticism of the crimes of the Stalin era played a part in undermining the power structure. It soon became clear that it was naive to divide Soviet history neatly into Lenin and Stalin periods because the latter was a natural outcome of the former. For this reason in 1989–90 the study of alternatives (Bukharin and so on) forfeited its appeal. Writers had to go beyond this and revive the traditions of pre-revolutionary historiography, throw off the chains of ideology and treat events in a more objective spirit. Unfortunately this radical tendency did not go far enough. Thus A.N. Yakovlev, the most progressive member of Gorbachev's Politburo, headed a team charged with producing a new history (modestly called *Sketches*) of the CPSU, which just carried on the earlier practice whereby each new ruler authorized his own particular variant. The new version, in two volumes covering the period to 1921, was ready for press by 1990 but never saw the light.[83]

Work on this project ceased the following year when the CPSU itself disintegrated. As for the ten-volume official history of the Soviet–German war, of which General Volkogonov was chief editor, it failed to appear because military leaders and orthodox Party historians regarded Volkogonov's interpretation as subversive, and in 1991 he lost his post as director of the Military History Institute in the Defence ministry.[84]

Gorbachev's policies were inconsistent, not to say, contradictory. On one hand he recalled A.D. Sakharov from exile, stopped the senseless war in Afghanistan, and gave the green light for the dismantling of the USSR's security belt in eastern Europe. On the other he retained controls over scholarship (for example, university appointments still required approval by the local Party *obkom*) and used troops to quell disturbances in Tbilisi, Baku and Vilnius. Publicly Gorbachev and Yakovlev claimed they had not authorized these shootings, just as they said that they did not know the truth about the Nazi–Soviet pact or the Katyn massacre.[85] The main lesson of perestroika is that it was impossible to reform a Soviet-style totalitarian state unless one curbed the power of the secret police and introduced a market economy – thereby causing it to collapse.

Looking back, Afanas'ev describes Soviet historiography as "a unique scholarly and political phenomenon, smoothly adapted to serving the ideological needs of the totalitarian state".[86] Much the same view is taken by N.I. Pavlenko and, in the West, by George Enteen.[87] These views strike me as excessively categorical and in need of correction because Soviet historiography was never monolithic. After all, Zimin, Nekrich, Volobuev, Tarnovsky and many others were also Soviet historians, yet they did not fit the stereotype. Moreover, the dissidents also wrote history: one thinks of A. Amalrik's essays, of works by national-minority historians like the Kazakhs O. Sulemeinov or A. Kalmyrzaev, and especially of Solzhenitsyn's *Gulag Archipelago*. The extent of politicization varied from one individual writer to another, in inverse proportion to his degree of professionalism.

In April 1993 a conference on historiography was held in Moscow. Several speakers, including I.D. Koval'chenko, V.P. Danilov, Yu.A. Poliakov and A.N. Sakharov, said that the discipline was in a state of crisis, but the first-named was the only speaker to realize how important historical *schools* are, and even he did not see that a school is not just a group of students but includes all those who appreciate and apply the methodology of a master such as Kliuchevsky. Danilov contended that historical writing since 1989 had a surrealistic character since the collapse of the old myths had gone hand in hand with the creation of new ones designed to bolster the current post-Soviet order. The positive aspects, he thought, were the publication of previously suppressed works, closer co-operation with colleagues abroad, and the beginnings of new historical *Weltanschauungen*.[88] Poliakov for his part saw progress in that post-Soviet historians now knew a lot of what Westerners had been writing about for decades: the famines of 1932–3 and 1946–7, for example, or the Terror, but this knowledge was being manipulated for their own interests by various political parties and national élites in the CIS. The main dangers came from dogmatism, dilettantism and following fashion ("conjuncturalism"); historians were drifting towards "a new view of the past" but progress to date had been slow, even though many had cast off the shackles of Marxist methodology.[89]

The British scholar R.W. Davies's authoritative two volumes on historiography under Gorbachev and Yeltsin have been generally well received in Russia, although they are not beyond criticism for over-reliance on newspaper reports, which are inevitably biased.

During the Gorbachev "thaw" the scope of historical investigations broadened appreciably. A number of works appeared on, for example, Stalin's deportation of the "punished peoples" or the 1937 census.[90] But the forces of inertia were still strong and no fundamental revisionist monographs saw the light. Military history in particular remained a backward field. It all amounted to little more than settling accounts with what had been written earlier. Some people were already saying that one should not throw the baby out with the bath-water; after all, had not medieval science prepared the way for the Renaissance?

Unfortunately the Russian renaissance has yet to dawn. Not all the obstacles to independent research have been removed. Financial stringency has prevented scholars from getting grants to work in the archives; as a rule their pay is minimal and irregular. Davies is right to point out that, despite material hardships, valuable monographs and documentary collections are appearing[91] – although one should add that most of them relate to pre-revolutionary Russia and are written in conjunction with foreign historians (and also to some extent financed from abroad!).[92]

Since August 1991 Russian archives have been opened up to scholars and, as noted above, those of the Party and KGB placed under the state archive administration's control. A law passed on 7 July 1993 set a thirty-year rule for access to public documents; for those of a personal nature the term is seventy-five years; researchers wishing to work in institutional archives need permission from the body concerned.[93] Later, on 17 March 1994, President Yeltsin issued a decree detailing the "special procedure" to be followed for access to papers of the security service, the ministries of Foreign Affairs and Defence, and some other government agencies; in this way a large number of documents are still restricted. A.S. Prokopenko, former director of the Special

Archive (which holds material from twenty European countries taken as "trophy" after the Second World War), and A.O. Chubar'ian, chairman of the Russian archivists' society, have both noted that limitations have recently begun to be reimposed.[94] One gets the impression that the authorities, having opened the doors sufficiently wide to replace old ideological clichés with new ones, are hastening to close them again lest information leak out that could harm them.

In an article setting out historians' tasks as the new millennium dawned, A.A. Iskenderov, editor-in-chief of *Voprosy istorii* since 1989, expressed the hope that "for the first time in a long while history may take its rightful place among the sciences", enriched by new ideas, its crisis finally resolved; researchers would enjoy guaranteed free archive access.[95] One cannot but welcome his acknowledgement of the previous crisis that denied Clio her proper standing, but should add that this was not just the fault of the political authorities, who sought to exploit her for their own ends, but in many cases also of the historians themselves, who succumbed to their pressure.

Summing up the present situation, Davies writes that: "Historians are deeply divided in their political allegiances. But many historians now seek to write history which is informed but not distorted by their outlook on the world. And – perhaps most important of all – historians of different outlooks, at least in the younger generation, respect each others' professional competence. European and North American historians would often fail this test.'[96] Indeed, a new generation is coming to the fore in Russia: men and women who were never repressed and who never felt afraid to say what they thought. Their outlook is pragmatic and professional – no less so than among their colleagues in the West. For the moment at least they are free to express their opinions without restraint, able to overcome outdated stereotyped thinking, and to see things objectively. They can hold their own in discussions with historians abroad, and their recently published works, mainly on the early twentieth century, are of high quality.[97]

G.A. Bordiugov, who has edited one of several new collections of essays, makes the point that the young historians are linked solely by generational ties and do not belong to any particular historical conception or school.[98] Of course such independence is fine, but what about continuity of historical tradition? This matters more than Bordiugov seems to think. Some of the contributors to his volume appeal for adherence to academic standards, but to which ones: those of the Soviet era or those of the age of Kliuchevsky? The volume's reviewers were divided in their opinion of the new historical avant-garde.

In my view, although their degree of professionalism varies, they are united not just by their age (most being under forty) but also by their critical approach to the works of their forerunners. They are trying to solve the old "accursed questions" raised by nineteenth century Russian intellectuals: "who is to blame?" "what is to be done?" Their writing often leaves one with a sense of disappointment in that they just tell us what should be done instead of actually doing it themselves. Where are the major monographs that could bear comparison with those written in Russia before the revolution or those coming out elsewhere in the world?

In 1998 a report appeared on the work of the Institute of Russian History in the Academy of Sciences which noted that studies are in progress on the level of Russian civilization and the nature of its social structure in various periods, and especially on the interaction between state and society. This is a hopeful sign, as is the enormous number of Soviet-era documents published in recent years.[99]

A Hungarian critic, Gyuly Szvak, has written that after 1953 Soviet historians of "feudal" (that is, pre-1861) Russia dealt properly with the facts but stopped short of innovative conceptualization. He went on to note that some writers on the twentieth century (Heller, Nekrich) were interested primarily in correcting the distortions of Stalinism whereas others (A.N. Sakharov) were attempting to replace old interpretations by new ones.[100] Clearly it is more of the latter that we need. However, old practices die hard, as can be seen from Moscow University's two programmes of lectures on historiography and source criticism for the year 2000, which took up respectively 108 and 136 hours of the students' course work. The initiators of the programme admitted that the second series was based on an outline from the 1970s, updated in 1987; it now included documents about the dissident movement, but study of Lenin's political legacy still loomed large. The course in historiography likewise recommended a lecture on the development of the Marxist view of history, with Plekhanov and Lenin as key figures. All this was not so far removed from Stalin's *Short Course*.[101] Not a single Western work was featured on the reading list. Of course, in Moscow students can easily find such works for themselves in libraries, but one can imagine the situation in a provincial university where such literature is practically unavailable. Here everything depends on the instructor's personality, erudition and political views – more concretely, on his or her ability to keep up with what is currently being written at home and abroad.

Let me try to answer the question posed in the heading to this chapter. The pre-revolutionary historical tradition was seriously deformed in Soviet times, yet was never entirely suppressed. It *did* survive and now we are witnessing a gradual return to this tradition, which means that Russia is recovering its former place in the world-wide community of historians.

Part II

Fiction and Fact in Soviet History

2
Approaching the Past

Thousands of books and articles have appeared on Soviet history, and there are also countless memoirs and documentary publications. The quality of all this work is very uneven. It is not really surprising that so many Russian writers have taken the easy way out by swimming with the prevailing current. On the cover of R.W. Davies's study *Soviet History in the Gorbachev Revolution* there is a drawing which shows a cheeky schoolboy replying to a question by his history teacher: "Shall I give you the textbook version or the real one?" A Soviet child would indeed have had good grounds for doubting what was written in his textbook. But the fault lay less in the textbook, or in the historians who compiled it, than with the politicians who insisted that whatever scholars wrote, in history as in other disciplines, should accord with their own interests. These politicians were particularly keen on controlling school textbooks, for they saw them as a powerful means of moulding young people's minds.[1]

Gorbachev's perestroika called forth a great upsurge of popular interest in the country's past. A re-examination of the historical record got under way, but it proved to be an extremely difficult operation. Efforts to depict Soviet reality in a more truthful manner ran up against resistance from Stalinists. This was shown most clearly by the Nina Andreeva episode. On 13 March 1988 the paper *Sovetskaia Rossiia* published an article by this lady, who was a teacher at the Leningrad Institute of Technology, under the heading "I Cannot Forego My Principles". Andreeva defended

Stalin and accused "left liberal intellectuals" of kowtowing to Western values in their writings on Soviet history. She also took on the "traditionalists", that is, Russian nationalists, who were starting to praise the pre-1917 Imperial order. Three weeks passed before Gorbachev's advisers, notably A.N. Yakovlev,[2] came up with a reply in *Pravda* (5 April), in which they contested Andreeva's conclusions and said that the past should be looked at critically – but in the spirit of perestroika! In other words the Party was still issuing directives to historians, but the official line had been given a new twist.

In 1990 an American professor, E. Foner, after spending some time at Moscow University, summed up his impressions for *Harper's Magazine*. He noted that the "new history" emerging in the USSR was more thought-provoking and interesting to read but that it was just as politicized as before.[3] This view was also taken by Afanas'ev, of the Moscow Historical Archive Institute, who, at a meeting with American colleagues in January 1989 observed that, notwithstanding perestroika, Soviet historians were continuing to respond in an ideological way to the public's desire to be told the truth, since it was easier "to live with the familiar fraudulent myths" than to adopt a professional attitude.[4]

This politicization of scholarship, reflected in most of the work done during the Gorbachev era and since, continues a tradition dating from the late Imperial era, when the tsarist bureaucracy sought to promote a conservative intellectual climate in order to bolster the existing order.[5] The difference is that Soviet studies were directed towards preserving the revolutionary heritage; moreover, sources were selected for publication according to much stricter political criteria than before.

As was pointed out above, the old "accursed questions" (who is to blame? what is to be done?) are still with us – especially the first. A number of works have appeared lambasting the Bolshevik regime, but their authors adopt a tone more suitable for a public prosecutor in the courtroom and fail to address the major issues impartially. These themes were taken up instead by journalists and politicians. It is not really the historian's job to allocate blame or to forecast the way the country ought to develop. He or she should rather try to explain and analyse the causes of historical events and their consequences. Assessing them from a juridical point of view is a task for the legal profession, while sensationalism is best left to the media.

The public's readiness to accept a mythological interpretation of the past is due to poor historical education. This in turn stems from the enforced changes of direction in school textbooks and from the ignorance displayed in this respect by members of the ruling *nomenklatura*.[6] The Party cadres' lack of knowledge was painfully evident at the top-level conference on historiography in May 1944, mentioned in the previous chapter. One of those present, the medievalist K.V. Bazilevich, complained that applicants for entry into the prestigious Higher Diplomatic Academy – all of them politically reliable graduates with degrees in engineering, jurisprudence and so on – were ignorant of the most elementary historical facts. One man, when asked who the Roman Pope (*papa*) was, replied "father of the king of Rome". Another thought that the eighteenth-century empress Catherine II had reigned prior to the Mongol conquest in the thirteenth century. A third candidate, when asked who Karl Marx was, called him "a dialectician" who had lived in sixteenth-century France. All this showed how poorly history was being taught in secondary schools.[7]

Of course this was the "post-purge" generation that was going through the tribulations of the Great Patriotic War, but the intellectual level of the *nomenklatura* was always inferior to that of the population as a whole. In 1927 only 1.06 per cent of Party members had received a higher education, and two-thirds had attended nothing better than elementary school.[8] In 1940, 41 per cent of provincial Party secretaries (*obkomsecs*) had less than secondary schooling, and at the next level down the hierarchy (city and district) the proportion was 71 per cent.[9] This is understandable since the regime's propaganda played up the virtues of the "simple man or woman" who made up for lack of formal education by keen "class sense". Gorbachev was the first Soviet leader to have had a regular university education.[10] By contrast, in the fifth State Duma (1993–5), 33 per cent of deputies had higher degrees (candidate or doctor), and in the next parliament the proportion was 31 per cent. This did not mean that the people's representatives had had a proper dose of history at school. Even in the mid-1990s pupils in Russian schools had simply replaced one set of myths with another; this at least is the view of A.V. Golubev, who studied the textbooks in use and found them sadly defective.[11] School-leavers today do not have to sit an exam in history, since it is an optional subject. Incidentally, it says much about the way this discipline was taught in Soviet times that in 1956, after the XXth Party congress, and again in 1988, examinations in history had to be cancelled because of the confusion induced by the sudden change in the official line.

On the other hand, perestroika and the subsequent Soviet collapse have brought a number of advantages. The relative freedom of opinion under Gorbachev's *glasnost'* meant that more source material could be published, including some documents from previously secret Party archives. Historians could begin to grapple with hitherto taboo themes such as the GULag and secret police, defence installations and desertion from the armed forces, political opposition to the Bolsheviks, and social problems such as prostitution. These issues had been studied by Western sovietologists, but they too were now in serious difficulty. Having started out in the shadow of the cold war, most of these scholars had moved on to a "revisionist" position that was more favourably disposed to the Soviet system. Martin Malia, lately of the University of California, writes: "Now that we have some idea of the way the Soviet system lost its dynamism, we should go back and redo our economic and social calculations, examining afresh each period of Soviet history from the October revolution to perestroika. Such a general revision is needed for the social sciences in general, because the failure of sovietology ... is also a failure of the social sciences as such."[12] This verdict suggests that, for all the differences of methodology and approach among scholars in various countries, they are prone to mythologize the past.

The quest for a more truthful picture of the Soviet experiment requires one to abandon the Marxist illusion that socialism is the most progressive "formation" in the onward march of world history – its climax, so to speak. This is a difficult step for intellectuals to take in Russia today. Some people praise Stalin while others condemn him; some want socialism but with "a human face", while others think any kind of socialism, national or international, is evil. Historical study is still so politicized that people say jocularly: "With the sort of historians we have, the past is unpredictable."

Reacting against such criticism, some scholars have cautiously started to rethink the major eras of Soviet history with the aim of reconceptualizing the entire phenomenon. The most promising approach is to leave behind the current emotion-laden debates and to go back to what the sources have to tell us, recognizing that they need careful study (and of course publication). It is in this spirit that Poliakov has recently noted that today, historians, with their vacillating opinions, have lost credibility, and that greater reliance is placed on documentary evidence: "the renaissance of historiography will begin when the records are published."[13] In this light let us now try to re-examine chronologically some of the most topical issues in Soviet history.

3
The October Revolution

Bibliographers have calculated that during the Soviet era no less than 20,000 historical works appeared on "Great October". It was seen as the twentieth century's principal event and a triumph of virtue over vice. Today some historians and publicists perpetuate the legend but with the signs reversed, representing the Bolshevik insurrection as the source of all the country's misfortunes. Neither approach can be considered fruitful.

Over the past decade the established view of the revolutionary epoch has been challenged and Russian historians' outlook has come closer to that of their Western confrères. International conferences have been held with animated discussions about the role of various parties and social groups, the "preconditions of revolution" and so forth. The theme of the first of these, which took place in St Petersburg in January 1993, was "Russia's 1917: Masses, Parties, Power"; two others were held in February and October 1997 in Moscow, devoted to the revolutionary events in each of those months seventy years earlier.[1] Yet another international colloquium was convened in St Petersburg in June 1998 on the subject of Russia's role in the First World War. There was a good deal of agreement on questions that had once aroused seemingly irreconcilable argument: for example, on the need to study social history, the psychology of different strata of the population in 1917, and the impact of the First World War. Differences arose as to how far the October overturn had been a "law-governed" event – Volobuev was in favour, Haimson and Hasegawa against – and whether the subsequent changes deserved to be labelled "socialist". Russian specialists are coming round to the view that these phenomena, and the civil war as well, need to be seen as part of a continuous process.[2]

Such non-confrontational gatherings could not have been held prior to the late 1980s, for in the Soviet epoch delegates to international scholarly conferences were bound to maintain a united front against "bourgeois falsifiers"; these meetings might even sometimes be cancelled at short notice for political reasons – as happened in 1972, when Trapeznikov, of the Party CC, stopped members of the "New Directions" movement from attending a colloquium in the United States organized by Haimson and others. But since about 1988, Russian participants have been on an equal footing with their foreign colleagues.

It was then that taboos were being broken as to what could be publicly discussed: for example, the role of freemasons in the Russian revolution. At first, Academician I.I. Mints (who was Jewish) had feared that discussion of this issue would encourage the anti-Semitic organization Pamiat', but V.I. Startsev, a leading authority on the period, took the initiative in opening up the matter.[3]

Was the October insurrection a logically predetermined event or the result of a series of chance developments? The first generation of Soviet historians had been none too sure, but from 1938, with the appearance of Stalin's *Short Course* of Party history, the schematic concept took hold that the Bolsheviks had been in charge of the revolutionary process throughout 1917; any element of spontaneity was ruled out *ex hypothesi*. Western historians maintained the reverse. Among the chance factors they cited were the last tsar's personality (another emperor might have been a more capable leader), or the First World War (which might have broken out at a less delicate moment in Russia's modernization); then again the Provisional government might have been run by politicians of a more resolute stamp, capable of embarking on land reform and concluding a separate peace.[4] But no Soviet historian could afford to countenance such "heretical" views. As late as 1990, Startsev, in a draft chapter of the new official Party history, argued that "in the autumn of 1917 socio-economic and political realities in Russia favoured the Bolshevik seizure of power over all other options."[5] The most obvious objection to this interpretation is this: if the masses had wanted Bolshevik rule, why was there such widespread popular resistance to the Reds during the civil war?

In the 1960s and early 1970s Marxist historians in the "New Directions" group, such as A.M. Anfimov, Volobuev and Tarnovsky, tried to refine the doctrine that the Bolshevik victory corresponded to the people's interests and was predetermined by the state of Russia's socio-economic development. They argued that in fact capitalism had *not* been so advanced in Russia as this theory implied. Several rival concepts were entertained, but were seldom articulated clearly: that Russia had been a semi-colony of the West (as Stalin had once claimed!); that capitalism had been at an average level of development overall (with some sectors of the economy being more advanced than others); and that Russia had still been an under-developed country. Depending on which view one favoured, October could be regarded as a great festival of the exploited, at one extreme, or else, at the other, as an event for which there was no good reason to celebrate at all.[6]

These arguments echoed those of Russian Marxists at the time. As is well known, Plekhanov then held that a transition to socialism necessitated a high level both of productive forces and of "consciousnesss" among working people; since neither of these conditions obtained in Russia, it was nonsense to dream of socialism. As he put it in June 1917, "Russian history has yet to thresh the grain from which the socialist pie will one day be baked."[7] Martov, the Menshevik leader, wrote similarly to N. Kristi that "it is senseless utopia to try to implant socialism in an economically and culturally backward country".[8] It is an odd paradox that the Mensheviks were truer to Marxist principles than Lenin's followers. As V.P. Buldakov writes: "Lenin was dogmatic about the fundamentals of the Marxist creed, but he was not hostage to theory. One could say that he won despite the doctrine, although he never acknowledged this."[9]

In the Soviet era "Great October" was celebrated with much pomp whenever its anniversary fell every ten years: apart from parades innumerable conferences were held, propagandist books published and so forth. On the fortieth jubilee the Academy of Sciences' Historical Division set up a learned council (*uchenyi sovet*) to promote – and control – study of the revolution; ten years later the occasion was marked by a three-volume standard work by Mints (1896–1991) for which he won a Lenin prize, the only one awarded to a historian. This was the high-water mark of Soviet historical apologetics.[10] At the tedious scholarly conferences which it was my duty to attend as a member of this learned council, the most interesting papers were by scholars from the provinces. They were permitted to criticize the doings of local Bolshevik activists provided that they could show that their "errors" were "corrected" by the central Party bodies.[11] However, I think Buldakov goes too far in maintaining that Soviet historians of October indulged in "monstrous mythologizing".[12] Certainly the work done was of uneven quality, but it was then that the minutes of the Petrograd Military-Revolutionary Committee were published *in extenso* and several other works appeared that can still be consulted with profit.[13]

Recent work on 1917

Several useful documentary collections have appeared recently: one contains 200 items on the February revolution, others deal with the Mensheviks and the Second All-Russian Congress of Soviets.[14] In 1997 Buldakov claimed that we now at last had an opportunity to appraise just what happened in October and what its international effects were.[15] This, alas, is over-optimistic. Not only are orthodox Communist works still being published – for example, *October Seventeen* (1997), by I.Ya. Froianov, dean of the history faculty at St. Petersburg University, or others with a nationalist slant (by M. Nazarov and E. Satton) which attribute the revolution to Jews and freemasons – but also, and this is the main point, there is so far little trace of any basic rethinking based on newly published documentary sources. Most present-day Russian historians are keen to expose the sins committed in the past, but the conclusions they draw are often the same as those previously arrived at in the West; either they repeat what their Soviet predecessors wrote or just say the opposite – in short, they are stuck in a blind alley. This is not really so surprising because, so long as Russia remains in such an unstable condition, confrontational views are bound to prevail among historians, too; the situation is not conducive to achieving consensus. This point has been well made in two articles by V.V. Zhuravlev.[16]

Another defect of this scholarly literature is that it is chiefly concerned with political history. It is a pity no one has tried to emulate or surpass the achievements of the "New Directions" movement, suppressed in the early 1970s, for Anfimov and his colleagues were right when they pointed to the different stages of economic development that coexisted in pre-revolutionary Russia. Scholars in St Petersburg such as Anan'ich and Ganelin, as well as some in the provinces, did notable work in economic history which ought to have been followed up once conditions became freer.[17]

Buldakov's book *Krasnaia smuta* ("The Red Turmoil") has caused quite a lot of fuss.[18] The title immediately makes one think of the seventeenth-century Time of Troubles and was deliberately chosen to underline the author's critical stance towards the revolution, which he sees as little more than an outburst of wanton violence by unruly mobs, whose mentality he tries to explore. Of course a "psycho-pathological" approach is not without merit, but Buldakov is too keen to score points off earlier historians, whether Soviet or Western, and dismisses their reasoning as intrinsically faulty. In his view the revolution, far from being a "progressive" phenomenon, actually had an "archaizing" or retrograde effect; Russian society reverted to a primitive state that facilitated the Bolsheviks' construction of a new centralized state order. Unfortunately Buldakov is unable to bolster his stimulating hypothesis with reference to sufficient new source material and so his argument remains unproven, as critics have correctly noted.

Another topic that has received attention of late is the once familiar question of whether the Bolsheviks received "German gold" and, if so, what influence this had on the revolution's outcome.[19] Soviet historians dismissed such allegations as sheer falsifications, but today opinions are more nuanced. Some think that although Lenin did take money this did not make him a German agent,[20] whereas others such as S. Lyandres maintain that there is not enough evidence to prove that these dubious transactions took place.[21] Another student of this problem, Startsev, takes the view that significant amounts of German money (50 to 60 million gold Reichsmarks) only reached the Bolsheviks after they had taken power, and that this helps to explain their regime's survival in 1918.[22] Probably we need to discover more material before this matter can be properly elucidated.

Lenin's role in the revolution is now regarded more critically than in Soviet times when, especially after 1956, he was turned into a sacrosanct iconic figure. There has been a curious debate as to whether he may have been partly of Jewish ancestry. Back in 1964–5 two Leningrad archivists, A.G. Petrov and M.G. Shtein, discovered documents showing that two brothers named Blank (the name of V.I. Ulianov's maternal grandfather) entered the capital's Medical–Surgical Academy in 1820, which meant that they had to convert to Orthodoxy. They reported the find to the writer M. Shaginian, and she asked Pospelov whether the documents might be published. The director of the Institute of Marxism–Leninism was horrified and referred the matter to the CC. Publication was ruled out. Shtein was summoned to the local Party *obkom*, where a functionary told him not to "dishonour Lenin". "So is it dishonourable to be Jewish?", asked Shtein. "The likes of you can't understand", the official replied. "But what about Marx? He was a Jew after all." "Yes, unfortunately he was." With that the hot potato was dropped.[23] By the way, the documents on Blank are preserved in the Presidential Archive.

Volkogonov's biography of the Bolshevik leader, also available in English, was criticized in Russia for its negligent treatment of the 3724 unpublished Lenin documents to which the author had access in RTsKhIDNI (now RGASPI); only 322 of these have so far been published.[24] The 1999 volume contains some items which appeared with cuts in the fifth edition of Lenin's *Collected Works*. Volkogonov and the American historian Richard Pipes were among the first scholars allowed to see copies of them. (I managed to get access to them a little later.) The former, an ex-general and once an orthodox Stalinist, commented that "in my mind the Leninist bastion was the last one to fall".[25] Pipes has published some of those he consulted in his book *The Unknown Lenin* (1996), which aroused considerable controversy.[26] If one compares Pipes's commentary with that by V.T. Loginov in the Russian edition, it appears that both authors allowed political passions to get the better of them. They take contrary positions, for example, on the subject of German subsidies to the Bolsheviks.[27] Which of them is nearer the truth, it is not yet possible to say.

Another welcome recent development is the biographical treatment meted out to leading Bolsheviks in 1917 whose names were unmentionable for decades: Trotsky, Bukharin, Zinov'ev and Kamenev. Most attention has been paid to Trotsky, as is understandable since he played the leading part in organizing the October insurrection (and later the Red Army); he was also the only top-ranking Bolshevik to refuse to serve under Stalin. Many of Trotsky's works have been published in Russia, as has Isaac Deutscher's well-known life. Russian authors have made a contribution to Trotsky studies, too. Unfortunately Volkogonov's biography of Trotsky is too politicized and journalistic to be considered definitive.[28] In the Gorbachev era the Party leadership was still committed to the "socialist option" but with the flood of literature critical of Soviet communism it became ever harder to defend the regime's ideals. Trotsky could not serve as a positive identification figure because he had backed the "Red terror" in the civil war.

Nor were Zinov'ev or Kamenev suitable as "heroes", since they had helped to promote the rise of Stalin. Instead, Bukharin, who although Stalin's associate had at least the reputation of a "moderate", enjoyed a brief vogue of popularity. In 1988 he was rehabilitated, just fifty years after he had been put to death by Stalin; his essays and speeches were published; and youth clubs were formed which adopted his name. The idealization of Bukharin got a fillip from the appearance, in Russian translation, of Stephen Cohen's study.[29] From 1990 onwards there was a sobering up as people came to realize that Bukharin had been linked to the harsh policies of "War Communism" and in 1919 had even been a leading official of the Vecheka (security police); he could not therefore really be thought of as an advocate of "socialism with a human face". Public opinion turned against the Soviet regime, seen as incapable of reforming itself and modernizing the country. If the whole system needed changing, then clearly the Old Bolsheviks were of no use and could be consigned to the dustbin of history.

It was at this time that historians began to question the legitimacy of Soviet rule, founded as this was on dictatorship and revolutionary expediency. As respect for the principle of the rule of law gained ground, attention turned towards the "White" governments that had resisted the Bolsheviks (Reds) during the 1918–22 civil war. Soviet historians, naturally, had argued that the regime in Moscow alone had enjoyed popular support, from which it derived its legitimacy; its rivals had sought to usurp power from the people, and that was why they had been soundly defeated. It was suggestive that in the elections to the Constituent Assembly, over 85 per cent of the vote had gone to left-wing parties; and the Second Congress of Soviets (25–26 October 1917), which had endorsed the Bolshevik takeover, had represented the will of the workers and soldiers.

However, this was by no means the whole story, as present-day historians have pointed out. In the first place, the peasants, who at the time comprised some 80 per cent of the population, took no part in the congress's deliberations. Secondly, the All-Russian Executive Committee of Peasant Soviets refused to recognize the Second Congress or its decisions. Likewise the All-Russian Central Executive Committee of Soviets (VTsIK), elected in June, refused to cede its powers to its Bolshevik-controlled successor. It was even doubtful whether the Bolsheviks had had a quorum at the Second Congress when it had taken its crucial vote on "Soviet power". For not all the delegates had yet arrived, and some who had been there (Menshevik Internationalists, front-line soldier delegates) had already left the gathering. Given a quorum of 726, the decision to back Lenin's government had been taken by only 625 delegates, which was not enough to confer legitimate title.[30]

Today historians no longer counterpose February to October; rather they view the events of these two months as turning-points in a lengthy and complex process of transition from one socio-economic system to a new one in the course of which power passed from one elite group to another. Solzhenitsyn has had some influence here. While the professionals were squabbling over "spontaneity and consciousness" in the February revolution, the great writer's epic *The Red Wheel* stressed the destructive character of these events and portrayed the masses as being in the grip of some elemental madness; this had been the start of eight months in which the country had plunged into ruin.[31] On 2 June 1999, speaking to the Russian Academy of Sciences after being awarded the Great Lomonosov medal, Solzhenitsyn reiterated his view that the February revolution, not that of October, had been the source of all Russia's woes.[32] To be sure, this is a writer's approach, too coloured by emotion to be considered a contribution to scholarship. Any revolution is bound to be destructive; the real question is why the Russian one took the course it did. After all, the overthrow of autocracy did open up unprecedented opportunities for the country to evolve in the direction of democracy. Unfortunately, for reasons that are largely familiar but deserve to be explored further, these opportunities were allowed to go by default and we landed up with a "dictatorship of the proletariat". The root of the problem was that in 1917 Russians lacked experience in democratic ways of thinking and acting, for civil society was still feebly developed.

At present, historians are seeking fresh theoretical approaches in an effort to understand what happened in that crucial year and why. Little reliance can be placed on the accumulated store of knowledge, and people are suspicious of the new information that has become available. Where once excessive emphasis was placed on the degree to which the Bolsheviks directed the course of events, now the prevailing view stresses the role of chance. Much less attention is paid to the role of organized labour, which was the focus of attention under the Communists, since the USSR was ostensibly a "workers' state". Now the working class is portrayed rather as having been antagonistic towards the Bolsheviks.[33]

There is also greater interest than before in what went on in the provinces, regional particularities and the workings of organs of local self-government.[34] Moreover, historians outside Moscow are also looking at the "centre" from a fresh perspective or developing their own approach to the general course of events.[35] The renewed interest in the Russian revolution is no longer just a matter of celebrating anniversaries but has an academic character, and this is most promising.

4
The Civil War

Causes and consequences

When I was a boy we used to sing a popular ditty about valor-
ous commissars in dusty helmets doing battle with the revolution's
enemies so that working people should enjoy a bright and joy-
ous future. Nowadays the songs are different and the civil war
of 1918–20 is often referred to in Ivan Bunin's phrase as "the
accursed days". In Soviet times the history of those years was
treated from the standpoint of the victors. Now it is seen as part
of the "Red Turmoil" – although the forces involved included
Whites and Greens as well as Reds. For Soviet historians it was
obligatory to see the civil war as simply a struggle between classes,
as Lenin had done; thousands of books and articles were written
in this spirit. This interpretation is now being revised, not least
because the struggle still going on in various parts of the former
Soviet Union clearly cannot be explained in class terms.

Today it is hard to make sense of much that occurred in that
terrible time eighty years or so ago, because in a sense the strife
that rent the country apart never came to an end but was continued in other forms. The confrontation between contending
armed forces gave way to a long drawn-out conflict between the
Party-state and its citizens, characterized by mass repression and
constant pressure on the people: economic, political, moral, ethnic
and fiscal. The main features of the civil war – its cruelty, violence, disregard for human rights – survived into later epochs.
Such a war boils down to a struggle for power between political
parties, clans and leaders who try to win support, with slogans

promising the people a better life in the future, although these promises lead in reality to tragedy and incalculable losses. Civil wars break out in countries where the economic and political order has broken down. They would be unimaginable in happy, secure lands. Alas, twentieth-century Russia did not enjoy stability or good fortune; on the contrary, its lot was permanent civil war. The populace was disadvantaged economically, and most people were discontented with their miserable material conditions. When someone is pushed into a tight corner he tends to react either by "storming the heavens" or by giving up in despair. Violence is the solution of those who see no light at the end of the tunnel.

Where brother turns against brother the result is a national tragedy. During the five years 1918–22 Russia lost 13 million people, of whom about 2 million emigrated and another 2 million or so fell in action. The victims of the terror numbered about 1.5 million, including 300,000 Jews killed in pogroms carried out by Reds and Whites alike. The rest, some 7.5 million, died of starvation and disease. In Tatarstan alone, according to a secret GPU report, in May 1922 over 500,000 corpses lay unburied.[1] During the famine of 1921 there were even cases of cannibalism. Famines occurred elsewhere in Europe too, but I doubt whether any country lost so many lives from starvation as did post-revolutionary Russia, where everything was supposedly being done for the benefit of ordinary folk.

State terror began in 1918 with summary executions and the setting up of concentration camps – by Whites as well as Reds. It was a mass phenomenon. Individual life ceased to count for anything; human beings were treated simply as material for social experiments. Some zealots, intoxicated by having freedom to do whatever they pleased, felt it was time to give their enemies a bloody lesson.

For many years, the prevailing view of the civil war in the USSR was that given in Stalin's *Short Course* to the effect that "the victorious Red Army, born on 23 February 1918 in the battles of Narva and Pskov, under Bolshevik leadership routed the in-terventionists and White Guardists". Efforts to get away from this simplistic treatment began in the late 1950s and early 1960s, as part of de-stalinization. The first cliché to come under attack was the so-called "Stalin plan to crush Denikin" in the autumn of 1919. The former practice had been to claim that all the main decisions, including strategic ones, were taken by Stalin, rather than by Trotsky as chairman of the Revolutionary Military Council. Under Khrushchev, and later, these decisions were attributed to Lenin and other members of the Politburo. Which view, if either, was correct? Clearly, what was needed was to study the documentary evidence. This shows that the plans to drive General Anton Denikin's forces back from the approaches to Moscow were drawn up by I.I. Vatsetis and S.S. Kamenev, two leading Red Army commanders, and not by any of the Bolshevik leaders. A close look at Stalin's correspondence reveals that he backed the plan but did not initiate it. Incidentally, it was also discovered that there had not been any engagement with the Germans near Narva or Pskov on 23 February 1918, the date officially celebrated as that of the Red Army's foundation.[2]

However, one had to wait until the late 1980s and 1990s for any substantial reconsideration of the civil war. Two scholarly conferences on the subject were held in December 1989 and October 1990, the first in Moscow, at the Institute of Marxism–Leninism, and the second at Simferopol' in the Crimea, under the auspices of the Ukrainian Academy of Sciences. Although most speakers still hewed to the "class line" in their interpretations, Volobuev, Poliakov and others put the accent on the cruelties inseparable from civil strife. Moreover, L.M. Spirin, who had been commissioned to write the relevant chapter in the new edition of the official Party history, was willing to lay the blame for the war not only on "counter-revolutionary Whites", as hitherto, but also on Lenin and the Bolsheviks who, he wrote, had been guilty of "a number of serious errors": for instance, they had taken a dogmatic ultra-left stance towards peasants and Cossacks, had artificially forced the class struggle by setting up *kombedy* (committees of village poor), had confiscated grain by force and engaged in repressive acts.[3]

Some historians' views continued to evolve, as became clear at another conference in June 1993, organized by the Moscow State Pedagogical University. By this time the country was facing the dangerous possibility of a new civil war which the public could do little to avert. Volobuev, V.L. D'iachkova and others argued that it had been the Bolsheviks' fault "that the war had gone on for so long and that it had been so brutal and destructive". This view was shared by certain Western historians. Martin Malia maintained that, while it was true that the first shots were fired by soldiers of General Kornilov's Volunteer Army on the Don, the war's outbreak was actually due to the Bolsheviks' determination to monopolize state power and to exclude all other political tendencies.[4]

It is hard to say precisely who was responsible for starting the war, for the question is so politicized. Soviet writers used to put all the blame squarely on the Bolsheviks' foes, especially the "foreign interventionists". They propagated the notion of the Soviet Union as a fortress under siege by "world imperialism". The Comintern's revolutionary activities were represented as a reaction to attack by "the armies of fourteen imperialist states".[5] But already then, and more especially later, scholarly studies appeared on specific episodes in the war, such as the Anglo-American landings in North Russia, which offered a more nuanced interpretation, one that was less ideological and monolithic. It took account of the economic and military interests of the various foreign powers involved, and showed that these were often in conflict.[6]

Yet it took time for the realization to dawn that the civil war was primarily a struggle between Russian citizens, all of whom, to the extent that they were involved, were in various degrees responsible for its scope, cruelty and duration. This view was not to the liking of those who sought to pin responsibility on to specific individuals. A.I. Ushakov and V.P. Fediuk argue that the "everyone-was-partly-to-blame" approach closes the door on further historical research and blurs the dividing line between the two sides, so that one cannot identify oneself with either.[7] But in my view it is precisely by avoiding such one-sided identification that one can hope to arrive at objective conclusions. Looking for the "guilty men" leads only to political results, not scholarly ones.

This is clear if one looks at the Reds' measures to "de-cossackize" the Cossacks in 1919–20. In October 1917, Russia had eleven Cossack hosts with a total population of 4.5 million, over 70 per cent of whom lived on the Don, Kuban' and Terek. In return for military service they were granted privileges by the tsarist state in the form of large land allotments, free health care and schooling. On the whole the Cossacks opposed the Bolshevik takeover, although the Reds had support among the under-privileged elements and there were even a few "Red Cossack" commanders such as B.M. Dunenko and F.K. Mironov, who led sizeable cavalry detachments in the Red Army; they were both shot in 1920–1 after being fraudulently denounced. The Bolsheviks mistrusted the Cossacks as "class alien". Already on 11 November 1917 (OS) the new government decreed the abolition of the old ranks and estates (*sosloviia*). This gave a legal pretext for physical elimination of the nobility and the Cossacks. Then, on 24 January 1919, the Party's Orgburo decided on a policy of "de-cossackiza-tion". (The minutes of this session were published in 1989.) "Taking account of the civil war with the Cossacks", the decision ran, "it is necessary to recognize as the only correct [course] the most merciless struggle against all the Cossack leaders by destroying them individually"; there followed recommendations as to how this should be done. The document was signed "Central Committee of the RCP".[8] Its authorship was subsequently attributed to Ya.M. Sverdlov, chairman of the Soviet Central Executive Committee and secretary of the Party CC, who was known for his radical hostility to the Cossacks. But from the Orgburo minutes for January 1919, it is clear that other CC members (M.F. Vladimirsky, N.N. Krestinsky, and Sverdlov's wife K.T. Novgorodtseva, the "techni-cal secretary") were the most assiduous in attending its meetings, and therefore they, too, bear some responsibility for its deci-sions. Conceivably they may have acted without seeking prior approval from Lenin and Trotsky. On 16 March 1919 the CC suspended implementation of this decision, but it was never repealed,[9] and in the meantime tens of thousands of Cossacks had been summarily liquidated.

Two reviewers of the volume on Mironov point out that the text of the introduction was emended, presumably by Yakovlev's editorial team. The first draft contained a reference to an inci-dent in 1960, when Marshal S.M. Budennyi intervened to prevent Mironov's rehabilitation, which was under consideration at the time. The draft also exposed as false the story that Trotsky was Mironov's chief adversary. These cuts and changes were evidently made in accordance with the old Communist tradition of doing whatever one wanted so long as it improved the Party's image.[10]

Such malpractices should forewarn us that the history of the civil war is still an ideological minefield. Not everyone has as yet understood that "the madness of the past was worse than the stupidities of the present", but rather something dangerous we need to free ourselves from as quickly as we can, for truth is not a commodity to be administered in measured doses. I rang Danilov to confirm whether Kabanov was right. When I asked him why he hadn't refused to authorize publication of the truncated version of his foreword, he replied: "then the volume wouldn't have appeared at all and the contributors would have toiled in vain." That is what he was told very clearly by Yakovlev. Danilov gave me permission to make our conversation public, and I do so here.

Recent writers of general works on this period tend to pull their punches. They argue that we should erect "a common memorial to all those, whether Red or White, who fell during the civil war years".[11] This is just a moral appeal to citizens' emotions which will go unheard so long as most people adhere to "class principles". Far more productive, in my view, are the investigations undertaken of late into anti-Bolshevik movements and socio-economic conditions during this era.

The Whites

The military fortunes of the Whites and the programmes of their governments have been studied more extensively by Western and emigré historians; the same is true of the resistance offered to Bolshevik rule by peasants and workers. Among these sources are the memoirs of Generals Denikin and Wrangel. These have since been reprinted in Russia (1991, 1992).[12] So, too, have historical works by Miliukov and S.P. Mel'gunov.[13] What is more, emigré activities and writings have become an object of study in their own right in post-Soviet Russia.[14]

Abroad, the Russian civil war received more intensive attention in the 1980s, when US "revisionists" came to see it as the key factor in explaining the violent character of later Soviet history.[15] I do not agree with Peter Kenez's assertion, in an article on Western historiography of the Russian civil war, that "historical scholarship in the West and in the Soviet Union scarcely influenced each other". After all, as he himself concedes, "Western historians made much use of Soviet works written in the 1920s on the civil war"; and he goes on to state, correctly, that both Western and Soviet historians preferred to study the actions of the Bolsheviks rather than those of their adversaries, because they were more interested in the victors than the vanquished.[16]

By the 1990s the situation in Russia had changed completely. Historians and journalists rushed into print on the White movement, and in the process were prone to whitewash its leaders whom they had previously excoriated. Instead of seeing them as "Russian Bonapartes" engaged on a hopeless adventure, they hail them as democrats who "were the first to struggle against . . . the Bolshevik experiment in forcing socialism on a peasant country".[17] There is even a tendency to idealize such leaders as Admiral A.V. Kolchak and Ataman G.M. Semenov. Of course, one may be touched by the story of Kolchak's love affair with Anna Timirevaia, but one should not forget his brutal system of military justice; Semenov was certainly an extraordinary man, yet he signed a number of execution orders and had several thousand people tortured.[18] Semenov was arrested by the Soviets in Harbin, Manchuria, on 26 August 1945 and interrogated for nearly a year before being hanged. The investigation record fills twenty-five volumes in the security services' archive (TsA FSB RF). *Inter alia* he stated that he had tried to kill Lenin in late 1917 and gave details of how he disposed of his share of tsarist Russia's gold reserve.[19]

There has been some approximation of views between Russian and Western historians concerned with this period. Norman Pereira's study of the civil war in Siberia adopts much the same approach as P.N. Dmitriev's and K.I. Kulikov's account of the exploits of the Izhevsk-Votkinsk workers' division, which fought on Kolchak's side against the Bolsheviks. Several historians have pointed out that we need to do more to foster the exchange of information and to combine post-Soviet Russian, Western and emigré research into a single body of scholarship that idealizes neither Reds nor Whites.[20]

Socio-economic aspects

A more promising avenue of inquiry is the comparative study of the socio-economic policies of the various White military regimes with "War Communism" on the Red side. This is especially important if one wants to find out why the civil war turned out as it did. It means that scholars have to abandon their political or ideological preconceptions and base their arguments on concrete historical data. Yu.D. Grazhdanov has put forward the bold assertion that "during the Russian civil war all the rival regimes employed War Communist methods, in the shape of violent measures and economic coercion for the sake of 'state interests'"[21] – a statement that may be right but needs further research to substantiate it.

For many years, students of "War Communism" justified its harsh policies on the grounds that they had been essential to sustain the Soviet regime. They played down their harmful economic and social effects, such as the corruption engendered by criminalization of normal market relationships and the unparalleled proliferation of officials who employed martial methods against the people. I recall attending several conferences on the civil war at which, if one voiced the slightest criticism of "War Communist" methods, one was immediately faced by the question: "how else could an army of several million have been supplied with the bare minimum of what it required?" Nobody showed any concern about the effect of requisitioning and mass mobilization on the civilian population. Unfortunately present-day scholars have not yet departed very far from this attitude.[22] One exception is S.V. Yarov, who has studied popular reactions in the Petrograd region to the ruinous policies imposed by the country's new masters.[23]

These policies were adopted because they fitted the political and economic model of the new society that was in the Bolshevik leaders' minds and not just as a desperate response to the crisis brought about by enemy attack, as many historians believed, even in the West. Their ideological outlook predisposed Lenin and his associates to try to solve economic problems by violent, arbitrary methods. The main elements of "War Communism" (a name it did not acquire until later, by the way) were the forced requisitioning of foodstuffs, the nationalization of industry, and compulsory labour service by all able-bodied citizens. The adverse consequences, when they became apparent, went unheeded because they did not fit the leaders' preconceptions. By the end of 1920, peasants were being deprived of their entire crop – with only nominal compensation or none at all – and even that was only half of what was needed to feed the towns and the armed forces. Total grain requirements were put at 744 million puds (12.2 million tons). The amount of grain and forage collected by the requisitioning squads was as follows (m. puds):

1918–19	107.9
1919–20	212.5
1920–21	367.0

The peasants reacted to these seizures by rising in revolt, curtailing the sown area, and reverting to a subsistence economy.[24]

Nationalization of industry, extended even to small-scale plants and artisans' workshops, implied militarization of the economy. In 1919, out of a total of 1.4 million workers, 862,000 were employed on war production; yet even they could not provide enough weapons for the Red Army, which was short of rifles by 35 per cent, of machine-guns by 65 per cent, and of artillery pieces by 60 per cent.[25] Meanwhile the number of officials was growing exponentially. By 1920 they comprised 40 per cent of the working population in Moscow and Petrograd. Some 200,000 people were employed in various departments of the provincial soviets, yet there were still over 70,000 jobs waiting to be filled. The cost of maintaining this vast apparatus was enormous, yet attempts to curb it led nowhere.[26] Some of the appointments made were curious. In 1919, peasants in Penza wrote to Lenin imploring him to end their oppresion by ex-criminals and horse-thieves who had been elected to their soviet on the grounds that "they were used to being in jail".[27]

Forced to introduce the New Economic Policy in 1921, Lenin admitted that "we went too far in nationalizing trade and industry, stopping the local exchange of goods, . . . but we were compelled to do so by necessity."[28] It is worth noting that he only criticized certain aspects of the earlier policies (now christened pejoratively "War Communism") in order to appease an aroused public opinion, but refrained from condemning it *in toto*. So one can hardly take the view that these policies came to an end in 1921. The ruling Party was obliged to replace crop requisitioning with a tax in kind, and small enterprises were denationalized. But this was only a limited, temporary retreat. From the mid-1920s, when the course was set for a great leap forward (industrialization, collectivization, and a heightening of the state's punitive role), this heralded a return to "War Communist" policies, which were applied with even greater brutality than before. This time the tightening of the screw could not be explained away as a response to armed resistance, yet the state behaved still more mercilessly. The "Stalin revolution" led to the famine of 1932–3 and to a permanent shortage of foodstuffs and basic commodities.

It is worthwhile reflecting seriously about the lasting traces which "War Communism" left on the whole of later Soviet history. They help to explain the present-day nostalgia among the needy for a system whereby goods are distributed by the state instead of by the market forces of supply and demand. This attitude goes back to the civil war, which was a national tragedy in more senses than one. The victors never forgot that they won by subjugating the people to famine conditions, and so to a degree of dependence on the state that gave the latter a powerful lever over their minds. This is why it deserves to be seen as *the* key period of Soviet history.

In the 1990s, specialists on the civil war began to investigate problems that had hitherto been taboo because of censorship and the closure of the archives. Documentary volumes have appeared on the peasant risings in Tambov province and western Siberia;[29] and the first instalment has appeared of a four-volume series of security police records on conditions in the countryside, dealing with the years 1918–22.[30] I had the honour to take part in the latter project, due for completion in 2000. The documents show that the peasants were far from impartial spectators of the fighting. They comprised the bulk of the rival armies. Not only was there a rising against Kolchak in 1919, but also insurrections on the Red side, which broke out as early as 1918 – and not just when the Whites had been defeated, as O. Figes mistakenly asserts; they culminated in the massive rural protests of 1920–1.[31]

At the beginning of Gorbachev's perestroika there was a resurgence of interest in the introduction of NEP in 1921–2, as it seemed to offer parallels to the current efforts to reform the command economy. But this interest evaporated as Gorbachev's "neo-NEP" failed to bring positive results and it became clear that the Soviet system was unreformable.[32]

Most of the work done recently on this topic, both original research and documentary publications, has served to expose the real character of the Bolshevik policies that led to the 1921–2 famine. In the latter year, nearly 36 million people were starving yet 50 million puds of grain were exported.[33] Lenin wrote to Kamenev on 3 March 1922: "It is a great error to think that NEP has put an end to terror. We shall still revert to terror and to economic terror."[34]

The Cheka and its successors

The 1990s have led many historians to seek novel approaches to the Soviet past. The religious factor has begun to receive due recognition, and there are several studies of the painful relationship between the Russian Orthodox Church and the atheist state.[35] Equally new are studies of "Russia abroad".[36] For reasons of space we shall concentrate on a few key topics. No one can doubt the importance of the Cheka, the name familiarly given to the All-Russian Extraordinary Commission for Struggle with Counter-Revolution, Speculation, Sabotage and Misconduct in Office (the full title, adopted in August 1918; the body was set up as early as 7 December 1917). Its chairman was Feliks Dzerzhinsky. During the Soviet era this institution was the subject of many apologetic works romanticizing the deeds of the stout-hearted "Chekists" and spreading the myth that (as used to be said in the 1930s) "the organs are always right". Even the wave of Red Terror in 1918 was treated as a harsh necessity imposed on the Bolsheviks by their enemies' hostility. Abroad, the Cheka earned itself a bad press for its brutalities, but even the most knowledgeable studies, such as that by George Leggett, suffer from lack of reliable first-hand information about this secretive body.[37]

Now, the Cheka's archives have been declassified and its register made available to researchers.[38] One may familiarize oneself with the minutes of the VChK's governing Presidium, which give an idea of the main directions of its work, and reports submitted by local organizations. But there is a fundamental problem in interpreting these materials: written regulations were supplemented by numerous internal secret rules or oral instructions. There was a great gulf between the Soviet government's declarative pronouncements and actual reality. In the judicial system as a whole much scope was left to officials' "revolutionary consciousness", which opened the way to arbitrary actions.

In December 1997, for the first time in the history of Russia's security organs, an international scholarly conference was held in Moscow under the title "Russia's Special Services: Past and Present". I was invited to give a paper on the Red and White terror during the civil war. The young Chekists who spoke at the meeting argued that in the 1930s the NKVD had been a helpless tool of the political leadership; it was the latter that had set up the purge trials and established the GULag as part of its drive to bolster its own power by waging war on ordinary citizens. The NKVD, they inferred, had been just an executant of policies decided elsewhere and so bore no responsibility for mass executions, deportations and other crimes. These speakers conveniently forgot that, if the Party turned to the "punitive sword of the proletariat" to undertake these missions, this was for the very good reason that "the organs" were prepared to carry out criminal deeds.

There is another angle to this: in 1956 Khrushchev defended the ruling Party and laid all the blame for the purges on the NKVD, which he claimed had "put itself above the Party".[39] Now, after the dissolution of the CPSU in 1991, the Chekists maintained that the reverse was true. Professor V.P. Yeroshin, of the Federal Security Services Academy, stated at the conference that the topmost leaders of the Soviet Union were often intellectually deficient and had prevented "the organs" from doing their job properly. The same idea was expressed, in a more civilized way, in a book called *No. 2 Lubianka*, which gave an account of the most successful operations carried out by the Cheka. The Party leadership was criticized for its lack of professionalism; it had allegedly used the security police as "an effective instrument to bring about the enforced transformation of society".[40]

At the conference a very different point of view was expressed by N.V. Petrov, who represented the civil rights organization Memorial. Noting that many Chekists had fallen victim to repression under Stalin, he stated that from 1933 to 1939, 21,000

NKVD employees had been arrested – but most of them for criminal conduct, not on political grounds; in 1936–8, the figures were 3200 arrests, of which 1800 were for political and the rest for criminal offences. A biography has appeared of the first chairman of the KGB, General I.A. Serov, and its author has also helped to compile a useful handbook listing the principal officials in the security police between 1934 and 1941.[41]

The 1990s witnessed publication of several documentary volumes, books and articles on the security services.[42] Characteristically, they were concerned mainly with the activities of their local branches. They also discuss cases where the Chekists were unsuccessful. Some of these authors are officials of the present-day Federal Security Service (FSB RF); they are critical of illegal repressions carried out by their Soviet predecessors, both at home and abroad, such as the assassination of the former White generals A.P. Kutepov and E.K. Miller, emigrés in France who were kidnapped and abducted to the USSR in 1930 and 1937 respectively.[43] Post-Soviet researchers have been able to consult documents in the former KGB and the Presidential archives. The latter contains the personal files of Stalin, Voroshilov, Yezhov and other leaders who had much to do with security matters.

The minutes of the Cheka's Presidium reveal that the first extra-judicial *troika* (triumvirate) with the power to sentence people to death was set up on 15 June 1918. It consisted of Dzerzhinsky, P.A. Aleksandrovich and M.I. Latsis; if they were absent, three other men could act as substitutes: Ya.Kh. Peters, V.V. Fomin and I.I. Il'in.[44] According to their personal files, Latsis and Peters were shot in 1938 on false charges of – absurd as it may seem – Latvian nationalism.

One of the most interesting Cheka operations that can be reconstructed with greater accuracy in the light of new documentary information is that mounted against B.V. Savinkov (1879–1925), a prominent SR who had been an assistant minister under Kerensky and was later an active anti-Bolshevik. In 1921, aided by Western secret services, he set up in Paris a National Union for the Defence of Freedom and the Fatherland which attempted to organize a resistance movement within the USSR. Many of its agents fell into Cheka hands and were "turned". In August 1924, Savinkov was arrested as he tried to cross the Polish border and was sentenced to death. Subsequently the sentence was commuted to one of ten years' imprisonment; Savinkov published a penitent article in *Izvestiia* which suggested that, under duress, he had reached an accommodation with his captors; then, on 7 May 1925, came an announcement that he had "committed suicide" in the Lubianka. People have often wondered whether he really fell from a window of the building or was pushed. Now we have details of what happened. That evening Savinkov was taken for a drive by three leading Chekists: S.V. Puzitsky (head of counter-intelligence), V.I. Speransky and G.S. Syroezhkin. On returning to the Lubianka at 11 p.m., they went up to Puzitsky's office in Room 192 on the fifth floor, where they waited for a convoy to arrive that was due to take Savinkov to the OGPU's internal prison. Speransky lay down on the divan because he had a headache – or so he testified a few hours later; Puzinsky left the room to get him a carafe of water, while Syroezhkin sat in an armchair listening to Savinkov reminisce about life in exile at Vologda. Suddenly, at 11.30 p.m., Savinkov walked to the window, which was open, and jumped out.

His death was investigated by an OGPU commission under V.D. Fel'dman, a top-flight police official. He reported on 11 May that Savinkov had recently become depressed at his imprisonment and had often said: "it's either freedom or death for me". Once he had decided to commit suicide, he would have found a way whether the window had been left open or not; accordingly there had been no lapse by his escort and "I terminated the inquiry."[45] Of course, this official Cheka account is not conclusive evidence, but it does make suicide look more probable than murder; for the Chekists could have finished him off more easily than by chucking him out of an office window.

The civil war, as I have already stated, crippled Russians in mind and body. It would take ages for society to recover, for people's souls to be cleansed from hatred. Unfortunately even today that moment is still far off . . .

5
The Age of Stalin

Reconsiderations of Stalinism

I grew up deprived of parental care and so I know what it is like to be a pariah, the son of an "enemy of the people" and a Jew to boot. I find it hard to write dispassionately about that era, the more so since Mikhail Gefter's question of 1988, "Did Stalin die yesterday?", must even today be answered in the affirmative. A whole generation of men and women are still alive who in their nostalgia for Stalinist "order" carry his portrait aloft during street demonstrations. Yet others are alive who as a result of that "order" drank the bitter cup to the dregs. For them a return to that past is simply unthinkable. Stalin's name has become a kind of litmus paper for young people too, including historians. His popularity among some Russians today has probably the same cause as the neo-Nazi fashion in more fortunate European countries: Hitler and Stalin symbolize the desire to resolve problems by violence. They were both animated by nationalism and in the last resort by fear of their fellow men.[1]

Much has been written on Stalin in recent years, in Russia as in the West. Some writers, in the tradition of Trotsky, represent him as a traitor to socialism, and his regime as essentially bureaucratic, "anti-popular", whereas others have detected a dynamic interaction between the Party-state authorities on one hand and upwardly mobile elements in Soviet society on the other.[2] There are several fresh biographical studies, notably those by D.A. Volkogonov and Robert C. Tucker.[3] Volkogonov, who died in 1995, conceived his study in 1979 when he was still a senior official in the Soviet Army's Main Political Directorate; it came out ten years later, at the height of *glasnost'*, when the exposure of past abuses was all the rage. At the start Volkogonov was still a Leninist and saw Stalin's rule as a despotic degeneration of authentic Communism. Later he wrote: "Like most of my compatriots, I was deeply mistaken in thinking that all our misfortunes came from forgetting Lenin."

Stalin's two most recent biographers are in agreement about the sources of his system of rule. "Stalinism flourished on Leninist soil", writes Volkogonov; for Tucker, "the essence of Stalinism is a mix of tough War Communist policies and Great Russian chauvinism".[4] This consensus has not stopped Russian historians from pursuing a rather scholastic discussion as to whether the "personality cult", as allegedly in principle alien to socialism, was inevitable in Soviet conditions. The debate led nowhere for, in practice, as experience shows, a leader cult is an inseparable feature of all totalitarian regimes, whether of the right or of the left.

Western historians have been prone to seek the roots of Stalin's dictatorship in Russia's autocratic past, in its lack of democratic institutions and civic culture, whereas many of their Russian colleagues argue that it was a consequence of the attempt to realize a Marxist-style "proletarian dictatorship" in a single country. In support of the former view one may cite Vasilyi Grossman, who in his well-known novel *Life and Fate*, written in the 1950s, noted that "for a thousand years Russians looked at a lot of things, including national grandeur, but one thing they never set eyes on was democracy."[5] But probably those who stress the ideological roots of Stalinism have the better case. It should be seen as one of the variant forms assumed by totalitarianism. This at any rate was the view taken at an international seminar held in Novosibirsk in July 1992.[6]

It is curious that Russian historians choose to write mostly about the work done on Stalinism by their Western colleagues, while the latter are to the fore in offering critical analyses of Russian writings on the subject. One Western observer noted in 1995 that the accumulation of factual material was currently being supplemented by more interpretative studies, and that attention was shifting away from the political leadership towards studies of society, which raised the question of the responsibility which ordinary people, and especially members of the intelligentsia, bore for the excesses that had occurred.[7] Michal Reiman published an article ostensibly devoted to the historiographical treatment of Stalinism, but actually he just advanced his controversial hypothesis that Stalinisim came about simply as a response to the structural, economic and political crisis that faced the Soviet regime in 1928.[8] Joachim Hösler remarks that the term "Stalinism" was used only in Western propaganda until 1988, when Volkogonov introduced it into Russian historical discourse. Hösler distinguishes between those who see Stalinism as a digression from Marxism and those who see it as a counter-revolutionary "Thermidor"; however, this distinction is no longer accurate as historical thought has moved on since the Gorbachev era.[9]

In 1998–9, I.V. Pavlova wrote two articles on Western historiography of the Stalin era. She took issue with the "revisionists", charging them with excessive reliance on Soviet sources and a reluctance to recognize the regime's totalitarian essence.[10] Her interpretation evoked criticism from Yu.I. Igritsky, I.N. Olegina, N.V. Shcherban' and A.K. Sokolov, who thought she took too ideological an approach, whereas from abroad Martin Malia took the opposite line, defending the ideological factor as basic to the Soviet system of rule.

I find myself in agreement with Malia, but must admit that the question is complex. We do not yet have enough documentary material to reach definitive conclusions. After all, there are no less than 1703 files, with a total of several hundred folios, in the Presidential Archive's Stalin collection (*fond*) which have yet to be declassified and studied.[11] The Stalin *fond* in RGASPI is relatively thin, but even of this material little has so far been published – what we have are, notably, his editorial emendations to his official biography and the list, compiled by his guards, of visitors he received in his office.[12]

Stalin's personal life

No modern dictator wielded as much personal power as Stalin, who was praised to the skies during his lifetime (no less than six cities proudly bore his name), so it is not surprising that there should be enduring interest in details of his biography. Incidentally, even at a time when one could be put in jail for the slightest criticism of the Leader, jokes used to be told about him.[13]

During Stalin's lifetime and for many years thereafter, it was taken for granted that he was born on 21 December 1879, but this date was false. In 1921, when filling in a biographical questionnaire, Stalin pretended that he was younger than he actually was. Why he did so is unclear, but he evidently knew that since he controlled Party records no one would dare point out the error. The fact was brought to light by L.M. Spirin, who in 1990 published the real date: 6 December 1878.[14]

His official biography contained untruths about his early years too. For example, his expulsion from an Orthodox seminary in May 1899 was said to have been for circulating Marxist propaganda, whereas actually, as the pertinent document shows, it was for "failure to turn up for an examination without sufficient cause". Later he told a tsarist police officer that he left school because he was fed up with the miserable material conditions there.

Spirin went on to publish eleven letters which Stalin wrote to his mother between 1922 and 1934. Once a year he would send her a terse note, polite but formal and in a jerky style, written in Georgian (for his mother did not know Russian). On 16 September 1930, for example, he wrote:

> Greetings, dear Mama! I was ill. Now I feel better. Nadia [Allilueva, his second wife] has left for Moscow and I shall go to Moscow soon. May you live for a thousand years. Yours, Soso.

He last saw his mother in 1935, when she was seventy-nine; she died two years later and was buried in consecrated ground in a Tbilisi cemetery. Stalin did not attend the funeral[15] – probably because he was afraid of assassination; after all, this was the height of the Terror and he knew how vengeful people could be in the Caucasus.

After Nadezhda Allilueva's suicide in 1932 Stalin did not re-marry. He took no interest in his relatives and ordered several of his two wives' kinsfolk shot. He had affairs with other women, including Moscow actresses such as Vera Davydova and Marina Semenova, whom he treated politely, inviting them by phone to come to the Kremlin for a glass of good Georgian wine.[16] None of them seems to have turned down an invitation.

In 1993, some documents were published from Stalin's personal archive dealing with members of his family. Among them was some correspondence with Nadezhda Allilueva. Also published, but only in part, was the record of the interrogation by the Germans of Yakov, his son by his first marriage, after his capture in July 1941, as well as papers on the investigation carried out in Moscow on 9–11 May 1953 into Vasilyi's affairs shortly after his father's death. The diary kept by Maria Svanidze between 1922 and 1937 also contains a good deal of information on the Soviet leader's personal life.[17]

Stalin's family life was marked by tragedy. He quarrelled frequently with his second wife, who was twenty-two years younger than he was. Her suicide, on the night of 8/9 November 1932, apparently came about after he had publicly humiliated her at a dinner party held to mark the fifteenth anniversary of the Revolution.[18] According to Svetlana Allilueva, her mother left a suicide note – it has not survived – that he found infuriating; during the civil leave-taking ceremony he pushed the coffin aside and walked abruptly out of the building; he neither stayed for the actual funeral nor visited her grave subsequently. His son Yakov also attempted suicide because his relationship with his father was so strained. Brought up in his late mother's family, he did not even meet his father until 1921, by which time he was fourteen. In 1941, when the Germans invaded, he was a senior lieutenant in command of an artillery battery. Captured on 16 July, he was put to death in Sachsenhausen concentration camp on 14 April 1943.

Svetlana, born in 1926, enjoyed a happy childhood but found life troublesome as she grew up. At the age of seventeen she fell in love with a thirty-nine-year old film producer, A.Ya. Kapler. Her father was furious and slapped her; Kapler got a ten-year sentence as an "English spy". In 1967 Svetlana defected from the USSR and eventually took up residence in the United States. She gave a personal account of her difficult life, and also of her father and his entourage, in two books, *Twenty Letters to a Friend* (1967; Russ. edn. 1990) and *Only One Year* (1969).

As for her brother Vasilyi (1921–62), his career was meteoric but marred by scandal. At twenty he was an air force captain and at twenty-four a lieutenant-general. But after his father's death his fairy-tale life came to an abrupt end. First he was thrown out of the armed forces without the right to wear uniform – equivalent to dishonourable discharge – and on 28 April 1953 was arrested, tried and sentenced to eight years behind bars for "abusing his service rank, wasting a large amount of state funds, forging documents and misappropriating objects of value". After a spell in prison, where he was treated as a privileged inmate, in 1961 he was sentenced to five years' exile in Kazan'. The rumour soon circulated that Vasilyi Stalin had been victimized lest he should become a figure-head in a pro-Stalinist *coup*, or even the organizer of one. There is no truth in this version, for he was not at all interested in politics. He was just a playboy who owed everything to the fact that he was the dictator's son. If Stalin was a mediocrity, as Trotsky called him, then Vasilyi was a mediocre mediocrity.

Vasilyi lived in Kazan' from 29 April 1961 until his death on 19 March 1962. The local KGB didn't let him out of its sight for a moment – a listening device was hidden in his room – and compiled no less than eleven volumes of surveillance reports, which I have been through in connection with my work in the Tatarstan Rehabilitation Commission.

The KGB records show that he continued to drink to excess and became a human wreck. On 14 March 1962 he had a visit from a Georgian who brought him a lot of wine, and even after his guest had left Vasilyi continued to put back red wine and vodka until, on 19 March, his heart gave out. An official investigation attributed his death to "arteriosclerosis due to intoxication with alcohol". There was no trace of any other poison in his body. Semichastny, the KGB chairman, at once informed Khrushchev. Vasilyi's funeral took place on the third day after his death, in conformity with Orthodox tradition. Some 250–300 people turned up at the cemetery, including his civil wife, Katolina Vasil'eva, and their two children; the bill for the funeral was footed by the local KGB.[19]

Soon after Vasilyi's remains had been buried, a band of Georgians tried to dig them up and take them back to Georgia. To prevent any similar attempt, the coffin was immured in concrete! Many years later, on 30 September 1999, the case against Vasilyi Stalin was reconsidered by the Military Collegium of the Russian Supreme Court. All the political charges were declared null and void, but the others were left in force.

Stalin had ten grandchildren, and some relatives of his wife are still alive. They have gone on record publicly as defenders of the Stalin era. In this they are like the children of other Soviet leaders, such as Sergei Khrushchev, Andrei Malenkov and Sergo Beria; they have only good things to say about their fathers who, they claim, had nothing to do with any illegal repressions.[20] This attitude is understandable psychologically, but the documentary evidence does not bear them out and their books cannot be regarded as reliable sources.

Stalin's personality was complex. He had a strong character and stopped at nothing in trying to achieve his goals. His detractors have called him paranoid – a diagnosis arrived at as early as 1927, when he was examined by the well-known psychiatrist Professor V.M. Bekhterev.[21] Others have alleged that he was at one time an agent of the tsarist secret police, the Okhrana,[22] and that this explains why he set up a police state based on intimidation, denunciation and the GULag. The American scholar Adam Ulam sees Stalin as exercising hypnotic powers, which prevented people from realizing how inhuman and absurd his system was. Valentin Berezkov, Stalin's personal interpreter, wondered to the end of his days how it was possible for Stalin to "bewitch" an entire people without at the same time improving their living standards, as Hitler had managed to do before the war.[23]

A number of memoir writers have remarked how extraordinarily suspicious Stalin was of others. Admiral I.S. Isakov (1894–1967) told a journalist how he once met Stalin in the Kremlin and walked with him the length of a brilliantly lit and well-guarded corridor. When he commented on the lighting and guards, Stalin replied: "That's not the point: the real problem is that I don't know when one of these rascals will put a bullet in the back of my neck."[24] Stalin was certainly very vengeful.

Kamenev, who had once been his close comrade-at-arms, recalled that on one occasion, when the Bolshevik leaders were chatting about what they most liked doing in life, Stalin, who was tipsy, said: "Eye one's victim, prepare everything, take revenge mercilessly, and then go to sleep."[25]

Opposition

One naturally asks oneself as a historian whether there were any attempts on Stalin's life and why his colleagues, aware of his dictatorial inclinations and readiness to destroy his opponents physically, did not get rid of him first. It is known that during the Second World War, German and Japanese intelligence agents did try to bring about his assassination. It is also known that in Stalin's Politburo it was considered "good tone" for each member to have been the object of at least one alleged attempt on his life by the "brutalized class enemy". Matters were taken to a point of complete absurdity when masses of innocent people were accused of plotting to murder the country's leaders. In 1937 Evgenia Ginzburg (subsequently famous as the author of *Into the Whirlwind*, memoirs of her experiences in the GULag) asked the chairman of the tribunal trying her which politician she was charged with trying to kill. His reply had a perverse logic: "They say the Trotskyists killed Kirov in Leningrad; you failed to resist them in Kazan'; therefore you must be dealt with as a terrorist."[26]

Only one genuine attempt was made on Stalin, so far as historians are aware. A soldier, Savelyi Dmitriev, on duty in Red Square on 6 November 1942, opened fire with his rifle at a black limousine leaving the Kremlin. He did not know that its occupant was not Stalin but Mikoian. Anyway, his bullets could not penetrate the car's armour-plate. Dmitriev was a priest's son who wanted to take revenge for the humiliations that he, and the peasantry generally, had been through. He turned his gun on himself but only inflicted a wound, whereupon he was arrested and subjected to frightful tortures before being shot years later, on 25 August 1950, on the false charge of having set up a terrorist organization.[27]

On no less than seven occasions between 1923 and 1952 Stalin offered to resign. These were acts of political blackmail, for he never had any intention of stepping down. Each time, he became even more certain that he was irreplaceable as leader.[28] Of course he did have to face opposition: not only from top-level Bolsheviks or national-communist leaders like Budu Mdivani in Georgia or the Tatar Mirsaid Sultan-Galiev,[29] but also from members of the scholarly community, whom he dealt with by discrediting them as political deviationists. One such was M.I. Frumkin (1878–1938), a deputy Finance commissar, who in 1928 sent letters to the Politburo protesting that the Party's agrarian policy was causing the ruin of the peasantry; Stalin labelled him a Trotskyite.[30] Once the Stalin cult got under way any statement the leader made became an absolute truth for scholars and scientists, whether they were geneticists or cyberneticists, linguists or sociologists.

Stalin's last scholarly opponent was the economist L.D. Yaroshenko, a Gosplan official who in November 1951 dared to criticize the official textbook on political economy – and for his pains landed up in the Lubianka. He recalled his experiences in 1989, having reached the age of ninety-three. He had termed the introduction to this work "unscientific" and called for a less politicized approach – not knowing that the book had been edited and approved by Stalin! The next year the dictator produced a screed of his own, *Economic Problems of Socialism in the USSR*, in which he called Yaroshenko "a Marxist who has gone out of his mind". Fortunately for him, Stalin died soon afterwards and at the end of 1953 Yaroshenko was released from jail.[31]

In 1961 a group of librarians working at the Institute of Marxism–Leninism was summoned to the Kremlin and given the job of sorting out Stalin's personal library. It was in two locations, his Kremlin apartment and suburban *dacha*, and contained over 20,000 volumes. Over half of them were literary works, which were transferred to the Russian State (then Lenin) Library. Among them were some books which had been the property of Bukharin, Zinov'ev and Kamenev prior to their arrest. Unfortunately a number of Stalin's books went missing, but several hundred of those on which he made marks or comments have been the object of historical inquiry.[32]

Many people – politicians, military leaders, writers and artists – who met Stalin have left us impressions of the man. They often noted that he dressed and lived modestly. One of his body-guards, A.T. Rybin, observed that his suspiciousness became more marked over time, and the same point was made by A.N. Poskrebyshev, who served as his personal secretary from 1935 to 1952.[33]

Stalin's death

Stalin died at 9.50 p.m. on 5 March 1953 at his *dacha* of Kuntsevo near Moscow. Did he die naturally or was he killed? His son Vasilyi thought the latter, as did A. Avtorkhanov, who identified Beria as the culprit. Likewise Poskrebyshev, interviewed in 1992, remarked:

> The circumstances of comrade Stalin's death were rather strange. His closest associates did not call for medical assistance at once, despite the entreaties of his guards, and he lay uncon-scious for over ten hours – this after being paralysed by a stroke! . . . I am firmly convinced that only Beria, who was eager to take power, had an interest in bringing about his demise.

Khrushchev also mentions this point in his memoirs, while others have suggested that Kaganovich might have disposed of Stalin to save Soviet Jews from being deported to Siberia. Svetlana Allilueva considers it odd that immediately after her father's death all documents in the Kuntsevo *dacha* were removed and the staff dismissed.[34]

During his lifetime, Stalin's state of health was a state secret – after all, he was supposed to be the Immortal Leader! Not until the 1990s did Volkogonov mention the fact that he suffered sev-eral strokes that caused him to lose consciousness. The first time this happened was in 1949. But when his doctor, V.N. Vinogradov, suggested he should slow down, Stalin took his advice as ma-licious and had him arrested. He was ageing fast, and long periods without any medical aid did not help his condition. The stroke that killed him occurred between 8 and 9 p.m. on 1 March. He was discovered lying unconscious at 11 p.m. but it was not until the next morning that he was examined by several doctors.

Professor A.L. Miasnikov (1899–1965) was a member of this group, which included experts in neuropathology and therapeutic medicine. He writes:

> Stalin, who was short and fat, lay in a cramped position, his face contorted, the fingers of his right hand stretched out like the thongs of a whip. He was breathing heavily ... Thankfully, there was no doubt about the diagnosis: an effusion of blood in the left hemisphere of the brain due to high blood pressure and arteriosclerosis.

On the third day the doctors came to the unanimous conclusion that the patient's death was inevitable. Their diagnosis was confirmed by a post-mortem conducted on 6 March. Stalin had been a very sick man for several years.[35]

Within an hour of his death a commission was set up under Khrushchev to organize the funeral. It was decided to embalm Stalin's body and to place the casket next to Lenin's in the mausoleum on Red Square. The funeral ceremony was lavish but marred by tragedy: several dozen people in the crowd were crushed to death. The corpse did not stay in the mausoleum for long. On 31 October 1961, at dead of night, it was removed from the casket to a wooden coffin; the gold buttons of the uniform were replaced by brass ones; and eight officers of the Kremlin guard regiment bore the body from the mausoleum to a grave that had been dug by the Kremlin wall. It was covered by a marble tombstone and later a bust of Stalin was erected on top.[36]

Stalinism

Nearly fifty years have passed since the dictator died, but his place in history is still questioned. In 1988 a retired legal official, I.T. Shekhovtsev of Khar'kov, laid charges against the writer A. Adamovich and the historian V. Polikarpov for insulting Stalin's honour and dignity by calling him a criminal, on the grounds that there was no judicial verdict to this effect. The court turned down the plea.[37] Even today many people would endorse Molotov's statement, made in the 1970s to the journalist F. Chuev, that the 1937 purge had been necessary.[38]

Discussions are still going on about the Stalinist political and social system. In my view one should begin by recognizing the plain fact that Stalin had the mind of an Oriental despot: he would smile at someone and reward him while simultaneously ordering the man to be kept under surveillance and false documents prepared to compromise him and justify his liquidation. No one was safe, however close they might be to the Leader. Stalin also deliberately promoted the cult of his own person; in this he differed from Napoleon, who did not become an object of worship until after his death.

What then was Stalinism? Above all it was a way of controlling and directing society – politically, ideologically and socially – on the basis of universal state ownership, single-party rule and contempt for human rights. In my view it was indeed totalitarian – one of several variants of this modern system of government, which had political, economic and moral dimensions; in the Russian case it can be explained, at least in part, by the people's lack of democratic traditions and their low political culture. It is significant that Stalin jotted down, on the last page of his copy of Lenin's *Materialism and Empiriocriticism*, the criteria he used in judging others. In red pencil he noted: "1) weakness, 2) laziness, 3) stupidity are the only vices." And later: "if a man is 1) strong (spiritually), 2) active, 3) clever (or capable), he is good, whether or not he has other 'vices'." These were the principles on which he operated – which did not, of course, stop him signing the death warrants of large numbers of clever people who, by his own criteria, were good.

Perhaps the most awesome aspect of the Stalinist system was that so many people, in Russia and abroad, came to believe in it, or at least to accept it. He was widely thought to be a just man, if not a genius; the official view of history was credited, though it was really no more than myth; the slogans that governed most people's public conduct were absurd and utopian; and if anyone failed to do what was expected of him or her – let alone questioned the dictates of authority – they risked exposure as "enemies of the people" and harsh punishment. Stalin made a favourable impression on such foreign politicians as (Sir) Winston Churchill, Franklin D. Roosevelt and Harry Hopkins, as well as several Western writers: Henri Barbusse, Romain Rolland,

Lion Feuchtwanger, H.G. Wells, to name just a few. Robert Conquest is surely right to say that not the "cult of the individual" but terror and lies were the essential features of Stalinism, and he deplores the gullibility of so many Western intellectuals who failed to discern what lay behind the mask.[39]

Take the case of H.G. Wells, whom Stalin received on 23 July 1934 for a chat lasting nearly three hours. We now know that Stalin edited the text of his replies to Wells's questions before they were published. It is also true that when Wells learned of the 1937 purges he changed his opinion of the Soviet leader and in his novel *Holy Terror* (1939) depicted him as a traitor to socialism and the revolution. It is unclear whether Stalin read this novel, or how he reacted to news of Wells's death in 1946.[40] Probably he took no notice of either. As for the German writer Feuchtwanger, who was granted a three-hour interview in January 1937, his book *Moscow 1937*, published soon afterwards, was a justification of everything that was going on in the USSR in that dreadful year. Modern critics have pointed out that his praise of Stalin and Soviet might was designed to alert westerners to the possibility that "Stalin's fist" could keep Hitler at bay.[41]

The Stalin files

The key source of information on the dictator's private life, and Stalinism too, is the leader's personal archive. Unfortunately access to its treasures is still restricted. Many papers were destroyed, first on Stalin's instructions and then on Khrushchev's. When Beria was arrested in 1953 his personal archive was also impounded. It contained material on Stalin's relations with the NKVD. Eleven sacks of these documents were promptly burned. Khrushchev ordered General I.A. Serov, the head of the KGB, to destroy the lists drawn up in 1937–8 of persons to be shot, the so-called *rasstrel'nye spiski*, which had been signed by other leaders besides Stalin, for Khrushchev was anxious to get rid of evidence about his own role in the purges. A few months later Serov gave Khrushchev a file of documents which were likewise destroyed.[42] It is regrettable that even today records from Stalin's archive are being removed for disposal. The only historian who has so far managed to get permission to see the papers in this collection is

A.A. Fursenko, academic secretary of the History Division of the Russian Academy of Sciences. But even he has been unable to see Stalin's correspondence with the NKVD and its commissar, Yezhov.

What is worse, when some of these materials were recently transferred from the Presidential Archive (APRF) to RGASPI, some important documents were removed. Fursenko wrote an angry letter to the head of the Russian Archive Service in which he noted: "A very important document has been taken out of [the records of] the history of Stalin's illness, the medical journal containing the conclusions reached by the doctors who were consulted about Stalin's illness and death on 2–5 March 1953." Fursenko saw only a file entitled "History of the Illness of J.V. Stalin (based on journal notes on the course of his illness from 2 to 5 March 1953)", bearing the signatures of the Minister of Health and nine doctors, but undated. On the draft of this was the date "July 1953". In other words, the file had been "gone over"; its internal register (*opis'*) had been compiled on 5 April 1990, although the register of the collection to which it belonged had been completed in 1978. The numeration of the folios had been changed and traces of corrections were visible. There were pages missing from the "Notes on Medicines Prescribed and Duty Rosters" and the cover was torn. Fursenko thinks that the papers removed did not accord with the conclusions reached by the doctors.[43]

The newly discovered documents are of some help in dispelling the myths and lies that were the legacy of the Stalin era. The Soviet dictator was spared the fate meted out to Hitler and Mussolini, and was buried with honours. But the world was a better place without any of the three. Overcoming the heritage of the totalitarian past is, however, a more complicated business than just publishing documents about it. Given the distrust with which Russians today approach anything on paper, other measures are required to educate the public to appreciate the evil that was done in its name and to make amends, even if only symbolically, on behalf of the innocent victims.

6
The "Great" Terror

Stalin's terrorist policies have been studied most thoroughly by the British historian (and poet) Robert Conquest. The most famous of his many books on Russian history, *The Great Terror* (1968) and *Harvest of Sorrow* (1972), have been translated into Russian.[1] I first came across the former in the Lenin Library's special repository. It made a great impression on me as a general study of what went on in Moscow during the 1930s. But there were two things about the book that disturbed me. One was the absence of any reference to Russian archival sources. This was because at that time objective research on the Soviet period could only be done abroad. I also had reservations about the title. By calling the terror of the late 1930s "great" was it not implied that the 1.5 million victims of the terror, Red and White, in 1918–22 were somehow less important? In fact, as I argued above, terroristic measures against fellow-citizens were a feature of the whole of Soviet history. Incidentally, the same arguments apply to Michael Parrish's study of the post-war era, entitled *The Lesser Terror . . .*, published in 1996.

Collectivization

Conquest's *Harvest of Sorrow*, which deals with collectivization and the famine of 1932–3 (which was most acute, as the author emphasizes, in Ukraine) led to a polemical exchange with V.P. Danilov, the leading Russian agrarian historian, about the number of victims. Danilov put this at 3–4 million, much lower than the 14.5 million (for 1930–7) estimated by Conquest. The latter revised his figure downwards to 11 million, of whom he thought 7 million had perished in the famine, and the rest during collectivization (including millions of Kazakhs who were deported or emigrated). Danilov apologized for having misunderstood Conquest but continued to insist on a much lower figure, a position shared by R.W. Davies and other Western specialists.[2]

Most present-day Russian scholars are convinced that forced collectivization after 1929 and the 1932–3 famine, caused by excessively harsh state grain procurements, were part and parcel of the same policy, designed to bring about the enserfment of the peasantry; for this is what the recently published documents show.[3] The peasants resisted administrative pressure to join the new collective farms (*kolkhozy*) but their uprisings were brutally repressed. An edict of 7 August 1932 made it a capital offence to steal "socialist property". Under its provisions, as we now know, 103,000 people were convicted, of whom six thousand were shot. Under another decree of 27 December 1932 it became obligatory to carry an internal passport and to have a residence permit; but such passports were not issued to citizens "not engaged in socially useful labour" or to peasants, even if they had joined a *kolkhoz*. Peasants were thus openly discriminated against in law; not until 1976–81 were they entitled to receive such passports, and to change their place of residence, on the same basis as other citizens.[4]

Historians have pointed out that it was precisely when collectivization began, at the end of 1929, that the population of the forced-labour camps grew spectacularly. From April 1930 they came under the GULag, or Main Administration of Camps, an enterprise of the OGPU (later NKVD) made familiar by Solzhenitsyn. By 1940 the GULag "archipelago" consisted of 53 camp complexes containing thousands of sections and "points" (that is, camps), as well as 475 colonies (industrial, agricultural and so on), 50 colonies for children, and 90 infant homes. (On 1 March 1940 the latter contained 4595 children whose mothers had been sent to camps.) The GULag administrative network did not include prisons, whose population was twice as large as the number of places available. There were also over two thousand "special komendaturas" which controlled the lives of millions of special or labour settlers (*spets-* or *trudoposelentsy*). The latter two branches of the penal system came under the NKVD's Prison Administration and its Special Settlers Department respectively. Most inmates of prisons or settlements were peasants.[5]

In June 1994 a scholarly conference was held in Moscow on "Mentalities and Russian Agricultural Development". Two of the speakers, V.V. Kondrashin and V.V. Babashkin, maintained that the 1932–3 famine "had dealt a mortal blow to the peasantry" and that these years had seen "the peak of peasant resistance to the regime".[6] This was not so. Soviet peasants were definitely not turned into dumb slaves, even though they were subjected to death from hunger by the million, but continued to protest in manifold ways: by escaping from the settlements, which were located in remote areas, refusing to pay taxes or to subscribe to state loans, and leaving the collective farms under various pretexts. Between 1945 and 1958 alone, Russia's rural population declined by 23.5 per cent. Finally, they wrote countless complaints or petitions to the authorities and disregarded many of the authorities' appeals and instructions.[7]

How many victims?

One of the most complex and controversial problems in the history of Soviet repression is in establishing the number of victims, their social status, ethnic allegiance and so forth – as well as giving an account of the GULag inmates' resistance to the regime. Contradictory figures have been advanced for the number of those executed, arrested and sentenced to deprivation of liberty; this is partly because there is no agreement on the best method of counting them. Such a methodology could of course be drawn up, but this is made difficult by the political situation and the inability to check the various figures advanced against archival documents.

On 1 February 1954 R. Rudenko, the procurator general, S. Kruglov, minister of Interior, and K. Gorshenin, minister of Justice, presented a memorandum to Khrushchev – a five-page typescript that gave the following figures for the OGPU collegium, NKVD *troiki*, its Special Board, the Military Collegium of the Supreme Court, and military tribunals for the years 1921–53:

convictions   3,777,380
of these sentenced to:

                              death   642,980
          detention in camps and prisons 2,369,220
                              exile   765,180[8]

This calculation left out extra-judicial arrests and shootings
carried out by the Cheka in 1918–21, an omission due to the
post-Stalin leadership's desire to legitimate itself by idealizing
the Lenin era.

In February 1963 a commission appointed by the Party Presidium, consisting of N. Shvernik, A. Shelepin, Z. Serdiuk, R.
Rudenko, N. Mironov and V. Semichastny, presented a final report,
10 pages long, on the victims of repression, which gave the
following figures:

1935–40:	arrested	1,683,671
	of whom shot	687,903
1941–52:	arrested	1,076,563
	of whom shot	4,464[9]

Clearly these data do not corroborate the earlier ones. The figure
for those put to death in the late 1930s is higher than that given
in the 1954 document for the *whole* period 1921–53.

I tried to locate in the Security Services Archive (TsA FSB) the
calculations by region, carried out by the KGB on 16 June 1988,
for the number of people arrested and convicted by extra-judicial
organs (*troiki, dvoiki* and so on). The total figures are:

1918–53:	arrested	4,308,487
	of whom shot	835,194[10]

These figures cover only those persons for whom the KGB
was willing to take responsibility. But of course there were other
courts and tribunals, as well as unrecorded deaths in camps and
prisons . . .

Take the case of the *Indigirka*, a steamer which sank in the Sea
of Okhotsk in December 1939. Of the eight hundred on board
who drowned, most were prisoners. Yet they are not included in

any statistics of prison deaths, and the fact that they perished did not become known until fifty years later.[11] No doubt other such cases will come to light in time. For this reason one can only speak of *approximate* figures for the victims of Stalin's repressions, and one should not assume that those put into circulation by V.N. Zemskov, in co-operation with two Western "revisionist" historians, in 1993 are more than what the authors claim, a "first approach".[12]

Studies of this melancholy subject that have appeared in Russia over the last decade give various figures for different periods. This makes it very hard to arrive at a total score. From 1928 to 1937 inclusive, about 7.9 million individuals died in the famine and in places of detention. In 1939 alone at least 525,000 died in prisons and camps. The same source gives some financial data as well. In 1937, 26.4 million roubles' worth of cash and valuables was confiscated from individuals under arrest or in detention; and a credit line in the amount of 27.2 million roubles was opened for the maintenance of those in captivity – so that, broadly speaking, these people were being kept from their own confiscated resources.[13]

V.N. Zemskov is one of the most prolific Russian writers on the GULag and special settlers. His articles are based mainly on an analysis of official documents such as reports compiled by the security police, and subordinate officials of the punitive organs, for their political chiefs. For this reason V.P. Popov takes the view that their reliability is doubtful. He argues that the security police officials' figures were those for the *capacity* of the various installations rather than for the actual number of detainees they held. He worked out that the number of people arrested for "counter-revolution" was 4.1 million, not the 3.8 million given by Zemskov.[14] Despite these objections Zemskov continued to hold that the number of people sentenced for political offences was over 3 but under 4 million. Of these 1,344,923 had been convicted in 1937–8, of whom 681,692, or 50.7 per cent, had been shot.[15]

The years 1937–8 are generally regarded as the climax of the terror on account of the large number of people arrested and executed.[16] What this meant in practice is best described on the basis of the records left by the extra-judicial *troika* that operated in the Tatar ASSR, which I have been able to go through. It comprised the secretary of the Party *obkom*, the republic's commissar of Interior, and a special procurator. Its materials for 1935–6 show that over one thousand residents of Tatarstan were arrested and convicted in each of these two years, but so far as I have been able to discover, none of them was sentenced to death. This practice began in August 1937, and was the result of an order from Stalin and Yezhov to commence an operation "to repress former kulaks, active anti-Soviet elements and criminals", which was entrusted to such *troiki*, whose powers and membership were confirmed by the CC. They were told to divide the people who were to be repressed into two categories: 1) those to be shot, and 2) those to be sent to a forced-labour camp for eight to ten years. In addition an instruction (*raznoriadka*) was sent to each republic or province giving the *number* of individuals who were to be shot or sentenced to deprivation of liberty. In the case of the Tatar ASSR, 500 were to be shot and 1500 detained; in Leningrad province the figures were 4000 and 10,000; in Moscow 5000 and 30,000; and so on. The troikas kept to an abbreviated, simplified procedure, and passed verdicts in the absence of the accused, let alone any defence counsel.[17] Details of the "work" accomplished by the team in Tatarstan from August to December 1937 are given in Appendix A.

These figures show that peaks of cruelty were reached in August–September and December 1937. Most of those convicted – 60 per cent of them peasants – were accused of harbouring sympathy for Trotsky, Sultan-Galiev and Tukhachevsky, or else of doubting "the stability of Soviet power"; they were all dubbed "enemies of the people".[18] In the following year, 1938, the Tatarstan *troika* sentenced 627 people to be shot, mainly for "espionage". As well as Russians, Ukrainians and Tatars they included Finns, Jews, Chinese, and people who had either been born abroad or had relatives outside the USSR. Among the 212 people put to death in Kazan' between January and June 1938, 94 were alleged to have spied for Poland, 14 for Romania, 11 for Finland, 6 for Germany, and 4 for Estonia.[19] Their execution was linked to the NKVD's orders to repress political emigrés; for it was then that Béla Kun and eleven other commissars of the 1919 Hungarian Soviet republic were executed, along with leaders of the Polish Communist party, 113 Comintern officials, and a large number of foreign specialists who had taken up employment in the USSR.[20]

Mass repression had been a feature of the Soviet scene since February 1918, when extra-judicial organs and procedures were instituted. In December of that year came the trial of the Left SRs, the first in a long series of quasi-legal proceedings, some public and others secret, of the Bolsheviks' political opponents and then of members of the ruling Party itself who were considered objectionable by the Stalin regime. The "show trials" reached their climax in the late 1930s, when the accused were charged with fantastic crimes that even the prosecution knew they had not committed. The first move came after the assassination on 1 December 1934 of S.M. Kirov, the Party's leading man in Leningrad. This was followed by an edict ordering the use of accelerated procedure and the immediate execution of "politicals" and alleged spies. It is still open to debate whether Kirov's death was engineered by G.G. Yagoda, head of the NKVD at that time, on Stalin's order, or whether the assassin, Leonid Nikolaev, acted on his own, either from a desire for revenge (the story goes that Kirov had an affair with his wife) or because his mind had become unhinged. Whichever version is true, it is clear that Stalin utilized Kirov's assassination to tighten the screw of repression. Kirov's murder led to five trials in Leningrad, as a result of which seventeen defendants were shot and seventy-six jailed; over one thousand people were exiled from the city, most of whom were supporters of Zinov'ev, then in disfavour and soon also to be shot.[21] There is no confirmation of the hypothesis that Kirov was Stalin's rival. Like others in the dictator's entourage, he behaved with extreme cruelty, as is shown by his brutal suppression of the Astrakhan' insurrection in 1919 or by his role in the construction by forced labour of the White Sea-Baltic canal.[22]

The orgy of terror that began in August 1937 was connected with the decisions taken at the CC plenum held in February–March of that year, with Stalin's desire to renew the ruling élite, and the need for slave labour to solve the serious economic problems facing the country. A climate of fear was created in which people were brought to see enemies everywhere and to denounce them.

Estimates of the total number of victims are continuing to rise. To the "politicals" sentenced under Article 58 of the penal code, one may add common-law offenders, victims' wives (who were also liable to arrest), the ethnic groups that were deported *en masse*, and repatriated Soviet prisoners of war – to name only the principal categories; apart from all these groups, there were those who perished during collectivization or died of starvation during the two famines of 1932–3 and 1946–7. According to A.N. Yakovlev, chairman of President Yeltsin's commission on the rehabilitation of victims of political repression, between 1918 and 1956 the Soviet authorities shot or destroyed over 15 million citizens in prisons and camps; between 1923 and 1953 some 42.5 million people passed through such installations. Yakovlev added, half-jocularly, that if one multiplied this figure by three to account for family members, under the Communists, half the population was "sitting" in jail while the others were either guarding them or about to join them.[23]

To arrive at a complete balance-sheet, one would also have to include the political prisoners of the post-Stalin era, for the last of their camps, Perm-35, was not officially closed until 1991. Article 58 of the penal code, of unhappy memory, which came into force in 1926, was replaced in the new code of 1960 by Article 70, covering "anti-Soviet propaganda and agitation". It served as the legal basis for the despatch of dissidents to camps in Mordovia, Perm' or Chistopol', in which hundreds died,[24] or to psychiatric hospitals; some died or were killed in confinement.

The GULag

A fair number of documentary collections, memoirs and studies have now appeared on the GULag. To the well-known works by Solzhenitsyn, Ginzburg, Shalamov and Razgon, one may add those conveniently listed in a 1995 bibliography compiled by the civic organization "Memorial".[25] The most important collections are a four-volume work on settlers (deportees) in Western Siberia, life in the GULag during the Second World War (studied in the West by Edwin Bacon), and in Karelia.[26] Historians have begun to move away from depiction of the horrors to an analysis of the GULag's place in the totalitarian system, the organization of surveillance, and the various types of labour performed by the inmates.

The idea that the camps should be economically self-sufficient originated in 1932 with N.A. Frenkel', head of Belomorstroi (the organization responsible for building the White Sea–Baltic canal). Prisoners worked without pay on the construction of numerous canals, railway lines, towns such as Noril'sk, Magadan, Vorkuta, Cheliabinsk-40 and Tomsk-7 (the latter two "secret" towns!), Stalin's reserve military headquarters at Kuibyshev (1941), atomic facilities, uranium and gold mining, timber-felling and so on. In 1940, NKVD enterprises produced 46.5 per cent of the nickel, 76 per cent of the tin, 40 per cent of the cobalt, 60 per cent of the gold, and 25.3 per cent of the timber in the country.[27] In the camps for top-flight scientists and engineers, the so-called *sharagi*, one could find such famous figures as the aircraft designers A.N. Tupolev and V.P. Petliakov, or the man who built the first Soviet rockets, S.P. Korolev. These scientists of world repute toiled for a ration only a little higher than the normal one: professors were entitled to forty grams of butter, and engineers twenty grams, with black bread in their canteens. Commenting on this horrendous distortion of socialist economics, A.D. Sakharov noted that "This barbarism was part of the wasteful extensive econonomy of that era and had far-reaching effects in that it destroyed the country's human potential."[28]

It has since become known that in 1937, NKVD personnel, including internal security forces, numbered 270,730 men; by 1939 the figure had risen to 365,839. GULag guards were ill-educated and behaved aggressively toward prisoners. The latter were far from passive and, especially after the Second World War, frequently put up organized resistance. Armed uprisings broke out at Arzamas-16 in 1947, Ukhta in 1951, Ekibastuz in 1952, Noril'sk in 1953, the Steplag (Kazakhstan) in 1954, and Taishet in 1956. This aspect of the GULag still awaits its historian;[29] perhaps on account of the archives' make-up, far more attention has been paid to the machinery of repression.

The security chiefs

Beria's role, and the degree to which he deserves to be rehabilitated, were first explored in post-Soviet Russia by B. Starkov and

O. Khlevniuk. Starkov credited Beria with plans for far-reaching reforms after Stalin's death; he is said to have tried to reduce the size of the GULag and to shift decision-making power from Party to state institutions. Khlevniuk holds that, "whatever may be said of Beria as reformer, some reappraisal of Beria is essential". Amy Knight, his American biographer, also sees him as a pragmatist, "a policeman turned liberal" in the manner of Andropov.[30]

However much evidence there may be to support such claims, one must stress that Beria and his associates were guilty of grave crimes against humanity, for which they were not tried (as were the Nazi war criminals at Nuremberg), but instead for political offences. The charges were not supported by legally valid evidence. The proceedings were conducted in the Stalinist spirit and included the ritual charge that Beria had been an "English spy"!

As for Yagoda and Yezhov, both were among Stalin's victims. On 4 February 1988 the USSR Supreme Court rehabilitated Bukharin, Rykov and the others convicted on 12 March 1938 at the end of the third great show trial, but did not include Yagoda. Fifty years later the Russian procuracy had no trouble in establishing that the evidence given by the accused at this trial had been falsified, that they had been tortured, and that in 1939–40 their investigators had themselves been convicted of abusing their powers. It was also ascertained that none of the accused had been in contact with foreign espionage services, or involved in terrorist acts, as had been alleged; that Gor'ky, Menzhinsky and Kuibyshev had died a natural death, as had Gor'ky's son, M.A. Peshkov.[31] So in that case Yagoda should have been rehabilitated as well. After all, if he had not committed the crimes which he was charged with in 1938, these charges should have been legally voided and he should have been re-tried posthumously for all his *other* crimes, and be refused rehabilitation on these grounds. But this was not done, perhaps because it would have meant initiating a host of other proceedings, which it was not in the Yeltsin regime's interest to do. Maybe it was also thought that offences committed so long ago were no longer justiciable. But there is no more reason to extend the period of prescription in the cases of Yezhov, Beria and their underlings than there is in respect of Nazis accused of crimes against humanity.

Rehabilitation

The rehabilitation of those repressed under Stalin began in 1954, but was more or less halted after Khrushchev's fall. Under Gorbachev, in 1987, the commission headed by Yakovlev was set up, but it has yet to complete its work. In 1990 Gorbachev decreed the rehabilitation of all those sentenced by extra-judicial organs; later Yeltsin did so for the Kronstadt mutineers of 1921 and for the insurgent peasants (1992, 1994). The commission rehabilitated almost all those involved in the four main Moscow show trials of 1936–8, and discovered that sixty other trials had been held in Moscow alone during the 1930s. In supplying more precise data on the number of victims, the "White Books" published in various cities and regions are useful; these contain lists of names of those repressed.

The RSFSR law "On the Rehabilitation of the Victims of Political Repressions" of 18 October 1991 does not do much to clarify the situation. One article states that persons who committed offences against the judicial order do not qualify for rehabilitation.[32] But what juridical order does the law-giver have in mind? The Soviet state was no *Rechtsstaat* and officials who committed crimes against humanity during the Soviet era were acting in accordance with the laws. It was the whole system of "socialist legality" that made their crimes possible and, so, is to be blamed for them. The legal responsibility for acts of terror committed under this system rests with each individual who took part in them, to a varying degree according to the gravity of his offence and the position held in the power hierarchy. Juridically, rehabilitation is an unsatisfactory measure because it does not condemn the system as such, but simply recognizes its destructive effects, exposes its secrets and shows how it can be reformed. It leaves a legal vacuum. This could be filled only if judgment were passed on the criminal regime itself and on those who did its bidding. Only then could it become possible to establish which decision-makers and executants of policy deserve to be rehabilitated, that is, acquitted, and which do not. In principle, one would need a Soviet version of the Nuremberg trial. Until such a court meets and passes judgment, we shall not have justice, and efforts will continue to rehabilitate the executioners and the GULag too.

On 28 April 1998 *Izvestiia* reported that a judicial review had been conducted four years earlier into the case against General V.S. Abakumov, head of the MGB from 1946 to 1951, who was shot in December 1954 during Khrushchev's purge of the security apparatus after Beria's fall. It was found that he had not been, as charged, a traitor guilty of committing terrorist acts against Soviet leaders, and so the sentence was retroactively amended from death to twenty-five years' jail. In this way Abakumov was turned from a state criminal into a mere official guilty of an administrative offence. But this posthumous reduction of sentence did not make his crimes any less serious. He was among those responsible for staging the "Leningrad affair" in 1949, as well as for the death of Raoul Wallenberg and thousands of others who had done no wrong.

This judicial review served as a precedent for a revision of the charges laid against other mass murderers. On 4 June 1998 the Military Collegium of the Russian Supreme Court initiated a review into the case against Yezhov, the NKVD chief shot in Moscow on 4 February 1940 for treason, sabotage, espionage and so forth. The legal basis for this review was the RSFSR rehabilitation law of 1991, which allowed a victim's surviving relatives to ask for a case to be re-opened – as did Yezhov's adopted daughter, Natalia Khaintina, who now lives near Magadan. An examination of the twelve bulging volumes of "Case no. 510" in the security services archive showed, as one might expect, that Yezhov had neither been a Polish and German agent nor engaged in subversive activities with a view to effecting a *coup*, as the indictment stated. Among these documents is a record of the search carried out at the time of his arrest in Yezhov's office, where the investigators discovered a parcel containing the very revolver (a Colt) and bullets used to kill Zinov'ev, Kamenev and I.N. Smirnov. Yezhov admitted everything demanded of him, even to having been a pederast. The fresh investigation by the Russian procuracy comprises an entire volume; among the documents it contains is an NKVD memorandum showing that in 1937 one in three of those arrested were shot, and in 1938 one in two (cf. the Tatarstan data in Appendix A). This was why the Military Collegium refused to rehabilitate Yezhov, although it did annul the charge of espionage.[33]

In May 1998 there were reports in the press that Beria, too, might be rehabilitated.[34] This did not come to pass, but there is a persistent tendency in Russia to gild the past and to try to find something good in the deeds of even the most odious Bolshevik leaders. The composer T. Khrennikov recalls meeting Stalin and finding him "intelligent"; the historian A.N. Yakovlev describes Beria as "a very charming man".[35] Meanwhile the major who was detailed to guard Beria after his arrest on 9 July 1953, M. Gurevich, has published memoirs with details of his ultimate fate: Gurevich himself fired the second shot, after General Pavel Batitsky; Beria's body was cremated, whereupon Gurevich gathered his ashes and strewed them into the air with the aid of a powerful fan.[36]

Naturally all this is bound to engender alarm among former prisoners, dissidents, and other citizens who do not harbour any nostalgia for Stalinism. As early as 1994 Sergei Grigoriants, a former political detainee, sent an open letter to the Procurator General stating that he had no wish to receive a rehabilitation voucher such as had been issued to Pavel Sudoplatov, a former KGB general who served a ten-year term for his crimes but in 1992 was recategorized as a victim of political repression.[37] Another ex-*zek*, the writer Lev Razgon, who celebrated his ninetieth birthday on 1 April 1998, gave an interview to a newspaper correspondent in which he said bitterly that Russians were starting to forget what had happened in 1937. He noted that former murderers like Abakumov were being partially rehabilitated under pressure from their relatives, anxious for a higher pension – this at a time when the Duma was refusing to increase the meagre compensation paid to former political prisoners! Razgon alleged that many people in positions of influence had either themselves been involved in crimes against humanity or were related to such persons, and so the authorities were not interested in re-establishing historical truth.[38]

Rather unexpectedly, this point of view was echoed by a high-ranking Chekist, Anatolyi Safonov, who in 1994–7 was first deputy director of the Federal Security Service. When asked by an *Obshchaia gazeta* reporter whether there could be another 1937, he replied that in the early 1990s he had thought such an eventuality impossible but now, "ten years later, I am not so certain."[39] In another interview published in the same paper in November 1999, Russia's senior military procurator, Yuryi Demin, stated that the number of people convicted of political offences by military tribunals alone had been 1.5 million. Over the past eight years, since the 1991 rehabilitation law, the cases of 86,000 individuals had been reviewed; of these, 57,000 had been rehabilitated whereas another 20,000 had been refused rehabilitation, including Yezhov, Beria, M.P. Frinovsky and Abakumov. He added that at this rate the job would take at least another twenty years.[40]

This juridical muddle of course does not ease the task of would-be scholarly biographers of the NKVD chiefs and other Soviet leaders involved in these crimes. There have, however, been a number of books and articles about Yagoda, Yezhov, Beria and Vyshinsky, the procurators who served in Leningrad/St Petersburg, and Soviet jurisprudence as the dictator's political instrument.[41]

Victims: the military

Over the past decade a lot of literature has come out on the victims of Soviet repressive policies: military personnel, Party and soviet officials, writers and scholars, as well as people from various social backgrounds. Even high-ups were not safe: the wives of Molotov and Kaganovich were arrested and detained, as was Stalin's secretary Poskrebyshev. Of 267 individuals who served as members of the Party's Central Committee between 1917 and 1934, no less than 197 perished.

Let us look a little more closely at the repression unleashed against the armed forces. In the early 1930s some 10,000 officers were discharged who had served under the tsar, of whom over 3000 were arrested. The total number of ex-tsarist officers thrown out of the army between 1924 and 1936 was 47,000. Then it was the turn of the victorious Reds of the civil-war era. During the year beginning on 1 March 1937, over 17,000 men were discharged on political grounds. When officers' ranks, from colonel to marshal, were reintroduced in November 1935 there were 837 such appointments, but of these individuals no less than 720 were repressed. They included 3 out of 5 marshals (Tukhachevsky, Yegorov, Bliukher); 3 out of 5 first-rank army commanders (Yakir, Uborevich, Belov); all 10 second-rank commanders; all 16 first-

or second-rank political commissars (including Gamarnik and Grishin, who committed suicide); 25 out of 28 corps commissars; 58 out of 64 divisional commisars; and 401 out of 456 colonels. Or take the Military Council set up in 1934–5 under the USSR Defence commissariat. Of its 85 members 68 were soon shot; one was locked up in jail and forgotten until he died there. March 1938 saw the establishment of a Main Military Council of the Red Army; of its 13 members 7 had been shot by 1941. During the Great Patriotic War the army lost 180 senior commanders (from divisional commander upwards) to enemy action, a figure that should be set beside the 500-plus senior officers (brigade commander to marshal) who were arrested on false denunciations in 1937–8, of whom 29 died while under arrest and 412 were shot.[42]

A number of proscription lists have survived, bearing Stalin's and Molotov's signatures, which authorized investigators to beat and torture prisoners under interrogation. There is also the well-known CC resolution of 10 January 1939, signed by Stalin, confirming that torture had been authorized since 1937 and laying down that "physical pressure should still be used obligatorily, as an exception applicable to known and obstinate enemies of the people, as a method both justifiable and appropriate".[43] Razgon, who was tortured several times, recalls in his memoirs appalling details of the methods applied.[44]

Historians who work on investigation records from this era face several "technical" problems, the chief one being to establish whether a document is genuine and reliable. There is still a debate going on as to whether the denunciation of Marshal Yegorov, concocted in January 1938 and signed "G. Zhukov", was really written by the famous marshal-to-be or by someone else with the same name.[45] In one's research one encounters a mass of absurd charges levelled against innocent people, which cannot be taken at face value since they bear witness only to the investigators' lamentable ignorance and complete indifference to their victims' fate. Let me give just one example. In 1938 an officer named Landsberg was arrested. From his service record the investigators discovered that he had been a student at the Charles University in Prague from 1922 to 1927. That automatically made him a "spy". To avoid being beaten, Landsberg confessed to "espionage activity" and stated that he had been recruited by Palacký (the great Czech scholar who died in 1876) and that his co-conspirators were Havliček-Borovský (a writer, d. 1856) and Götz von Berlichingen (d. 1562). These historical anachronisms were of absolutely no concern to his investigators or to the NKVD *troika* for Leningrad province, who without further ado sentenced Landsberg to be shot. Conquest tells of the Politburo member Eikhe, who in 1938 confessed to belonging to a criminal organization called "the Central Committee of the AUCP(b)"[46] – and he was not far from the truth!

In June 1997, several articles by historians and publicists appeared in connection with the sixtieth anniversary of Stalin's butchery of Marshal Tukhachevsky and other senior officers. Various explanations were adduced as to the reasons for this action and its consequences. There was some argument as to whether the Red Army leaders had indeed plotted to overthrow Stalin's regime or whether the whole case had been thought up by the dictator in order to get rid of a group of professional men who exercised authority and enjoyed high prestige. Some writers such as E.G. Plimak and V.S. Antonov take the view that there was no military conspiracy. They think that the affair was a provocation engineered by the Soviet intelligence service, which was manipulated by its German counterpart for its own purposes. Yu.N. Zhukov on the other hand maintains that Tukhachevsky had something to do with a plot in the early 1930s to remove Stalin and his clique.[47] Yet other writers have either argued that the repressions were justified ("V. Suvorov") or else pointed out that their consequences have yet to be studied adequately.[48]

Less interest has been taken in the 1990s than before in what happened during the Terror to officials in the Party and state apparatus or the Komsomol. So long as the CPSU held a monopoly of power, this aspect of the topic received exaggerated attention in order to show that Communists, too, had suffered from the "cult of the individual" and so, like the common people, deserved to be regarded as victims of Stalin's regime. However, this image of the Communist as martyr did not stick because, before they were shot, most of these functionaries had behaved just as brutally as those who were now executing them. For this reason the monographs and documentary collections published over the last decade have been less concerned with these victims' sufferings than with the reasons for the Terror and the way it was put into effect.[49]

Other victims

Meanwhile other writers have been endeavouring to trace the tragic fate of intellectuals who fell victim to Stalinist arbitrariness. Not only have survivors published memoirs, but documents too have come to light – this, despite the destruction of many that were pertinent. In 1989–90 the KGB burned 105 volumes of its "operational reports" on Solzhenitsyn (whom it referred to by the code name "Spider") and 550 volumes about Sakharov (known as "Ascetic").[50] Among the volumes of memoirs one may single out those by Nadezhda Mandelshtam and Petr Grigorenko.[51] A good deal has appeared on the Jewish Anti-fascist Committee[52] and there are also studies of specific groups of scholars such as historians and Slavists.[53]

It is still not clear whether Maxim Gor'ky died of natural causes on 18 June 1936 or whether he was poisoned. He had been under Cheka surveillance since 1922. His body was cremated and the urn with his ashes placed in the Kremlin wall. He had asked to be buried in Novodevichii cemetery next to his son, but when his first wife, Yekaterina Peshkova, asked Stalin to let her have at least a handful of ashes for this purpose her request was turned down.[54] By this time letters of denunciation had virtually become a literary genre among the Party faithful, and writers were obliged to declare publicly that they approved of the verdicts in the show trials. This was a means of enforcing uniformity of thought. In the circumstances it is especially significant that Boris Pasternak refused to make such a statement, as did the Siberian poet Pavel Vasil'ev who, like Osip Mandelshtam, had written anti-Stalin verse. Another resister was the physicist Leo Landau, the future Nobel laureate, who in April 1938 signed a manifesto critical of the Soviet dictator. Several scholars and scientists also submitted appeals on behalf of colleagues who had been arrested, but as a rule did not receive any reply; given the situation at the time, such interventions were acts of considerable courage. According to V. Shentalinsky, about two thousand writers alone were repressed during the Soviet era, of whom some three quarters perished in detention. He makes the point that leading officials of the Union of Soviet Writers – Stavsky, Gronsky, Pavlenko, Aleksandr Fadeev – played a key role in determining their fate.[55]

Confessions

Why did so many of those accused in the show trials of the 1930s confess so abjectly to crimes they clearly had not committed? A number of writers have tried to explain their behaviour. Among the reasons commonly advanced are: the effects of torture; psychological pressure; the wish to incriminate as many "enemies of the people" as possible in order to show how absurd the whole proceedings were; and Arthur Koestler's well-known version: in his *Darkness at Noon*, some Bolsheviks confessed because they deemed it their last duty to help their Party.[56] This problem still awaits its historian, as does that of assessing the degree to which their confessions were credible.

In the late 1950s and early 1960s I met a number of former inmates of the GULag. When I asked them why they had confessed under interrogation they replied laconically, and with some irritation: "We wanted to survive . . ." Valentin N. Astrov, a Party member since March 1917, and in the 1920s a member of the editorial boards of *Pravda* and the periodical *Bol'shevik*, was arrested in 1933 and sent into exile. In 1936 he was arrested for a second time in connection with the case mounted against Bukharin, Rykov and the other "Rightists". He was not tortured but his interrogator suggested he should give evidence against Bukharin. He duly did so, stating that Bukharin had been involved in terrorist activity. Next year, in 1937, he was freed on Stalin's personal order. Years later he was still unable to explain convincingly why he had acted in such a cowardly fashion. According to Stephen Cohen, Astrov was the only member of Bukharin's "school" to survive.[57]

After Stalin

State terrorism became less intense once Stalin was no more, but it did not come to an end. Khrushchev freed most GULag inmates, and the majority of camps were closed down, but some of them continued to exist until the late 1980s. A lot of Russians today ask themselves why this terrible bloodbath had to happen. Why did so many million innocent people perish? Briefly, because they were out of place in a totalitarian state – and there is not much of a place for them in present-day Russia either.

A joke recently went the rounds. In 1914 the gendarme Sidorov catches a member of the Bolshevik underground, Ivanov, and claps him in jail. In 1917 the revolutionary Ivanov is freed, joins the Cheka, and imprisons the ex-gendarme Sidorov. Twenty years later Ivanov is unmasked as an "enemy of the people" and sent to Kolyma. Twenty years pass. Both Ivanov and Sidorov are rehabilitated and emerge from the camps. Another twenty years. The Old Bolshevik Ivanov no longer receives his miserable pension and earns his living by selling hot sausages outside the Moscow metro station, "Square of the Revolution". Sidorov passes by, recognizes him and says: "Hey, Ivanov, didn't I tell you not to sell sausages when the Father-Tsar was still on his throne?"[58]

Unfortunately many Russians today shrug their shoulders and say: "Well, they shot millions of people, then they rehabilitated them because they had done no wrong, and that's all there is to it". However, one cannot just close the books so simply. Each year the 30th October is set aside as an official day of remembrance for victims of political repression. There are not too many such people left, even including relatives who shared their ordeal: about two thousand in Moscow, six hundred in Kazan'. They are all aged over sixty. Few people lay flowers on the memorials to the victims in cemeteries, or go to Moscow's Lubianka Square, where in 1988 a stone was brought from Solovetsky Island to serve as a symbol of remembrance. Those who turn up are mostly the survivors themselves – so long as they can make it. Last year I went to such a gathering in Kazan'. An official came along, uttered a few sympathetic words, then a band struck up and each of us was given a polyethylene bag of tinned food and biscuit. *Izvestiia* marked Remembrance Day with an article headed "Memorials No One Goes To".

7
World War II

The Great Patriotic War, as the Soviet–German war is still called in our country, was treated by Soviet historians in isolation from what was going on in other theatres. Thousands of books and articles, memoirs and documentary volumes were produced to show that the USSR played the decisive role in the defeat of fascism. Emphasis was laid on the fact that we suffered the heaviest losses and that operations on the eastern front were on a greater scale than those elsewhere.

Now that over half a century has elapsed since VE-Day, it seems extraordinary that there should have been such a fuss in the mid-1960s over the publication of A.M. Nekrich's book *22 June 1941*,[1] in which he discussed Stalin's errors that led to the initial Soviet setbacks. To the ideological watchdogs, this was heresy since it undermined confidence in the current Party leadership too. Nekrich was expelled from the CPSU and soon had to emigrate. Few people today bother to read the memoirs (often expurgated by the censor) written by leading Soviet commanders. It is absurd that in successive editions of the official six-volume history of the war, first Khrushchev and then Zhukov were credited with the victory at Stalingrad.[2]

Oblivion has thankfully likewise descended on Leonid Brezhnev's propagandist memoir *The Little Land*, in which some engagements of limited scope on the Taman' peninsula were represented as decisive battles just because the current Soviet leader had played a part in those actions. In 1973–82 the earlier official history of the war was replaced by a new one, in twelve volumes. In it

Stalin re-emerged as the principal architect of victory. Then on 13 August 1987 the Politburo decided to prepare yet another version, this time in ten volumes, to be called "The Great Patriotic War of the Soviet *People*". The work was entrusted to a team in the Institute of Military History, which came under the Defence ministry, but the enterprise collapsed in uproar, for when the draft of the first section was discussed, several generals accused the authors of lack of patriotism, slandering the Party, white-washing the Wehrmacht, and so on. Volkogonov lost his post as the institute's director and not a single volume has yet seen the light.[3]

Soviet historiography of the war has been fairly well studied.[4] The first casualty of any war is truth, and to arrive at an under-standing of what really went on in those tragic years will take a long time. Yet a start has been made. When the fiftieth anniver-sary of VE-Day was celebrated on 9 May 1995, the tone was rather pessimistic. The dominant emotion was not pride but sorrow. Relatives of those who had been killed went to place flowers on the graves of fallen soldiers. Parades were held, attended by nos-talgic veterans, but many other ex-servicemen who had suffered poverty and discrimination after the war wondered what they had fought for. Owing to official neglect over the years the bodies of many soldiers who fell in battle in marshy land near Smolensk and Novgorod still lie unburied. Of the 2,757,127 soldiers buried in military cemeteries, only 1,467,416 have been identified by name.[5]

Casualty figures

The figures given for the total toll during the war have varied over the years. Stalin stated that it had cost 7 million lives; Khrushchev raised the figure to 20 million; and the calculations of the demographer Yu.A. Poliakov have shown that it was really somewhere between 26 and 28 million.[6] Since he wrote in 1995, the data have been refined. In 1998 the Russian General Staff put the army's "irrecuperable losses" in 1941–5 at 11,944,100. Of these 6,885,000 were killed, died of wounds or disease or in accidents, or else committed suicide. Missing or captured accounted for 4,559,000 (according to other data 5.7 million). In addition about half a million reservists lost their lives on the way to the front, or from other causes, and were not included in the figure for the active forces. Since total fatalities were given as 26.6 million, civilian losses (killed or died) were 17.4 million – considerably more than those of the armed forces.

Some other information has also become available recently. When the war ended, the armed forces had 12,839,800 men on the rolls, of whom 11,390,000 were on active duty, 1,046,000 in hospital, and 400,000 in "labour armies" or other civilian formations under the authority of the Defence commissariat. The number of war invalids was 2,576,000, and of servicemen sentenced for various offences 994,000. Of the latter, at least 157,593 were shot by military tribunals alone; of the remainder roughly half were sent to penal units and to places of detention respectively; 212,000 deserters remained unaccounted for. It is now known that in the initial fighting, from June to November 1941 inclusive, the daily loss rate was 24,000 (17,000 killed, *ca.* 7000 wounded), and at the war's end (January 1944 to May 1945) 20,000 (5200 killed, 14,800 wounded).[7] Estimates of the toll are continuing to rise. V.G. Pervyshin has now put the figure for total population losses at 38,794,000, of whom about 17,774,000 were members of the armed forces.[8]

The published documents reveal other equally terrible and grievous facts about the impact of the war. During the siege of Leningrad, in the twelve-month period between 1 July 1941 and 1 July 1942, hunger and disease took the lives of 1,093,695 civilians.[9] But the siege went on for another year and a half! For a long time we were told that Leningrad's total death toll was less than a million, but now we have the above data, compiled by the city's Burial Trust. Other historians have come up with a lower figure than either the Burial Trust or that officially announced earlier. V.M. Koval'chuk calculates that after evacuation and call-up the besieged city had a population of about 1,329,000 (as against 3.3 million before the war), of whom some 700,000 died.[10] The militia counted 2057 cases of cannibalism and necrophagy. Historians discovered plans for "Operation D", whereby the city was mined and could be blown up if the local army commanders considered this necessary.[11]

Owing to the surprise nature and speed of the German attack, a large number of Soviet armed forces personnel were taken prisoner during the first few months. The figure has now been put at 3.8 million, of whom nearly half perished in German camps. On 16 August 1941 Stalin signed Order no. 270 prohibiting Soviet troops from surrendering on pain of execution. The fate of those prisoners who survived was tragic, for they were treated as a potential security risk and punished. At the end of 1944 a secret report stated that after "filtration", 354,592 servicemen had been freed from enemy captivity, or after being surrounded by enemy forces; of these, 249,416 were sent to the army, mainly to penal battalions, and 57,257 to forced-labour camps. In accordance with the Yalta agreement (11 February 1945) about two million Soviet ex-prisoners of war who did not want to return home were handed over by the Western allies to the Soviet authorities and either killed outright or sent to the GULag.

Such prisoners and members of their families remained politically suspect for many years thereafter. Right up to 1992, if one applied for a job or a place at a university, one had to answer the question: "Were you or any of your relatives in captivity, interned or on enemy-occupied territory?" This practice was not formally ended until 24 January 1995, when President Yeltsin issued a decree "on the restoration of the legal rights of Russian citizens who had been Soviet prisoners of war and civilians repatriated during and after the Great Patriotic War".[12]

June 1941

In the past decade Russian historians have dropped the propagandist approach, which stressed heroic achievements at the front, in favour of a critical examination of the circumstances that led to the outbreak of the Soviet–German war and the reasons for the heavy reverses suffered over the next few months. It has been agued that the USSR actually entered the war some two years *before* the German attack on 22 June 1941, by signing the Soviet–German non-aggression pact (23 August 1939) and then invading Poland on 17 September of that year;[13] this was followed by a joint parade of Soviet and German troops in Lwów, the Soviet attack on Finland on 30 November, the incorporation of the Baltic states, Bessarabia and northern Bukovina in the summer of 1940, and the supply of strategic war materials and foodstuffs by the USSR to Nazi Germany.[14]

Both Russian and Western historians have provided fresh information about the role of the surprise factor in the Wehrmacht's early successes. Several intelligence officers have written memoirs from which it is clear that their service at least was well-informed that invasion was imminent, but that Stalin (and Beria) did not trust their reports.[15] Marshal Zhukov maintained, in the draft of a speech for a CC plenum in 1956, which he could not deliver because the gathering was not held, that "there was no surprise attack by the Hitlerite forces. We knew the attack was coming but Stalin pretended it was a surprise in order to cover up his own mistakes". Later, when a censored version of his memoirs was published, the blame was shifted from Stalin to F.I. Golikov, the head of military intelligence, who submitted reports he received from agents in the field with critical comments alleging that they reflected the views of either the British or the Germans, that is, that their information was really "disinformation". There are documents showing that Stalin knew the Germans were already planning to attack a whole year before they did so.[16]

Generals who held senior positions in the military districts along the frontier have testified in their memoirs that the troops were not put on a state of alert to repel the invasion. It is also known that on 22 June 1941 Stalin conferred all day long, from 05.45 to 16.45 hours, with military and civilian leaders, and that this conference issued conflicting orders. The first directive called for resistance to the German attack but without crossing the border, the second for destruction of enemy forces wherever they were to be found. In between these two messages Stalin tried to come to terms with Hitler.[17]

In the last few years there has been a lively debate about the writings of V.B. Rezun, a Soviet intelligence officer who defected to Britain in 1978 and was thereupon sentenced to death *in absentia* by the Soviet authorities as a traitor. Under the pseudonym "V. Suvorov" he has endeavoured to show, in several popular books, that Stalin was preparing to attack the Germans on 6 July 1941 and that Hitler's invasion two weeks earlier was designed to forestall such a blow.[18] One of the first to disprove this version was Volkogonov; he was later followed by others, among them Gabriel

Gorodetsky, the Israeli historian, who has produced two fine studies of this issue.[19] Suvorov's books evoked tremendous public interest as they made it appear as though the whole of Soviet history in 1939–41 needed reassessment; and he has found quite a few supporters.[20]

Let us just note two points here: first, the arguments on both sides in this discussion rely on the same sources; and second, the German note to the Soviet Foreign Affairs ministry on 22 June asserted that "Bolshevik Moscow was about to stab Nazi Germany in the back", so that "the Führer has ordered the German armed forces to respond to this threat by all available means".[21] The two documents most frequently mentioned in this connection are Stalin's speech of 5 May 1941 to graduates of the military academies[22] and one entitled "Considerations on the Plan for Strategic Dislocation of the Soviet Armed Forces in the Event of War with Germany and her Allies", which was drawn up – but not signed – by top Soviet army commanders. These two sources were both mentioned by Marshal Zhukov in 1965 when he spoke to V.A. Anfilov, who had written a book on the outbreak of the war:[23]

> The idea of forestalling the German invasion was taken up by Timoshenko in connection with Stalin's 5 May speech . . . in which he said one should act in an offensive spirit. Concrete measures were proposed by A.M. Vasilevsky [then first deputy head of the Operational Department of the General Staff – A.L.], who on 15 May submitted a draft directive to me and the [Defence] commissar. However, we did not sign this document but decided to submit it first to Stalin. He went off the deep end when he was told of a [possible] blow against the German forces. "What's the matter with you, have you gone out of your minds, do you want to provoke the Germans?", he exclaimed angrily. We drew his attention to the situation that was developing on the Soviet border and to the ideas expressed in his speech of 5 May. Stalin snarled: "I said that in order to encourage those present, so that they should think of victory and not that the German army was unbeatable as papers were saying the world over" . . . Now I think it was

just as well that he didn't agree with us. Otherwise there could have been a catastrophe, given the state our forces were in.[24]

No doubt Zhukov was right. The Soviet leadership favoured an aggressive posture but at that moment it was not prepared for war with such a powerful adversary as the German Wehrmacht.[25] Stalin's intentions are thus debatable but of course we know what transpired: on 22 June German forces crossed into Soviet territory and millions of people were drawn into war. They had no time to wonder whether they were fighting and suffering in order to avoid a preventive blow or not . . .

New issues

Characteristically, Russian historians have recently taken up a number of novel problems, such as what character the war had once the victorious Red Army crossed the western border. Afanas'ev and V.L. Doroshenko point out that at this stage the conflict can no longer be described as a patriotic war, yet it was not a "war of liberation" either, since the USSR introduced a totalitarian regime in the countries it occupied rather than a democratic one – which, as Afanas'ev noted, was why Russia was not invited to send a delegation to the ceremonies marking the fiftieth anniversary of D-Day in Normandy in 1994.[26]

Among the other new topics addressed by Russian scholars over the last few years are: Lend–Lease, the Katyn massacre of Polish prisoners of war by the NKVD in 1940, and the fate of Axis prisoners or internees in the USSR. On the latter point, it has been established that by 1950, 3,168,109 prisoners had been repatriated to Germany, Japan, Hungary, Romania and Austria, but some were still kept back in detention.[27]

Historians in Russia have also begun to tackle the sensitive issue of war-time collaboration with the enemy, in the first instance those men who actually fought on the German side. Their numbers are variously estimated at between a quarter of a million and one and a half million.[28] For some historians they are traitors, for others victims of circumstance (at least up to a point), and for a third group anti-Stalinists.[29] Study of this topic is still in its infancy, and many works are too ideological in approach or else lack a proper documentary basis. But quite recently the "filtration records" compiled by SMERSH (Soviet counter-intelligence) officers during and after the war, when they interrogated Soviet ex-prisoners, former Vlasovites, and those who had served in the pro-Axis national legions, have been declassified and transferred from the former KGB archive to state repositories. Analysis of these materials enables one to draw a more comprehensive social and political portrait of the typical soldier in the ROA (Russian Liberation Army, the official designation of Vlasov's followers) or legionary.

One also needs to bear in mind that fascism posed a greater or lesser threat to the various Soviet nationalities. For Jews, Roma and Sinti it meant physical annihilation, but for the Slavic peoples "thinning out" and assimilation. Although the Stalinist regime did not exterminate the Jews it discriminated against them by pursuing anti-Semitic policies; it deported a number of Caucasian and Oriental peoples (Karachai, Balkar, Ingush, Chechens, Crimean Tatars, Meskhetians and Kalmyks) who were alleged to have helped the enemy occupation forces. This was to apply a concept of collective guilt and was itself a criminal act. It would be worthwhile trying to find out what the actual extent of collaboration was among each of the groups that were deported.

Our historians recognize that people were led to collaborate for a variety of reasons, but Poliakov's effort to distinguish between those who did so out of nationalism, class allegiance, or on other political grounds cannot be regarded as satisfactory.[30] After all it is fairly well known that General Vlasov and his associates were of worker or peasant stock and had been Stalinists prior to their capture. I recall a scholarly conference in the late 1960s in the Institute of Marxism–Leninism at which two historians, N.I. Makarov and L.M. Spirin, said that there had been a little over one million partisans, underground agents and members of resistance groups, and about the same number in the pro-German units, occupation police and other collaborationist bodies. In the circumstances that prevailed under Nazi rule it was certainly more dangerous to throw in one's lot with the partisans than to play along with the occupiers.

Balance sheet

We still do not have a scholarly account of the USSR's role in
World War II. Time is passing and there are ever fewer people
alive who took part in it. My students treat it as ancient history
and feel that its problems do not concern them. They ask me,
for instance, whether Russians will forget Victory Day, celebrated
on 9th May, just as they have forgotten the day when the war
with Napoleon ended, which after all was also called "Patriotic".
I tell them, hand on heart, that my generation will never forget . . .

I sympathize with the writer Viktor Astaf'ev, who after reading several generals' memoirs about the war said that he, as an
ex-soldier, must have been in a different conflict altogether. For
hardly anything has been written as yet about what the war was
like for ordinary soldiers – or for refugees, who were billeted in
many towns, including Kazan' where I was then living as a boy.
I remember the blackout, the constant hunger, and the fear of
being deported, a fate that might be meted out at any time to
relatives of alleged "enemies of the people".

Part III

Russia and the Wider World

8
The Nationalities Problem

During the Stalin era and after the official formula ran that "the USSR has finally solved the nationalities question inherited from pre-revolutionary times". Writers as well as historians had to hew to this ideological line. The satirists Il'f and Petrov, touring the United States in the 1930s, were asked by someone: "How is the Jewish problem being solved in the USSR?" They answered: "It doesn't have to be solved. We do have Jews but we don't have a problem."

The mythological nature of the Communist outlook was ruthlessly exposed in the late 1980s. In vain did Moscow appeal for the Soviet peoples to live in amity with one another. Instead there was an international free-for-all: pogroms of Meskhetian Turks in Uzbekistan and of Armenians in Azerbaijan; hostilities between the latter two republics over the Nagornyi Karabakh region. The peoples of the union republics experienced an upsurge of national consciousness which local élites turned to their own account, taking advantage of the weakening of the central power. The three Baltic republics annexed in 1940 struggled to regain their independence; there were popular demonstrations in Belarus, Ukraine and Moldavia; and a number of hitherto autonomous republics or regions strove to win more rights. All this led in 1991 to the collapse of the USSR, which turned out to be an artificial construct. Yet even after this the process of disintegration continued. More fighting broke out in and around Nagornyi Karabakh; Abkhazia and southern Ossetia tried to win their freedom from Georgia; and in the Russian Federation, Chechens called for independence while Tatars, Bashkirs and Yakuts (Sakha) strove to improve their political status. Historians were faced with the problem of analysing the reasons for these cataclysmic events.

From the works that appeared in the early 1990s it was clear that several different approaches were possible in studying the history of inter-ethnic relations in the Soviet period. One was to highlight the deportation of so many non-Russian peoples under Stalin.[1] These writers' aim was to document the criminal behaviour of the Soviet authorities in this era, so supplementing the work done by emigrés such as A. Nekrich and A. Avtorkhanov.[2] Under the aegis of the law of 26 April 1991 "On the Rehabilitation of the Repressed Peoples", publication began of the pertinent sources.[3] These volumes, especially those appearing in the provinces, laid stress on the atrocities that had occurred – most notably in a book published in Grozny, the Chechen capital, in 1994, during the first round of fighting in that republic, which described what had happened fifty years earlier in the village of Khaibakh as the Chechens were being deported: no fewer than three hundred inhabitants, elderly folk and children who could not move fast enough, were herded into a barn and burned to death.[4]

Deportations were nothing new: already in 1920 the Bolsheviks had resorted to this drastic measure in regard to Cossacks and "kulaks". But in the 1930s and 1940s it was applied much more widely: 15 entire nationalities and members of over 60 ethnic groups (Russians, Jews, Iranians, Greeks, Bulgarians, and so on) were affected. The total number of people seized and exiled to other parts of the country at this time was no less than 3.5 million. In October 1946 the "special settlements" (*spetsposeleniia*) run by the NKVD in Siberia, Kazakhstan, the Urals and Central Asia contained 2,463,940 exiles. Of these 655,764 were men, 829,084 women, and 979,182 children aged up to sixteen. Their ethnic background was very varied. Apart from Russian or Ukrainian peasants designated "kulaks", there were people from the Caucasus and Baltic regions, Crimean Tatars, Kalmyks, Germans, Koreans and others. Later they were joined by so-called "parasites" who had allegedly shown slackness on the job and were banished to the east to make them work harder. In February 1948 Khrushchev, then first Party secretary in Ukraine, had over two thousand such individuals exiled.[5] The tradition lived on after Stalin's death: in 1964 the poet Iosif Brodsky, a future Nobel Prize laureate, was exiled from Leningrad for "parasitism".

We now know in some detail how the deportation of the "punished peoples" (Nekrich) was carried out, what consequences it had, and how poorly the process of rehabilitation functioned: many exiles could not return to their former dwellings because in the interim these had been allocated to new immigrants.[6] Some interesting points emerge from a comparison of the published documents on the exile of the Karachai in 1943 with an unpublished memorandum to be found in the former KGB archive in the Lubianka. This operation, codenamed "Seagull", was carried out by the NKVD with the express sanction of Stalin and Beria, who put I.A. Serov and A.Z. Kobulov in charge of it. They had the assistance of M.A. Suslov, at that time secretary of the Party committee (*kraikom*) in the Stavropol' region. According to the 1937 census the Karachai autonomous district, which was situated within this territory, had a population of 94,030. The order was given for all the Karachai to be deported, including even Party and Komsomol members. The charge against them was the hackneyed one of aiding the German occupiers – this although 20,000 Karachai soldiers were serving in the Red Army at the time and only 3000 Karachai at the most could be said to have collaborated with the enemy. The deportees were allowed to take with them foodstuffs and personal possessions to the limit of 100 kg each but not more than 500 kg per family. The NKVD force consisted of 20,000 police troops and 7000 "operational workers". In the course of two days, 2–3 November 1943, 70,000 Karachai were loaded into railway waggons and despatched to various regions of Kazakhstan and Kirgizia. Serov's reports indicate that they offered no resistance; his men "captured" 6 automatic firearms, 100 rifles, 59 revolvers and 1500 swords, knives and so on. The district inhabited by the Karachai was divided up between two Russian regions, Stavropol' and Krasnodar, and the Georgian SSR. In 1957 the surviving Karachai, like most of the other deportees (except, notably, Crimean Tatars and Germans) were allowed to return and the Karachaev–Circassian autonomous region was re-established. By 1995, 23,024 Karachai had been issued with rehabilitation certificates.[7]

When one studies the history of the "punished peoples" one realizes the extent of the human tragedy involved. Vast masses of adults and children were arbitrarily seized and deported to unfamiliar territories where they were treated as pariahs. Their experience naturally colours their attitude to the Russian state authorities today and explains why their historians have been vigorously pursuing research into their nation's history, so far as they are able to do so. Maierbek Vachagaev, a history graduate from Grozny, was admitted to Moscow's Institute of Russian History in 1990 to study the Chechen independence struggle in the nineteenth century, but the grisly atrocities by tsarist troops that he described led to pressure by A.A. Novosel'tsev, the institute's director, to make him abandon his dissertation on the grounds that it was inspired by "chauvinistic anti-Russian sentiments inimical to friendship between peoples". Nevertheless in 1995 he did sucessfully defend his thesis and went into politics as the personal representative in Moscow of the Chechen president Aslan Maskhadov. Arrested in October 1999 and physically abused in prison, he became a "prisoner of conscience" whose case was taken up by Amnesty International.[8]

Historians today have relinquished the Soviet formula justifying tsarist territorial expansion on the grounds that it represented a "lesser evil" for the conquered peoples than annexation by Western "imperialists". This formula is contested with particular vehemence by non-Russian historians whose peoples were forcefully incorporated into the Russian empire, such as the Tatars of the middle Volga basin who were subdued by Ivan IV. Each year on 15th October ceremonies are held in Kazan' in memory of the Tatar soldiers who fell during the siege of the city in 1552. In the early 1990s they were marked by stormy scenes when demonstrators burned portraits of Ivan IV and demanded demolition of a statue erected two hundred years ago to commemorate the Russian soldiers who had died in the battle. On 15 October 1999 some two thousand people gathered to protest the use of force against the Chechens; graffiti were scrawled in public places and so on. Many residents of Tatarstan regard Russia's nineteenth-century Caucasian wars as acts of aggression and hail the *imam* Shamil as a hero who defended the native peoples' right to freedom and independence.[9]

Prior to 1991 the history of the national republics was treated as subordinate to the development of the Russian empire and its Soviet successor. Today efforts are being made to tell the story from the viewpoint of each nation concerned. Take the case of Tatarstan: in the Soviet era there was an official *History of Tatariia* which went through several editions. It highlighted those facts and personalities that fitted into Moscow's scheme of things, especially when discussing relations between Russian and Tatar residents of the region (which was then an autonomous republic). Now most of the books published in Kazan' deal with the Tatar element in the population. At the university there is a chair of history specially devoted to the Tatars, and the tendency is to view their history in the context of Islamic–Turkic civilization rather than that of Russia. On the other hand, a new scholarly periodical, *Ab imperio*, recently saw the light in Kazan'. Edited by a board of reputed Russian and foreign specialists, it is devoted to the study of the history of all the nationalities in Eurasia.

The national historians in Tatarstan, as elsewhere in the CIS, see it as their chief task to bring out the contribution which their people have made to world civilization, not just to the history of Russia. Such writers are no longer concerned with what was achieved as a result of incorporation into Russia but with whatever was done that resounded to the credit of their own nation and of Russia, too. A lot of the material currently coming out in Tatarstan stresses the humiliations and sacrifices that non-Russians had to put up with in both tsarist and Soviet times, and exalts the struggle for national emancipation.[10]

Of course every nation has a right to its own history. However, it is a matter for regret that these new scholarly publications are so politicized and serve the interests of new ruling élites who play the "national card" in order to consolidate their own power. In 1996 an Institute of History was set up in Tatarstan. The person appointed to head it is not a professional historian but a political adviser to the republic's president. In 1992 Kazan' was the scene of an international conference of Turcologists, who passed a resolution recommending that an authoritative *History of the Turkic Peoples* be compiled. This gathering was followed the next year by one celebrating the seven hundred and fiftieth anniversary of the formation of the Golden Horde. Then in April

1996 there was an international symposium in Kazan' on the recent Islamic renaissance among the Tatars of the region.[11]

Publications dealing with the sort of themes now in favour receive state support, and this has led to a lowering of scholarly standards. There have been cases where extreme nationalists have gone overboard in praising their people's "exceptional" gifts to the world. This is a risk inherent in any historical work written from the standpoint of a single nation and counterposing its fate to that of its neighbours, because this is bound to involve an element of myth-making instead of being based on solid research into documentary sources. In 1994 a Kiev publishing house brought out a *Dictionary of Ancient Ukrainian Mythology* in which it was claimed that Ukrainians had founded Rome and Troy; indeed, they were said to have been among the ancestors of Jesus Christ! The following year the Ukrainian Academy of Sciences published in its *Vestnik* a book by an economist, Yu. Kanigin, under the title *The Aryan Way*. He asserted that the Ukrainians were descended from the Indo-European Aryans, who had borne on their standards a swastika symbol on a blue and yellow background. The vice-president of the academy, P. Tolochko, sharply condemned this work as "ukrainophilia taken to the point of absurdity".[12]

In 1998 Bashkortostan, the former Bashkiria, introduced its own system of honorific orders. They included an Order of Salavat Yulaev, named after a confederate of the eighteenth-century rebel leader Pugachev, which is to be awarded, of all things, for services rendered to science and culture! Not wanting to be left behind, the Chuvash have published works claiming that they are linguistically and genetically related to the ancient Sumerians or, in another version, are descended from the Huns. Advocates of the former theory hold that "the Chuvash language is the father of many others" and that one can find many Chuvash words in Hebrew – itself said to be a word of Chuvash derivation![13]

These excesses may be seen as a reaction to the integrative processes at work in the tsarist empire, which continued under the Soviets. As Andreas Kappeler writes in his classic study of the evolution of the Russian multi-national state, the Bolshevik revolution and its sequel merely delayed the natural process that was causing the tsarist empire, like those of the Western powers, to fall apart. After 1953 the worst excesses, such as forced deportation, came to an end but Stalin's successors held to the fundamentals of his policy, which was essentially imperialist but cloaked in the ideological garb of "developed socialism"; it amounted in effect to forcible, if gradual, assimilation. Thus in the 1970s, Soviet officials tried to promote the teaching and use of Russian in the minority republics. "As in the late tsarist era, official policy assumed a Russian nationalist colouring and even an anti-semitic one, although it distanced itself from the extreme nationalist and anti-semitic currents in Russian society at large."[14]

This led hundreds of thousands of Soviet Jews to emigrate, a trend that has continued since 1991. Germans and Greeks, too, have left the country in large numbers. There are several reasons for this. In the case of the Jews it is a response both to economic hardship and to the threat posed by fascist organizations; particularly alarming were the statements by extreme right-wing Duma deputies such as A.M. Makashov and V.I. Iliukhin. Whereas in Soviet times a myriad obstacles were placed in the path of would-be emigrants, now people have the right to leave the country if they have relatives abroad – causing some Russian Jews to engage in a frantic search for grandmothers and great-grandmothers living abroad! Ten years ago the Jewish community in Kazan', a city of well over a million inhabitants, numbered ten thousand; over half have since left and now at least a hundred do so each year, yet the community's strength remains stable at around five thousand. Since Jews have a relatively high birth rate, people joke that the more Jews leave, the more remain behind.

Historians of nationality affairs have focused their attention in recent years on rather traditional themes, such as the imperial Russian government's policy, national resistance movements, the administrative structure under Soviet rule, the merits of federalism as against separatism in various epochs, and the programmes of the new nationalist parties in various CIS states.[15] These writers have been assisted in their work by documentary publications,[16] but there are not nearly enough of these and they touch only on certain limited topics. In a survey of recent literature on this theme, Kappeler notes that not a single general work has yet come out in Russian on the polyethnic empire prior to 1917, although studies of particular problems have been undertaken.

He notes approvingly that more historians are now investigating regional history and trying to compare the way various territories were administered. In the late 1990s several conferences were held on these matters.[17]

Soviet historians used to be concerned pre-eminently with the doings of the Russian state. True, in the 1920s there was a genuine effort to advance the interests of the national minorities by developing their languages and cultures, promoting education and building up native cadres (*korenizatsiia*), but once Stalin was firmly in the saddle this liberalism gave way to a struggle against all forms of so-called "bourgeois nationalism" and to the physical elimination of national élites in the purges. As Marc Ferro notes, "nationality policy from the 1920s onward ensured that each republic should have its own official history, compiled according to a common pattern. This approach led to distorted treatment of the real history of these peoples. The impression was created that each of them had gone through the same stages of historical development, whose rhythm and tempo were prescribed by Moscow."[18] He is justified in his criticism of official Soviet historiography, but one can go further. After the USSR's collapse, the immediate appearance of distinctive national historical schools in each former republic (and even in minority regions within the Russian Federation) has provided fresh evidence that Soviet nationalities policy was a total fiasco.

All the preaching about "the unshakeable unity of the peoples of the USSR" was just balderdash. The idea that all these nations and ethnic groups, at different stages of development, were effecting a "transition to socialism" under the Party's scientific guidance was just a myth. This is clear from the fact that in Central Asia and the northern Caucasus many of these peoples have reverted to their earlier feudal or clan relationships. It was not at all scientific for Marxist–Leninists to classify the USSR's peoples into "elder brothers" (the Russians) and their supposedly less advanced juniors (the non-Russian minorities), leaving out of consideration other groups that lacked administrative divisions of their own, such as Jews, Germans or Greeks, or which had actually been rendered homeless (the deported peoples) and could scarcely be mentioned in public. Yet one has to add that the replacement of this uniform Communist outlook by the many different national historical schools we have today has produced unhealthy discriminatory tendencies, a narrow outlook that distinguishes between "us" and "them". It has destroyed with a bang the old "Russian Idea" with its exceptionalist implications.

It is important to stress the point that, although at present Russians comprise eighty per cent of the population of the Russian Federation, very few Russian historians look on their country's history from a nationalist perspective. One writer who does so is Solzhenitsyn. The existential question he posed in 1994, "will our nation survive or not?", has evoked responses by scholars as well as in the media.[19]

The emphasis placed by Soviet propagandists over the years on the theme of the Russians as "elder brother" of other peoples in the USSR did not bring any material privileges for Russians *vis-à-vis* their neighbours, all of whom shared the same difficult lot. What it did involve was, rather, moral support for Great Russian national chauvinism. This sometimes acquired a morbidly distorted form that was perceived as humiliating by non-Russians. All too often Russian regimes have resorted to a deceitful ploy in order to explain to their people why their lives are so grim, by blaming outsiders: "American imperialism", "international Zionism" or – as now – "persons of Caucasian stock". The Jews were targeted especially in the late 1940s and early 1950s, when there was an official campaign against "rootless cosmopolitanism" (popularly known as the *Zhdanovshchina*), which had a pronounced anti-Semitic component. The Stalinist clique prepared its own variant of a "final solution of the Jewish question": to deport the Jews to the east in the wake of the other ethnic groups that had already been sent there.[20] Stalin's death prevented this plan from being put into effect.

Some work has been done on these matters in conjunction with historians or publishers in Israel, and V. Levashov, notably, has explored the murder of Solomon Mikhoels, which set the scene for Stalin's anti-Semitic campaign.[21] A round table organized early in 2000 by the editors of *Otechestvennaia istoriia* concluded that, while state-supported anti-Semitism is not a factor in Russia today, there is a good deal of it at the popular level, which expresses itself in political, social and religious antagonism.

The authors of some contemporary Russian nationalist works

even regard Stalin's repression of the Old Bolsheviks and other revolutionaries, many of whom were Jewish, as an act of retribution for sins allegedly committed by Jews.[22] One also finds a contrary position expressed: that the 1937 Terror was *not* anti-Semitic and that, since the Jewish functionaries who helped to organize it were "odd men out" in Russian life, they bear less responsibility for their misdeeds than their Russian comrades.[23]

But this line of argument does not satisfy everybody. In 1997 the regional assembly (*duma*) in Voronezh decided to remove from local schools as "russophobic" a schoolbook published with the aid of George Soros's Open Society Foundation in which, so it was said, more space was given to the repression of the Jewish Anti-fascist Committee than to the (mainly Russian) victims of the "Leningrad case". In 1999 the US Jewish Anti-Defamation League took a poll of 1528 Russian respondents and found that 44 per cent of them had anti-Semitic leanings.[24] In the last few months the war in Chechnia and its antecedents have led to "Caucasians" replacing Jews as prime targets of Russian chauvinists. There are a lot of news items in the media about feelings of hatred entertained by Russians for non-Russians. This has sometimes led local authorities to intervene and to decide which newspapers or TV programmes citizens in their region should read or view.[25]

By 1995 or thereabouts, there had ceased to be much demand for popular literature exposing the evils of the Soviet era. This sort of topic was increasingly left to specialists among professional historians. In August 1996 President Yeltsin stated that the country needed a national idea; but it at once became clear that this national idea was not perceived in ethnic terms but as something that would build support for the state authorities. This notion was not well received in some national republics that were concerned to preserve their sovereignty and had worked out their own relationship to "the centre", even adopting constitutions that in certain points differed from the Russian one. The leaders of Tatarstan were the first to say that, if Russia formed a confederation with Belarus, they wanted their own republic to be an equal member of such a confederal state; in this way they posed a threat to the existing structure of the Russian Federation.

It is all too easily forgotten that in some minority republics the numerical relationship of the titular nation to the other residents is not in favour of the former. In Bashkortostan, for instance, Bashkirs comprise a mere 21.9 per cent of the population and Russians 39.3 per cent; in the Sakha republic (Yakutia) the figures are 33.4 and 50.3 per cent, in Tatarstan 48.5 and 43.5 per cent, and in Karelia 10 and 73.6 per cent.[26] This disproportion sometimes leads to tension; for example, residents of the Russian province of Samara, which borders on Tatarstan, are doing better economically than people living in the latter republic. Here school history textbooks contain tendentious remarks about the Tatars, which have led to protests by Russian teachers – and also by pupils who are keen to go on to college or university in Moscow, where they will not be expected to know much about the Tatars.

Soviet nationalities policy did not boil down all the Union's ethnic groups in a common pot and produce a homogeneous soup of "Soviet people". The forced assimilation policy engendered anti-Russian feelings which in turn contributed to the spread of the nationalist "Russian Idea". As a result we have a "we-and-they" attitude in history teaching and publications. This is perhaps a disease of adolescence inseparable from the growth of national consciousness, but it tends to last a long while. In theory separate national histories could be combined to create a new history of Russia – not of the state but of all the peoples who reside within its borders. But another, less agreeable, scenario is also conceivable: that each of the various national élites might create its own "new history", emphasizing the claims and privileges of its own ethnos. Such an exclusivist approach would rule out for many years any hope of writing a common history of all the peoples of Russia.

9
Soviet Foreign Policy

Soviet historians clung to a highly idealized view of the USSR's foreign policy. All the numerous studies they turned out on this subject, with many volumes of supporting documents, proceeded from the standpoint that the Party leaders' actions were unfailingly correct. Their intentions were peaceful and benevolent; if something had gone wrong, then it was the fault of the "imperialist" enemy, which was forever scheming to undermine and destroy the socialist system. An example of this simplified and indeed mendacious approach is the official *History of the Foreign Policy of the USSR*, edited by A.A. Gromyko and B.N. Ponomarev, which went through five editions.[1] Its approach became standard for all other writers on the topic. From the 1930s onward they were prone to extend it back in time and so to legitimize the doings of imperial Russian policy-makers and diplomats as well as Soviet ones, despite the aggressive and expansionist course which the tsars and their ministers often adopted.[2]

Since the USSR came to grief a number of former Soviet diplomats and other officials have published their recollections. These often contain important information about key moves, such as the introduction of Soviet troops into Afghanistan in December 1979. This rash step, like many others, was decided by a very narrow group within the leadership. The scene was Brezhnev's country *dacha*; those present, besides Brezhnev himself, were KGB chairman Andropov, Defence minister Ustinov, Foreign minister Gromyko, and Chernenko (who was then in charge of the General department in the Party's CC). The composition of this gremium is itself significant because in the Soviet system of government the CC, the Council of Ministers, the KGB and the Defence ministry were the most powerful agencies by far. They were all physically located within Moscow's Sadovoe Ring, the avenue that runs round the city centre. (Wits used to say that whatever was good for people living within this ring was good for the whole country.) In reality not more than three thousand individuals, members of the *nomenklatura*, ruled the USSR after World War II.[3]

The principal topics of attention among Russian historians of foreign policy in recent years have been the Nazi–Soviet pact of August 1939, Cold War origins, and how to safeguard Russia's national interests at the present time.

The pact

In so far as they dealt with the Ribbentrop–Molotov pact at all, Soviet writers viewed it favourably. This line has found adherents since 1991 as well. Some Russian historians argue that "although the pact was *de facto* imposed on us, yet it was quite natural and well founded", especially since it benefited the Soviet economy.[4] They base this argument on a resolution passed in 1989 by the Congress of People's Deputies entitled "On the Political and Legal Evaluation of the Soviet-German Non-Aggression Treaty of 1939", which put forward two propositions: 1) that the pact was in conformity with the norms of international law; 2) that the secret protocols dividing up the territory of other eastern European states were illegal and were therefore to be repudiated.[5] At the congress Gorbachev and Yakovlev declared that the originals of these secret protocols were no longer in existence.[6] The implication was that the texts that had been published back in 1948 by the Americans, who had access to German archives captured after the war, were fallacious.

But shortly afterwards the originals turned up in Moscow.[7] What were historians to do? Some preferred to ignore them, while others tried to justify the Soviet–German territorial deal by rather specious arguments. L.N. Nezhinsky, head of the Russia and International Relations Centre in the Academy of Sciences – which came under its Institute of History – holds that the carve-up was justified because after the 1917 revolution Russia had lost Finland, the Baltic lands, part of Poland and Bessarabia, but now she had an opportunity to get them back and even to extend the state boundaries. He speaks of "successes for Stalin's diplomacy" in this regard.[8] The same point of view is taken by M.I. Mel'tiukhov, who contends that the pact settled to the USSR's advantage the Anglo–German rivalry for Soviet assistance in ordering Europe's affairs: Moscow was able to stay out of the war and got a free hand in eastern Europe.[9] In this spirit several writers began to explore the antecedents of the Soviet–German *rapprochement* earlier in the 1930s.[10]

At first sight, it may seem there is something to be said for this approach. After conclusion of the pact Soviet–German relations were based on mutual interest: Germany got access to Soviet agricultural products and raw materials, while the USSR regained territory that in the main had once belonged to the tsars. But the real point is that in concluding this deal the USSR behaved as an aggressor state, like Nazi Germany, by forcibly annexing or seizing territory from independent countries. It is true, as R. Raack argues, that the pact created the conditions for both World War II and the Cold War: the Nazi and Soviet dictators "smashed the territorial settlement of World War I."[11] One may legitimately condemn the appeasement policy pursued by the Western powers and their reluctance to include the USSR in a collective security system. But this does not mean refraining from criticizing the cynical nature of the pact, its contravention of international legal norms, the aid it gave the Nazis as they took over most of continental western Europe, or the contacts it established between the NKVD and the Gestapo which led to thousands of German residents in the USSR, including some prominent anti-Nazis, being handed over to the latter. Nor did Stalin make the best use of the breathing space he won, as we have seen above. To be sure, the causes and consequences of the agreement still need impartial study. Some contemporary Russian historians appear to be working on the right lines[12] and good work has also been done on Comintern and its successor, Cominform.

The cold war

In 1946 the "hot" war gave way to a "cold" one which, accelerated by controversies over the fate of Germany and eastern Europe,
control of the atomic bomb, and other issues of the day, had its
ultimate origin in the Stalinist ideological concept of the world
being divided into two antagonistic camps;[13] it continued, in
varying forms and with periods of greater or lesser tension, until
the USSR collapsed in 1991. The early phases of this long drawn-
out conflict have received a lot of attention from Russian historians
of late,[14] who have shown that beneath the surface of the war-
time Grand Alliance there were divergences of interest that came
to the fore once hostilities were over. In 1992 a conference was
held in Moscow on "Soviet Foreign Policy, 1917–1991: A Retro-
spective". One of the *rapporteurs* recalled that at a conclave with
Stalin soon after the war ended, Marshal S.M. Budennyi declared
that it had been "a major error" by the Soviet leadership not to
have ordered the Red Army to advance westward beyond Berlin
and Prague. The bluff cavalry general said that "with our sabres
we ought to have smitten [our enemies] from their heads down
to where their legs start". Stalin's reaction came as a surprise:
"And how are we going to feed them?"[15] He objected not to the
idea of a Europe-wide Soviet republic as such but to the practical
economic implications of such an advance.

It is now known that on 18 November 1947 Stalin received
Maurice Thorez, the French Communist leader who was then
deputy chairman of the Council of Ministers in France, and in
Molotov's presence said: "If Churchill had delayed the Second
Front in northern France for another year, the Red Army would
have got as far as France." He thought for a bit and then added:
"We were even thinking of going on to Paris." Thorez told Stalin
that the French Communists had secretly stockpiled weapons and
radio equipment for communication with Moscow. Stalin confirmed that he was prepared to send further arms supplies. "We're
all Communists, and that says everything."[16]

The Soviet leadership's vast geopolitical ambitions naturally
worried the USSR's war-time allies. Russian historians have pointed
out that the advent of the nuclear age led to a sharp shift in the
country's domestic and foreign policies. In view of the world-

wide rivalry of two antagonistic systems, it became vital for the Soviets to acquire a nuclear capability. Without actually being used, the atomic bomb could be flourished as a "rhetorical deterrent" – notably by Khrushchev and also by his successors. More recently President Yeltsin trod the same path when, in response to justified Western criticism of Russian behaviour in Chechnia, he noted that Russia still had "a complete arsenal of nuclear weaponry" and thus did not need to fear international sanctions.[17]

There is clearly a causal relationship between Stalin's election speech of 9 February 1946 and Churchill's speech in Fulton, Missouri, on 5 March of that year. The Soviet leader said that he was ready for competition with the West; the former British prime minister called on the Anglo-Saxon powers to unite in face of the growing Communist threat.[18] Historians have also noted that the military–industrial complex played a major role in the policy-makers' calculations at this time and also after Stalin's death. It made possible the development of nuclear weapons, rocket technology and the space programme, naval expansion and a vast build-up of Soviet military power, but only at the cost of overburdening the economy and impoverishing the population, especially the peasants. In 1989, according to official data, the USSR was spending 73 per cent of its national income on military purposes; that is to say, the country's economy was militarized, much as it had been during World War II.[19]

Russian historians of the Cold War are greatly concerned with the acute international crises that risked igniting a new world war: the confrontations with the West over Berlin, the Korean War of 1950–3, and the 1962 Cuban missile crisis. Among the documents that have been published on these episodes is the record of a conversation in 1951 between Gustav Hilger, counsellor at the German embassy in Moscow from 1938 to 1941, and John Emerson, of the State Department in Washington, about Stalin's intentions in Korea. Stalin, he maintained, was "a prudent elderly man who respected US atomic might and knew that the Soviet Union was not yet prepared for such a war."[20] This assessment is borne out by fresh information on the conflictual relationship between the USSR and the Chinese People's Republic before and during the Korean War: Stalin egged on both Kim

Il-sung and Mao Zedong, but took care to avoid a direct clash with the UN forces.[21]

At the Twentieth Party congress in 1956 Khrushchev departed from the Lenin–Stalin line that wars were inevitable so long as capitalism existed. The balance of military power, he averred, was shifting in favour of the "socialist camp" and its friends in the Third World, and this was bound to restrain the belligerence of the "imperialists"; this implied that in the nuclear age there were limits to Soviet expansion as well. Despite this show of moderation he behaved aggressively over Berlin in 1958 and four years later decided to instal medium-range missiles in Fidel Castro's Cuba, a move that brought the world to the brink of thermonuclear catastrophe.[22]

There were several other potentially catastrophic situations, due to the secretive and unpredictable character of Moscow's foreign policy. More and more facts are coming to light about the Soviet leaders' willingness to take risks by brandishing the country's armed might. V.S. Kozlov, a former submarine commander, recalls in a recent article how in 1959 he was sent to reconnoitre the movements of US warships in the Mediterranean. He managed to place his craft in a position whence it could launch a torpedo attack on the flagship of the US Sixth fleet, the *Des Moines*, which, as it later transpired, had President Eisenhower on board! The Americans tried to take a sonar bearing on the submarine but were unable to fix its position. When Khrushchev was told of the incident he expressed satisfaction and ordered the submarine crew to be suitably rewarded.[23]

Russian historians have shown that similar adventurist, "forward" policies were pursued in the 1970s. The USSR unilaterally increased the number and destructive power of nuclear-tipped missiles stationed in the western regions of the country, so undermining the credibility of its supposed commitment to détente. This was followed by the invasion of Afghanistan, which dealt yet another blow to détente. Both decisions were presented by propagandists as expressing "the will of the entire Soviet people", although they were actually taken by a mere handful of individuals. Another provocative, destabilizing policy was to extend financial support to Communist parties in various Third World countries and even to terrorist organizations too.[24]

Recent developments

By the 1980s an economic and political crisis was brewing in the USSR, since the country simply could not afford to keep up the never-ending arms race. It was essential to reform the economy, curb military expenditure, and cut back the milliards of roubles being poured into African and Asian states with a "socialist orientation". After 1985, with Gorbachev and Shevardnadze, Soviet foreign policy embarked on a radically new course. In 1988 the new leaders decided to withdraw Soviet troops from Afghanistan, a move completed the following year. Later Gorbachev let it be known that he would not authorize the use of armed force to stop the push for democratization in eastern Europe. The Communist regimes in the latter states collapsed, the Berlin Wall was torn down, and Germany was reunited. As M.Ya. Geller has noted, the first biography of Gorbachev appeared in the West (New York) on the very day he was elected General Secretary, 11 March 1985, whereas Stalin had been in charge of the Party for nine years before he earned one. This showed that Soviet affairs had become far more important to people in the rest of the world than they had been half a century earlier.[25]

Gorbachev's perestroika was a failure. He tried to reform virtually everything, yet sought to preserve the essence of the Soviet system in a purified Leninist form. His foreign policy, directed towards a *rapprochement* with the West on the basis of "universal human values", brought him popularity abroad. But at home his meddling and continual appeals to the population to back his reforms cost him mass support, while the *nomenklatura* objected to his radical methods. Used to governing in secret, they were unhappy about *glasnost'* and disliked having to compete for office at elections.[26] Gorbachev's "new thinking" in foreign policy boiled down to forming a Soviet–German alliance as a way of winning entry into the international community. But his domestic policy led to the collapse first of the "world socialist system" and then of the USSR itself. He took many of the most important decisions personally.

Volkogonov writes that for Western opinion, Gorbachev symbolized the disappearance of the Communist threat. His frequent appearances abroad and many speeches – he was the first Soviet leader to utilize television effectively – helped to improve the USSR's image abroad. Over the six years from 1985 to 1991 Gorbachev met at least five hundred foreign heads of state, party leaders and so on; all this dialogue engendered greater mutual comprehension.[27] Gorbachev maintained good relations with states-men round the world; yet the goodwill of his Western friends could not avert his fall. On 30 July 1991 US President George Bush met Gorbachev at the latter's *dacha* and warned him that a *coup* attempt was in the offing, but the Soviet leader self-confidently flew off for a holiday at Foros in the Crimea without taking any precautionary measures. On 19 August the plotters struck. Their venture was stymied by Yeltsin, the Russian (RSFSR) president, who stood for a more democratic course than Gorbachev. The latter was freed from house arrest and returned to Moscow, but from then on was on the defensive *vis-à-vis* Yeltsin. He had to resign as Party General Secretary; the CC was disbanded; and on 29 August the Supreme Soviet formally suspended all CPSU activity pending clarification of the Party's role in the plot. Four months later the USSR ceased to exist; Gorbachev resigned as president and became an independent public figure.

Two years later Boris Yeltsin acted differently in a similar crisis. On 24 August 1993 the US ambassador, Thomas Pickering, passed a confidential message through an embassy official, Colonel Parr, to Volkogonov, one of Yeltsin's advisers, warning him that deputies to the Supreme Soviet were conspiring to remove the president. Yeltsin forestalled them by issuing a decree (no. 1400) of 21 September dissolving both the Supreme Soviet and the Congress of People's Deputies. The ensuing confrontation between president and parliament culminated in the armed clash of 3–4 October 1993, in which several dozen people were killed.[28] No documentary sources have been published from which one could judge whether such a tragic dénouement could have been averted. After all, Yeltsin had foreknowledge of the deputies' intentions. The affair showed that he preferred to settle conflicts by much the same forceful methods as had been applied by the Bolsheviks, rather than by political dialogue as in established democracies. Nevertheless Western opinion, concerned at the parliament's pro-Communist leanings, was inclined to give Yeltsin the benefit of the doubt and continued to regard him as the best hope for Russia's evolution in a democratic direction.

Foreign policy under Yeltsin pursued a contradictory course. At first the Foreign Affairs ministry was headed by Andrei Kozyrev, a democrat who did much to break down the barriers of mistrust between Russia and the West. He was followed by Yevgenyi Primakov, a former Party and KGB functionary who dreamed of restoring Soviet grandeur. He had a special interest in Near Eastern affairs and was instrumental in getting Russia to oppose the Western powers' measures against Saddam Hussein in Iraq. Later, Moscow backed Belgrade against the NATO action in Kossovo. The present Foreign minister, I. Ivanov, has taken much the same line. The media are being used by those in power to inculcate patriotic emotions among the populace. Yet many ordinary folk are well aware of the cruel methods employed by the military in the reconquest of Chechnia. Polls show that they are in favour of putting a stop to terrorism and banditry in that republic, but only so long as their own sons do not have to fight to do so.

Spokesmen for Russian foreign policy today declare that the country's interests are best served by helping to create a multipolar world, not one dominated by the United States. But how can we bring this about when our international prestige suffers from the continuing economic crisis and we are so dependent on foreign creditors? In this situation there is a temptation to revive Cold War rhetoric and to remind our presumed adversaries that we still have nuclear weapons!

Russian historians of the "patriotic" school maintain that NATO enlargement threatens our security and geopolitical interests. They envisage a variety of scenarios for our foreign policy: to withdraw into isolationism; to join the international community of industrialized states; to associate with the developing countries of the Third World; or to seek an equilibrium between North and South. The last of these alternatives seems to them the best one to pursue. It would mean giving up any messianic pretensions such as were entertained in Soviet times, for that would make Russia the focal point of the tension between North and South. They are probably right that Russia needs to decide whether she wants to preserve a European political structure, and that she should try as far as possible to adapt it, and her economic system too, to the norms prevalent in the West.[29]

Each country has the right to pursue its own independent foreign policy. But I hope that our future will lie with Europe. I would like to see the scope of the Schengen accords extended to include Russia, so that people may travel to and fro freely in a world without frontiers. All conflicts ought to be settled by negotiation, without resorting to violence, and government policy should give pride of place to the interests of the mass of its citizens.

10
Conclusion

One might have thought that by now, nearly ten years after the collapse of the USSR, Soviet historiography would have become something best left to specialists, yet it is still a matter of public discussion. More than that: the burden of the Soviet past is an insuperable obstacle to democratic transition in Russia. It is not just that people are still alive who were once Stalinists and retain their faith in Communist ideas. Nor is it simply the persistence of black-and-white thinking – who is not for us is against us – although many citizens do indeed either idealize or prettify the Soviet experience, while others curse it and try to forget it. As in the old proletarian song *Varshavianka*, they would like to "shake its mortal dust from our feet".

In January 1999 a scholarly forum was held in Moscow at which papers were presented on attitudes to the Russian past. The gathering was organized by Intertsentr, the Inter-disciplinary Academic Centre of Social Sciences, which is chaired jointly by Teodor Shanin of Britain and V.P. Danilov of the Russian Academy of Sciences. Shanin suggested that there was a homogeneous character to Russia's history, in that it had throughout been a Third World country with the general and specific characteristics associated with such a status. Danilov drew attention to the drive for social advancement that had been the real motive force behind Soviet economic and cultural progress in general and its scientific–technological modernization in particular. He referred to the critical comments on the Soviet bureaucracy made by Trotsky, who had pointed out that a new class of officials had come into being –

men keen to perpetuate and legitimate the minimal amount of property they had acquired. Danilov drew a parallel with the situation today, when 61 per cent of the Russian bourgeoisie now in process of formation comprises former Party, Komsomol and Soviet functionaries. It followed from his analysis that Stalin's chief legacy had been a bureaucratic dictatorship, elements of which had survived to the present.

V. Mezhuev, intervening in the discussion, contended that modern liberals ought to be grateful to the Communists "because no one had done more than the Bolsheviks to modernize the country, even if they had used illiberal, undemocratic methods."[1] He was here endorsing the old jesuitical principle that the ends justify the means. This barbarous "principle" is not somehow inherent to Russia. But it is a dangerous one and, alas, is held to by many Russians today.

On 21 December 1999 Stalin's surviving admirers celebrated the one hundred and twentieth anniversary of their hero's birth (actually one year too late: see above). Just prior to this, sociologists at the All-Russian Centre for Study of Public Opinion conducted a poll which showed that 32 per cent of Russian citizens considered Stalin to have been a tyrant responsible for taking the lives of millions of innocent people. The same percentage thought that it was only thanks to Stalin that the USSR had defeated the fascist invaders in World War II. Another question ran: "Our people cannot manage without a leader of the Stalin type and sooner or later one will appear and establish order." To this, 18 per cent of those polled responded in the affirmative. Asked to provide a general assessment of Stalin's role in history, 22 per cent replied that his rule had brought Russia "only good, or more good than bad"; 44 per cent thought it had been "good and bad in equal measure", while 25 per cent of the respondents considered it had brought "more bad than good, or only bad".[2]

The current legend has it that Stalin was a "great and terrible" ruler, capable of inducing fear abroad and attaining his ends. Gennadyi Ziuganov, the leader of the Russian Communist party (KPRF), calls Stalin "the greatest statesman in the whole of Russian history". The liberal politician Grigoriy Yavlinsky is convinced that Stalin was a murderer. In my opinion he was a police *provo-*

cateur and executioner of genius. I am therefore closer to the views of Yavlinsky and Anna Akhmatova. She would fly into a rage at the very mention of Stalin as a statesman. "It's all very well to say that: the man was a cannibal, but you can't help admitting that he played the fiddle well."[3] This was putting it rather emotionally, but the fact remains that we have yet to reach a scholarly consensus on the Stalinist phenomenon, despite the abundance of literature on the subject.

At the VIth World Congress for Central and East European Studies, held in Finland in the summer of 2000, a panel was devoted to reappraising the long-term influence of Stalin's *Short Course*. Historians from four Russian cities (Moscow, St Petersburg, Kazan' and Novosibirsk) all agreed that for half a century this work had served an effective means for the ruling Party to legitimate its image of the future, enforce uniformity in historical thought, and bolster the CPSU's version of what socialism meant against all contending views. They showed that the textbooks in use at Russian schools and universities still had the same structure, and dealt with the same problems, as Stalin's had done; there were even stylistic resemblances. Moreover, the liberal-democratic interpretation of the past which had prevailed ten or so years ago was now yielding to a state-centered, patriotic one that differed from its predecessor only in taking a more positive line towards the monarchy and the Orthodox Church.[4]

The wide variety of opinions that exists about the recent past has called forth a good deal of exculpatory or condemnatory literature with a sociological orientation. Books are coming out which in my view are scandalous panegyrics to the tragic experience of our country in Soviet times;[5] on the other hand there are also some well-documented works about the Bolshevik leaders and their criminal deeds.[6] Among the latter, one may include a translation from the French of *The Black Book of Communism* by Stéphane Courtois, Nicolas Werth and others.[7] This includes data on crimes committed by Communist regimes in other states as well as the USSR. In his chapter on repressive actions by the Bolsheviks, Werth says he makes no claim "to a new appreciation of the facts" and, to be sure, the facts he mentions are fairly well known, but to have them assembled and listed chronologically yields a fearsome picture of a state that liquidated its citizens on a massive scale. One cannot but concur in his conclusion that some guilt also attaches to the silent collusion of so many thousands of people who readily executed criminal orders they received from above. This point is made by Yakovlev in the foreword to the Russian edition: "All of us, voluntarily or involuntarily, directly or indirectly, were either involved in, or silent spectators at, the Evil that was done. Sooner or later we shall have to repent." But recognition of collective guilt does not exempt the individual from bearing his or her share of it. Not everyone can be held responsible for the Bolsheviks' crimes, of course – if only for the simple reason that so many millions of people were their victims. The question remains: who should express contrition for what, and to whom?

Pluralism has made advances in Russia and people are free to express their own point of view. Historians can work as they wish on all sorts of problems that were previously taboo. One of these, which I did not consider above, is the size and where-abouts of Russian assets abroad, including valuables belonging to the CPSU.[8] Journalists have researched this topic, but it has not yet been examined by scholars. I present some relevant information in Appendix B.

Thus the past makes itself felt in today's Russia in several different ways. It is impossible to forget it. It stirs the souls of ordinary citizens as well as historians. A recent issue of a leading profes-sional journal contained an article headed "Trying to Conceptualize the Soviet Past".[9] Prior to Gorbachev's glasnost' (indeed, right down to 1991) the state sought to remake man and society by applying repressive measures and insisted on strict uniformity of opinion in public. (Stalin is quoted as having said: "In our Party there are no personal views or opinions but only those of the Party.")[10] The main consequence of the Soviet Union's collapse has been the disappearance of the "Party line". Individuals are free to make up their own minds. Historians can present alter-native viewpoints and put forward their own opinions without having to worry whether they are "politically correct".

In this connection it is worth noting that in the introduction to his major study of Russian social history before the Revolu-tion, B.N. Mironov of St Petersburg states that he had long intended to write such a work but until 1991 the idea had remained "platonic"; now, however, "the time has come for Russian historians to write what they think significant and in the way they think right . . . to [conduct] research independently as our Western colleagues do, without fearing whatever reviewers, editors or censors might say – or, what is equally important, self-censorship".[11] Mironov won grants from Western sponsors to carry out his great project, which would have been unthinkable in Soviet times. This freedom to choose one's subject and to get one's work published independently is a sign that pre-revolutionary traditions in scholarship have revived.

This revival is also evident in historians' willingness to forsake the Marxist-Leninist canon that held sway in the USSR for so long. Back in 1909 the philosopher S.L. Frank (1877–1950) warned that "if we believe in Lassalle and Marx we are essentially giving credence to ideas and values that were put forward by philosophers of the late eighteenth and early nineteenth centuries: Rousseau and de Maistre, Holbach and Hegel, Burke and Bentham. But in taking over these worthy ideas, most of which are over a hundred years old, we do not take a firm, conscious stand on them as the roots of our *Weltanschauung*. Instead we just put them to use blindly, without even asking ourselves how these values originated and what they are really based on."[12] Now Russian historians once again find themselves in a similar situation. They are free to express doubt as to whether the assertions of Marx and Lenin were correct; they can criticize the decisions taken at successive Party conclaves, and base their reasoning on the scholarly principles that obtain in democratic countries. Since 1990, at least in law, there has been no political censorship such as existed under Soviet rule, or in the tsarist empire before it.

Another important development in recent years has been the greater readiness of Russian scholars to venture into the history of other countries and to take account of what foreign specialists have to say about ours. Of course, even in Soviet times we were able to refer to Western works on Russian history, especially on periods before 1917. For example, Kashtanov, in his work on diplomatics, could acknowledge his debt to the American medievalists Horace W. Dewey or Gustav Alef; in similar spirit Yuryi Afanas'ev, after a spell at the Sorbonne, dedicated the book that resulted to the *Annales* school.[13] But one could not go far without incurring criticism for being too reliant on "bourgeois" scholarship. Now Mironov can state frankly: "I have tried to write the social history of Imperial Russia relying on the achievements of Russian and foreign, especially American, historians, who are currently in the forefront of international scholarship in Russian studies, ... avoiding both a negative and an apologetic approach to our achievements as a nation."[14] He does not share the view of A.N. Sakharov, the present director of the Institute of Russian History in the Academy of Sciences, or the American historian Stephen Cohen, that Russia is currently going through a new "Time of Troubles" or an era of "constitutional chimeras";[15] rather he sees our problems as normal in the circumstances. He affirms that Russia is not exceptional among European countries in experiencing so many tragedies and dramatic changes.[16]

I think he is right here and that his approach is worth pursuing. Too many of our political scientists today, and a number of historians too, are driven by "conjuncturalist" considerations (that is, concern for the present constellation of political forces) when they try to account for our current difficulties by Russia's geographical situation on the divide between Europe and Asia, by climatic factors, by our lag behind the West and so forth. They should rather seek to explain things by examining our recent past objectively and looking unsavoury truths in the eye.

Russian historiography has always been part of world scholarship in the discipline. In the nineteenth century it received powerful stimuli from German philosophers and historians (for example, Leopold Ranke or Max Weber); the former helped to shape the Slavophile–Westernizer debate, while the latter did much to raise professional standards in regard to source criticism, the study of laws and institutions, and much else. One could say that, in so far as Marxism was a German creation, German intellectual influences continued into the twentieth century as well, since it formed the basis of Soviet ideology; however, there has been much argument as to the degree to which Lenin may have "russified" Marx.

In any case, since the Soviet collapse the main foreign influence on our historical writing has been French. The works of

Marc Bloch, Fernand Braudel and Michel Foucault have been translated and published in Russia, and the idea of human history as a succession of civilizations has been popularized through school textbooks. Russian scholars today consult the works of Western colleagues irrespective of their national provenance, wherever their expertise on a particular topic coincides with their own; we are moving towards a genuine meeting of minds on an international basis.

As I have already suggested, one of the main features of the current situation is that the state no longer places obstacles in the path of historical research – although it does not have much money to promote it either. A glance back at the old control system may be helpful here. Twenty years ago there existed, in the Institute of Marxism–Leninism attached to the Party Central Committee, a so-called "Co-ordinating Council". Without its imprimatur it was impossible to defend a Ph.D. thesis on any subject connected with Party history, and that covered a lot of ground. (Lists of the dissertations approved by the council were published periodically in the journal *Voprosy istorii*.) A co-ordinating role was also played in the choice of research topics by Scientific Councils, set up in the late 1980s; these bodies were attached to the Historical Divison (*otdelenie*) of the USSR Academy of Sciences and had responsibility for different subject areas: for example, the October Revolution (chaired by Mints and Volobuev) or historiography (chaired by Nechkina and Koval'chenko).

Censorship was exercised not only through the provincial offices of Glavlit (known in the singular as *obllit*) but also through Science sections (*otdely nauk*) in the Party Central Committee and its provincial committees (*obkoms*). These bodies issued instructions regulating archive access. Today, although the Russian Communist Party (KPRF) still has such *obkoms*, they do not have as much power as they used to. Neither is there any political censorship over what is published, nor any committees to co-ordinate research topics. The Academy's Scientific Councils have been turned into commissions, such as those for the study of revolutions and reforms (chairman: Academician G.N. Sevost'ianov) and for the study of historiography (chairman: A.N. Sakharov, a corresponding member of the Academy). But these commissions have far less influence over what goes on in the various regions than the old councils did. Owing to lack of funds, they cannot afford to invite scholars from the provinces to their meetings. Moreover, the national republics within the Russian Federation have their own academies of science. Finally, *regional* centres of science and scholarship, such as those in the Urals, Novosibirsk, Tomsk and the Far East, play a much greater role than before.

According to the current statute of the Academy of Sciences (RAN) it consists of leading scholars in various disciplines, who are elected to this prestigious body. These rules are generally enforced in regard to Russian history before 1917 or world history. As for Soviet history, the choice of leading specialists was always a Party matter: one need only recall the insistence of the central Party apparatus under Brezhnev in the 1970s that S.P. Trapeznikov, boss of the Central Committee's Science Division, should be "elected" as corresponding member of the Academy. Unfortunately there has not been much change in this respect since then. At the last elections to the Academy in 2000 the Scientific Council of the Institute of Russian History refrained from nominating one of the most eminent Russian agrarian historians, V.P. Danilov. But the practice of choosing less distinguished people as members undermines the Academy's prestige. As for the academies in the various constituent republics that were set up in the 1990s, their full members (that is, academicians) and corresponding members receive the same salaries as those in Moscow or St Petersburg; they have tended to attract the scientific élite of the local nationality – people who would stand no chance of getting elected to the RAN, where posts in the discipline of history are held mainly by scholars from Moscow, St Petersburg or Novosibirsk.

Summing up, one cannot truthfully say that Russian historiography in the 1990s has been marked by a return to the best pre-revolutionary traditions. To be sure, freedom has been regained as regards choosing one's topic and publishing research results, as I just noted; historians are no longer obliged to adopt a "class approach" and may be categorized as belonging to the state-patriotic or the liberal-democratic tendency. The former continue to live in the shadow of Soviet traditions and are closer in sympathy to the politicians currently in power. Those who adhere to the latter tendency had a measure of success in the early 1990s but they could not make their influence stick in works written for the general public or in textbooks; here it is the historians of the state school who set the tone.

The difference is clear from what appears in the professional journals published in the two chief cities. Many of them have been in operation since the 1950s: for example, *Otechestvennaia istoriia* (previously *Istoriia SSSR*) for domestic history, *Voenno-istoricheskii zhurnal* for military history, *Istoricheskii arkhiv* (which publishes documents on various periods and topics), and *Kentavr* (*Centaur*, formerly *Voprosy istorii KPSS*). Older than all of these is *Voprosy istorii*, whose antecedents date back to the pre-war era. This latter journal, *Otechestvennaia istoriia* and the foreign-policy journal *Novaia i noveishaia istoriia* may all be categorized as liberal-leaning. All the others, led by *Svobodnaia mysl'* (previously *Kommunist*), are in the state-patriotic tradition.

Coexistence of two schools of thought is a success for Russian democracy. When I talk to my students about such matters they are not at all surprised. They are turned off by the idea of imposing uniformity of thought. They would much prefer to communicate by Internet than to read books anyway, and cannot imagine how one could possibly study some problem without considering alternative views or harbouring doubts as to the right answer. People entering university today belong to a generation that never had cause to be afraid. They are open-minded about all theories and try to analyse factual material in detail. This cheers me, as I feel confident that the students of today are keen to become professional historians. They can defend their own opinion of what is right against any attempt to tell them what they ought to think. The future, I am sure, lies with these young researchers who, after carefully investigating the pertinent documents, can form their own views and stand up for them.

Appendix A: Decisions of NKVD Triumvirate in Tatar ASSR, August–December 1937

Date	Number arrested	Of whom shot
23.8	30	28
31.8	38	38
8.9	24	24
11.9	77	77
17.9	56	56
22.9	82	81
23.9	94	93
26.9	97	94
28.10	225	209
29.10	61	57
30.10	185	173
31.10	199	107
5.11	40	22
6.11	185	95
10.11	52	15
11.11	174	52
16.11	39	8
17.11	104	34
21.11	149	52
22.11	61	11
23.11	151	88
24.11	67	27
26.11	179	29
29.11	185	6
10.12	269	61
13.12	262	150
15.12	173	93
21.12	174	121
22.12	95	35
25.12	177	130
26.12	11	11
27.12	39	17
28.12	52	33
29.12	84	45
30.12	408	159
31.12	591	164
	–	–
Total:	4889	2495

Source: see ch. 6, n. 19.

Appendix B: The Hunt for the Party's Gold

This was the term popularly used for the criminal investigation launched in October 1991 by the Russian Procurator General's office into the financial and economic activity of the Central Committee of the CPSU. The inquiry soon revealed that the Party's finances were closely interlocked with those of the Soviet state, and that it was hard to distinguish the former from the latter because, as the ruling Party, the CPSU considered that its interests were the state's interests, too. One of the sources that threw light on these dealings was the personal papers of Nikolai Kkruchina, the Party's manager, who committed suicide a few days after the defeat of the August 1991 *coup*.

These and other documents from the CC's archive gave grounds for the belief that holdings of valuables and foreign currency had been illegally smuggled abroad. It turned out that at the time when it ceased to function, the CPSU owned 4228 administrative buildings, 181 social–political centres, 16 social and political research institutes, 112 Party archives, 41 training establishments, 134 hotels, 54 museums (houses and flats where Lenin had lived), 145 motor workshops, 840 garages, 23 sanatoria and rest homes, and – last but not least – 206 "objects", including stores of industrial goods and foodstuffs, shops, and even a small plant where precious metals were worked into ornaments.

The value of this vast hoard amounted to several milliard roubles. Some of the Party's money was invested in banks and companies headed by people enjoying its officials' confidence. Some was handed over to foreign Communists. Between 1981 and 1991 alone the CPSU funded 98 parties and movements abroad. Over this decade the French CP got $24 million, that of the USA $21.25 million, the Finnish $16.6 million, the Portuguese $9.5 million, and so on. The money was usually handed over illegally by Soviet intelligence agents. Tens of millions of dollars were (and are?) kept in various banks across the world, but the exact figure is not known. The investigating team discovered $256 million in the safes of the CC's Financial department, of which $14 million were in cash.[1]

In 1999 S. Aristov, the head of this team, gave an interview to a correspondent of the paper *Argumenty i fakty*, in which he stated that in 1990 the Party's treasury had held $53.7 milliard (at the exchange rate of the day). Party officials were at that time busily trying to conceal its property to avoid possible nationalization. Between 1980 and 1991 Gorbachev authorized expenditure of $117,383,765; KGB chairman V. Chebrikov (1985–9) spent $38,503,765, and his successor V. Kriuchkov

(1989–91) $22 million; Ye. K. Ligachev, CC secretary (1985–91), $60,658,765; so the list goes on. Aristov said his men had not been able to retrieve this money, which the Communists were using for their own purposes.[2]

While Yegor Gaidar was Russian prime minister, he set up another investigating team, under the journalist Mikhail Gurtovoy, a former associate of his, to try to get back "the Party's gold". The members of this group soon established that during the civil war, the Party had already secreted funds abroad "just in case". Later some of those Old Bolsheviks who had held bank accounts abroad on behalf of the Party were arrested and, while under investigation, agreed to help get the money back. The investigators found several bank accounts in Switzerland but were unable to get the money returned to Russia because the CPSU had not been declared a criminal organization by the courts and so its foreign holdings were legal.[3]

Notes

Preface

1 V.V. Bakatin, *Izbavlenie ot KGB*, Moscow 1992, 149.

1 Did the Scholarly Tradition Survive?

1 Nechkina, "V.O. Kliuchevsky", 345; idem, *Vasilii Osipovich Kliuchevsky*, 571–2; Khvylev, *Problemy metodologii istorii*.
2 Koval'chenko and Shiklo, "Krizis russkoi burzhuaznoi istor. nauki", 33, 35; Alekseeva, in *Istor. nauka Rossii v XX v.*, 9.
3 Cf. G. Hosking's positive remarks on Kliuchevsky in *OI*, 5/1997, 123.
4 Zankevich, *K istorii sovetizatsii*; Barber, *Soviet Historians in Crisis*, 11.
5 Gurevich, "O krizise sovremennoi istor. nauki", 35; Litvin, in *Anatomiia revoliutsii: 1917 god v Rossii*, 53, 165; cf. Danilov in *Rossiia v XX v.*, 22–6.
6 Tsamatuli, *Bor'ba napravlenii*; Emmons, "Kliuchevsky i ego ucheniki", 45–61; Pashuto, *Russkie istoriki emigranty*; Vandalkovskaia, *Miliukov, Kizevetter*; idem, *Istor. nauka ross. emigratsii*; Raeff, *Russia Abroad*, 156–86; Stockdale, *Paul Miliukov*, 23–6.
7 "Russia and the West stand on common foundations but are distinguished by certain particularities." Kliuchevsky, *Pis'ma. Dnevniki*, 264.
8 Miliukov, *Vospominaniia*, i. 160.
9 Dumova, *Liberal v Rossii*, i. 117–30.
10 Kliuchevsky, *Pis'ma. Dnevniki*, 201–2, 281.
11 Shcherban', "Nevostrebovannye traditsii", 75.
12 Kireeva, "Iz istorii sov. istor. nauki", 487–95.
13 G. Orwell, *1984: A Novel*, London. 1969, 199.
14 A.V. Lunacharsky, *Stat'i o literature*, Moscow 1988, i. 245.
15 RTsKhIDNI, f. 5, op. 1, d. 878, l. 3; V.I. Lenin, *PSS*, li. 176.
16 RTsKhIDNI, f. 2, op. 2, d. 1344, l. 12; *Rodina*, 3/1992, 49. Rozhkov's major work on Russian history did, however, appear in twelve volumes in 1923–6. Cf. Alekseeva, *Okt. rev. i istor. nauka*, 103, 220–3.
17 Ivanova, *U istokov sovetskoi istor. nauki*, 181.
18 See his note to A. Udal'tsov's sketch of the academy's history in *Vestnik Sots. akademii*, 1/1922, 41.
19 A. Avtorkhanov, *Stalin and the Soviet Communist Party: A Study in the Technology of Power*, ed. O.J. Frederiksen, Munich 1959.

20 *Organizatsiia sovetskoi nauki v 1926–32 gg.,* 233.
21 M.N. Pokrovsky, "Desiatiletie IKP", *Pravda,* 11 February 1931.
22 Solovei, "Institut krasnoi professury", 93, 97–8.
23 RTsKhIDNI, f. 347, op.1, d. 6, ll. 6, 54.
24 Fokeev, "Iz istorii . . . proizvedenii V.I. Lenina", 7.
25 *Istochnik,* 2/1994, 71–3.
26 See *Istoriia sovetskoi politicheskoi tsenzury: dokumenty i kommentarii,* Moscow 1997.
27 *50 let sovetskoi istor. nauki,* 83, 94, 102; RTsKhIDNI, f. 71, op. 3, d. 9, ll. 13, 15, 24; *Istorik-marksist,* 14, 1929, 6.
28 I do not wish to enter here into the discussion that has been going on in certain Western countries as to whether Stalin's USSR was or was not totalitarian, on which there is now a large literature. My own position is close to that of M. Malia, in his *The Soviet Tragedy* (1994). For post-Soviet literature on this theme, see Igritsky, "Snova o totalitarizme", 3–17; Sakharov, "Revol. totalitarizm", 60–71.
29 Starostin and Khorkhordina, "Dekret ob arkhivnom dele 1918 g.", 49–50; Khorkhordina, "Arkhivy i totalitarizm", 153–5.
30 See the cases of G.G. Ibragimov and O. Piatnitsky in Litvin, *Zapret,* 118–19; idem et al. (eds.), *Yagoda,* 80–7.
31 See the guides listed in the Bibliography under RTsKhIDNI. On destruction of Party documents: Yakushev, "Iz istorii", 50–65; idem, "Tsentral'nyi partiinyi arkhiv", 23–33.
32 RTsKhIDNI, f. 147, op. 1, d. 73, l. 7.
33 Ibid., f. 558, op. 1, d. 2983, l. 5. Volosevich got off with a stern reprimand but was not repressed, at least before 1939; what happened to him later is unknown but he lived until 1954. RTsKhIDNI, card index, no. 2707637.
34 RTsKhIDNI, f. 71, op. 1, d. 24, ll. 2–3.
35 *Vestnik Komm. akademii,* 1–2/1932.
36 Arkhiv Akad. nauk Rossii, f. 377, op. 1, d. 262, ll. 1–11.
37 The diary was filed among Piontkovsky's investigation records. Arrested on 7 October 1936, he was shot on 8 March 1937. TsA FSB RF (the former KGB archive), d. R-8214, l. 359. E.M. Yaroslavsky (1878–1943) was a leading Party historian of the 1920s.
38 *Rezhim lichnoi vlasti Stalina: k istorii formirovaniia,* Moscow 1989, 71–2.
39 N.V. Krylenko, *Vyvody i uroki iz protsessa "Prompartii",* Moscow; Leningrad, 1931, 42.
40 These were Vanag, Piontkovsky, S.M. Dubrovsky and S.G. Tomsinsky, who had been arrested for "terrorism" and "banditry". M.V. Nechkina was among those present who backed Shestakov. B.D. Grekov was the only historian who limited himself to confessing his faults without mentioning his colleagues' names. He said he had spent half his life under the old regime when Marxism had not influenced him personally or his teaching, adding that in the light of recent events

he would have some "re-working" to do. GARF, f. 5143, op. 1, d. 613, ll. 1–7, 27–43.
41 RTsKhIDNI, f. 147, op. 2, d. 45, l. 5.
42 M.N. Pokrovsky, *Kak i kem pisalas' russkaia istoriia do marksistov*, M. 1931; G. Zaidel' and M. Tsvibak, *Klassovyi vrag na istor. fronte*, Moscow, Leningrad, 1931; S.A. Piontkovsky, *Burzhuaznaia istor. nauka v Rossii*, M. 1931; RTsKhIDNI, f. 147, op. 1, d. 33, ll. 42–6, d. 42, ll. 5–13.
43 RTsKhIDNI, f. 147, op. 2, d. 11, ll. 1, 5. Tarle (1874–1955) had been arrested in January 1930 as a leading suspect in the "Academy case", fabricated by the OGPU. He had supposedly been designated putative Foreign minister in a Provisional government to be headed by Platonov. On Tarle see now Chapkevich, *Poka iz ruk ne vypalo pero . . .*, 89–95; Leonov (ed.), *Akademicheskoe delo*, fasc. 2.
44 *Pravda*, 12 April 1931.
45 RTsKhIDNI, f. 147, op. 1, d. 30, l. 176.
46 Keep, "Rehabilitation of Pokrovskii", 397, 404; Govorkov, *Pokrovsky o predmete istor. nauki*; Enteen, *Soviet Scholar-Bureaucrat*; idem, "Spor o Pokrovskom", 155–6; Litvin, *Bez prava na mysl'*, 13–16; Artizov, "Pokrovsky: final kar'ery", 138–40.
47 TsA FSB RF, d. R-8214, ll. 370–3.
48 L. Graham, *The Soviet Academy of Sciences and the Communist Party, 1927–1932*, Princeton, 1967; *Repressirovannaia nauka*; Perchenok, "Akademiia nauk na 'velikom perelome'", 163–235; *Akademicheskoe delo 1929–1931 gg.*, fasc. 1.
49 Solovei, "Istor. nauka i politika", 149–68; Sokolov, *Istoriia i politika*, 5–9.
50 Volkogonov, "Stalinizm: sushchnost', genezis, evoliutsiia", 12; Reiman, "Perestroika", 146.
51 Shteppa, *Russian Historians*, 380; cf. Alekseeva, "Okt. rev. i istor. nauka", 45.
52 Davies, *Soviet History in the Gorbachev Revolution*, 167–8; idem, "Sovetskaia istor. nauka", 69; Dzhimbinov, "Epitafiia spetskhranu?", 243–52.
53 *OA*, 1/1992, 3.
54 See Artizov, "Kritika M.N. Pokrovskogo", 107–8; "1937 god: IKP", 135, 143.
55 Litvin, *Bez prava na mysl'*.
56 Preobrazhensky, "Novosel'sky", in *Istoriki Rossii XVIII-XX vv.*, 122–32; Kobrin, *Veselovsky*; Chistiakova, *Tikhomirov*.
57 Krivosheev and Dvornichenko, "Izgnanie nauki", 143–58.
58 Zakharova, *P.A. Zaionchkovsky, 1904–1983 gg.*, 17, 19, 121.
59 D. Shturman, "Deti utopii", *Novyi mir*, 10/1994, 194–5; cf. P.G. Grigorenko, *V podpol'e mozhno vstretit' tol'ko krys . . .*, Moscow 1997, 295–7; A. Amal'rik, *Zapiski dissidenta*.
60 Sharapov, *Litsei v Sokol'nikakh*, 87; Poliakov, "Put' poznaniia istorii", 141–2.

61 Sidorova, "A.M. Pankratova", in: *Istor. nauka Rossii*, 419–36.
62 "Pis'ma A.M. Pankratovoi"; "Novye dokumenty o soveshchanii istorikov".
63 Hösler, *Die sowjetische Geschichtswissenschaft*, 35–40; Kan, "Anna Pankratova"; Gorodetsky, "Zhurnal 'Vop. istorii'"; Burdzhalov, "O sostoianii sovetskoi istor. nauki"; Sidorova, *Ottepel' v istor. nauke*.
64 *Izvestiia TsK KPSS*, 3/1989. It had been published in the West in 1956. There are differences between the two texts, since Khrushchev added some remarks written by D.T. Shepilov, a Party secretary (and earlier at least an ardent Stalinist). Barsukov, "XX s'ezd", 174. In 1999 Poliakov made what I consider to be an unsuccessful effort to present Pospelov (1898–1979), a leading ideologist, as a humane individual: "Shtrikhi k portretu (vosp. o P.N. Pospelove)", *OI*, 5/1999, 154–63.
65 *Istochnik* 2/1994, 78; Alexeyeva, *Soviet Dissent*; Bezborodov, "Istoriografiia istorii dissidentskogo dvizheniia", 401–23.
66 *OI*, 6/1998, 57–85; cf. Litvin, "Epistoliarnoe nasledie", 29–32. For more on Zimin see Kashtanov and Chernobaev, "A.A. Zimin", in *Istoriki Rossii XVIII–XX vv.*, 133–48; Kireeva, "Iz istorii sovetskoi istor. nauki", in *Rossiia v XX v.*, 487–95.
67 *1941. 22 iunia*, Moscow.
68 Nekrich, *Otrekshis' ot strakha*, 272.
69 Hösler, *Die sowjetische Geschichtswissenschaft,* 169–77.
70 Ibid., 177–84; Baron and Heer, *Windows on the Russian Past;* Volobuev, "Ot prirody", 11–13; Polikarpov, "Novoe napravlenie", 349–400. On Volobuev (1923–1997), Gefter (1918–1995) and Tarnovsky (1921–1987) see the articles by V.L. Telitsyin, E.I. Vysochina, V.A. Yemets and V.V. Shelokhaev in the recent volume *Istoriki Rossii: poslevoennoe pokolenie*, compiled by L.V. Maksimova.
71 Leiberov, "Kak my zashchishchali P.V. Volobueva", 27–33; Shelokhaev, *Proshchanie s proshlym*, 149–54.
72 Got'e, *Moi zametki*; "Dnevnik Druzhinina"; "Iz dnevnikov Sergeia Sergeevicha Dmitrieva"; Veselovsky, "Dnevniki 1915–1923, 1944 gg."
73 *OI*, 1/2000, 161.
74 *VI* 2/2000, 90.
75 Cf. Miagkov, *Nauchnoe soobshchestvo*, 160–1, 192, 216–19.
76 Markwick, "Volobuev i istoriki 'novogo napravleniia'", 495.
77 Tsamutali, "Glava peterburgskoi istor. shkoly", 542, 546.
78 Poliakov, *Istor. nauka*, 313–16.
79 Paneiakh, "Uprazdnenie"; Anan'ich and Paneiakh, "O peterburgskoi", 111–12.
80 Sidorova, "Shkoly", 202–3.
81 Troitsky, in *Istoriki Rossii o vremeni i o sebe*, ii. 14, 27; Shelokhaev, op. cit., 197–8.
82 *Inogo ne dano*, 318, 322.
83 *Izvestiia TsK KPSS*, 7/1990, 137; Shelokhaev, op. cit., 210–15.

84 Volkogonov, *Etiudy o vremeni*, 39–40. He is the author of notable critical biographies of Stalin, Trotsky and Lenin, all of which have been translated into English.
85 Actually Gorbachev, like other General Secretaries before him, had been shown when he took over power the top-secret Politburo decision of March 1940 to exterminate the interned Polish officers and other captives.
86 Afanas'ev, "Fenomen sovetskoi istoriografii", 37.
87 Pavlenko, "Istor. nauka v proshlom i nastoiashchem", 94, 96; Enteen, "Intellektual'nye predposylki", 151.
88 Danilov, in *Rossiia v XX v.*, 22–30. Koval'chenko's introductory remarks were not included in the published conference proceedings.
89 Poliakov, *Nashe nepredskazuemoe proshloe*, 11–13, 90, 115, 128; idem, in *Rossiia v XX v.*, 31–42.
90 *Vsesoiuznaia perepis' naseleniia 1937 g.: kratkie itogi*, Moscow 1991; Bugai, *From Beria to Stalin: In Accordance with Your Instructions*, Moscow 1995 and articles in *IS*, 1/1991, *VI*, 7/1990, *OI*, 4/1992, 4/1993; V.N. Zemskov, articles in *Argumenty i fakty* 45/1989, *SOI*, 11/1990, 2, 6–7/1991, *Rodina*, 21(1–2)/1994, *OA*, 1/1993 and later publications.
91 Davies, *Soviet History in the Yeltsin Era*, 118.
92 Among these volumes are, for instance, the minutes of the Constitutional–Democratic (Kadet) party's executive from 1905 to the mid-1930s (5 vols., 1994–7), three volumes on the Mensheviks in 1917 (1994–7), and Kashtanov's *Aktovaia arkheografiia*, 1998.
93 *OA*, 5/1993, 3–10. For the archival regulations issued on December 1998 see *OA*, 1/99, 3–8.
94 A. Prokopenko, "Arkhivy snova zakryvaiutsia: nas opiat' khotiat lishit' istoricheskoi pamiati", *Izvestiia*, 25 Sept. 1997; Chubar'ian, "Kazhdaia epokha imeet svoe prednaznachenie", in *Istoriki Rossii o vremeni i o sebe*, ii. 43.
95 Iskenderov, "Istor. nauka na poroge XXI v.", 26–9.
96 Davies, *Soviet History in the Yeltsin Era*, 220.
97 *Istor. issledovaniia v Rossii: tendentsii poslednikh let*, Moscow 1996; *Rossiia i reformy*, fascs. 1–4, Moscow 1991–7; cf. "Novoe pokolenie rossiiskikh istorikov", 104–24.
98 *Istor. issledovaniia*, 7.
99 *OI*, 4/1997, 106–9, 118; 3/1998, 195.
100 D. Svak [G. Szvak], "O nekotorykh metodologicheskikh problemakh", 91–2.
101 *Programmy distsiplin spetsializatsii po otechestvennoi istorii*, Moscow 2000, 8, 24, 30, 51.

2 Approaching the Past

1 Reiman, "Perestroika", 145–6, 158.
2 A.S. Cherniaev, *Shest' let s Gorbachevym*, Moscow 1993, 207.

3 Cited by Bolkhovitinov, "Sovetskaia amerikanistika", 4.
4 Afanas'ev, in *VI*, 4/1989, 102, 104.
5 V.I. Chesnokov, *Prav. politika i istor. nauka Rossii*, 185.
6 Good studies of the Soviet elite include A. Avtorkhanov, *Proiskhozhdenie partokratii*, 2 vols., Frankfurt 1973; M. Voslensky, *Nomenklatura: the Soviet Ruling Class*, tr. E. Mosbacher, NY 1984; cf. also T.H. Rigby, *Communist Party Membership in the USSR, 1917–1967*, Princeton NJ 1968.
7 "Pis'ma A.N. Pankratovoi", 72–3.
8 K.B. Litvak, "K voprosu o partiinykh perepisiakh . . .", *VI KPSS*, 2/ 1991, 86.
9 *30-e gody: vzgliad iz segodnia*, Moscow 1990, 27.
10 Lenin, to be sure, studied law as an external student at St Petersburg University, but soon became a professional revolutionary; Stalin and his successors received their training above all in the practical world of political struggle.
11 Golubev, "Noveishaia istoriia Rossii v uchebnikakh 1995 g.", *Istor. issled. v Rossii*, 65.
12 Malia, "Iz-pod glyb, no chto?", 107; idem, *The Soviet Tragedy: A History of Socialism in Russia, 1917–1991*, NY 1994, 491–520.
13 Poliakov, *Nashe nepredskazuemoe proshloe*, 124; idem, "Arkhivy – zolotaia kladovaia", 78.

3 The October Revolution

1 The proceedings were published under the titles: *Anatomiia revoliutsii. 1917 g. v Rossii: massy, partii, vlast'*, St Petersburg, 1994; *Fevral'skaia revoliutsiia: ot novykh istochnikov k novomu osmysleniiu*, Moscow 1998; *Oktiabr'skaia revoliutsiia: ot novykh istochnikov k novomu osmysleniiu*, Moscow 1998; *Rossiia i pervaia mirovaia voina*, St Petersburg, 1999.
2 *Anatomiia revoliutsii*, 38, 50–1; Buldakov, "Istor. metamorfozy", 182.
3 Mints, "Metamorfozy", 107–22; Startsev, "Ross. masony" and in *VI*, 3/1988, 39. Since then several studies have appeared such as O.F. Solov'ev, *Russkoe masonstvo, 1730–1917*, Moscow 1993 and A.I. Serkov, *Istoriia russkogo masonstva, 1845–1945*, St Petersburg 1997. Serkov shows that although there were masons in the Provisional government this was not a factor in the fall of tsarism. Another writer, I.S. Rozental', has more recently pointed out that some Social Democrats, too, were also masons: the Bolshevik I.I. Skvortsov-Stepanov and the Menshevik N.S. Chkheidze. "Masony i popytki ob'edineniia politicheskoi oppozitsii v Rossii nachala XX v.", *VI*, 2/2000, 52–67.
4 See, for example, E. Acton, "Novyi vzgliad na russkuiu revoliutsiiu", *OI*, 5/1997, 69.
5 *Kommunist*, 12/1990, 21.
6 "Interv'iu s akad. P.V. Volobuevym", *OI*, 5/1997, 118–20. For an earlier Western appreciation, Keep, "Soviet Historians", 405–15.

7 G.V. Plekhanov, *God na rodine*, Petrograd 1921, i. 129, 218.

8 *Martov i ego blizkie*, NY 1959, 48 (letter of 30 Dec. 1917).

9 Buldakov, *Krasnaia smuta: priroda i posledstsviia revoliutsionnogo nasiliia*, Moscow 1997, 215.

10 Mints, *Ist. Velikogo Oktiabria*, 3 vols., Moscow 1967–73 (2nd edn Moscow 1977).

11 The council was chaired in succession by Mints (1957–88), Volobuev (1988–97) and S.V. Tiutiukin (1997–). During the Gorbachev era attention began to be paid to the non-Bolshevik parties and voices were even raised in criticism of the "proletarian dictatorship" as incompatible with *Rechtsstaat* principles: see K.F. Shatsillo, '"Kruglyi stol'", 182.

12 *Istor. issled. v Rossii*, 179.

13 *Petrogradskii Voenno-revoliutsionnyi komitet: dokumenty i materialy*, 3 vols., Moscow 1966–7; E.N. Burdzhalov, *Vtoraia russkaia revoliutsiia*, Moscow 1971 (Eng. tr. by D. Raleigh: *Russia's Second Revolution . . .*, Bloomington; Indianapolis IN, 1987); L.M. Spirin, *1917 god: iz istorii bor'by politicheskikh partii*, Moscow 1987.

14 *Fevral'skaia revoliutsiia 1917: sbornik dok. i materialov*, Moscow 1996; *Petrogradskii Sovet rabochikh i soldatskikh deputatov v 1917 g.*, vol. I: *27 fevralia–31 marta 1917 g.*, St Petersburg 1993; *II-oi Vseros. s'ezd Sovetov . . .: sb. dok. i materialov*, Moscow 1997; *Men'sheviki v 1917 g.: dokumenty*, 3 vols., Moscow 1994–7. Characteristically, the latter contains material from newspapers of various political colouring, whereas its 1928 forerunner did not.

15 Buldakov, "Oktiabr' i XX v.", in *Okt. rev.* (see n. 14), 11.

16 Zhuravlev, "Ot smeny", 108; idem, "God 1917–y v kontekste", 237.

17 But see the proceedings of two colloquia held in St. Petersburg in 1990 and 1995: *Reformy ili revoliutsiia? Rossiia 1861–1917*, 1992; *Rabochie i intelligentsiia Rossii v epokhu reform i revoliutsii, 1861 – fevral' 1917 g.*, 1997; cf., by a British historian, David Saunders, "The Static Society: Patterns of Work in the Later Russian Empire", in G. Hosking and R. Service (eds), *Reinterpreting Russia*, London 1999, 126–41.

18 Buldakov, *Krasnaia smuta*; idem, "'Krasnaia smuta' na 'kruglom stole'," *OI*, 4/1998, 139–68.

19 Iu.G. Fel'shtinsky, "Kak dobyvalis' den'gi dlia revoliutsii", *VI*, 9/1988, 34–51; A.M. Sovokin, "Mif o 'nemetskikh millionakh'", *VI*, 4/1991, 69–79; V.I. Startsev, *Nenapisannyi roman F. Ossendovskogo*, 2 pts., St Petersburg 1994; S. Lyandres, "The Bolsheviks' 'German Gold' Revisited: An Inquiry into the 1917 Accusations," *Carl Beck Papers in Russian and East European Studies*, Pittsburgh 1995.

20 Fel'shtinsky, op. cit., 49–50.

21 Lyandres, op. cit., 94–6; idem, "Nemetskoe finansovoe uchastie v russkoi revoliutsii", in *Rossiia v 1917 g.: novye podkhody i vzgliady*, St Petersburg 1993.

22 Startsev, op. cit., i. 6–7.

23 N.I. Dedkov, "Kak ia dokumental'no ustanovil . . .", *Istor. issled. v Rossii*, 114–38; V.I. *Lenin: neizvestnye dokumenty 1891–1922*, Moscow 1999. For the archive's change of name (15 March 1999): *Informatsionnyi biulleten'*, 23/1999, 15–17.

24 Volkogonov, "Leninskaia krepost' v moei dushe pala poslednei", *Mosk. novosti*, 19 July 1992.

25 R. Pipes (ed.), *The Unknown Lenin: from the Secret Archive*, New Haven CT; London 1996.

26 On 6 January 1917 (O.S.) Lenin wrote to his friend Inessa Armand in Geneva that her fears about "German captivity" were excessive. Pipes thought this had something to do with secret financial arrangements, but Loginov holds, (rightly, in my view) that it simply refers to the possibility that, if Switzerland were to be drawn into the war, the French would occupy Geneva and the Germans Zurich, so cutting off communication between the two comrades. Pipes, op. cit., 34; V. Loginov, "O 'plombirovannom vagone' . . .", *Kommunist*, 5/1991, 124–6; *Lenin: neizvestnye dokumenty*, 200, 582. Incidentally, we now know that when the Soviet censor responsible for supervising the publication of Lenin documents, G.D. Obichkin, came upon one of Lenin's letters to Armand addressed "Dear friend" he would let it through, but if it was headed "Very dear friend" it went into the secret archive. See Yu.P. Sharapov in *OI*, 3/2000, 188.

27 A.V. Pantsov, "L.D. Trotsky", *VI*, 5/1990, 65–87; Volkogonov, *Trotsky: politicheskii portret*, 2 vols., Moscow 1992 (Eng. tr. by H. Shukman, *Trotsky: the Eternal Revolutionary*, London 1996).

28 See the critical appraisal by Pantsov and A.L. Cherevishnikov in *Istor. issled. v Rossii*, 100–14.

29 S. Koen [Cohen], *Bukharin: politicheskaia biografiia, 1888–1938*, Moscow 1988.

30 V.V. Yurchenko, "O nekotorykh pravovykh aspektakh resheniia II-go s'ezda", *Rossiia v XX v.*, 288.

31 Ts. Khasegava [Hasegawa], in *Fevral'skaia revoliutsiia* (see n. 14), 98–101; D. Shturman, "Ostanivimo li krasnoe koleso? . . .", *Novyi mir*, 2/1993, 150–2. A.I. Solzhenitsyn, *Krasnoe koleso*, Paris 1984. H. Willetts's English translation of the second "knot", *November 1916*, appeared in May 1999; two more sections of the work are to follow.

32 *Nezavisimaia gazeta*, 3 June 1999.

33 *Rabochie i ross. obshchestvo: II-aia pol. XIX – nach. XX v.*, St Petersburg 1994, 5; Buldakov, in *Istor. issled. v Rossii*, 188–9; Marsel' van Linden (ed.), *Konets rabochei istorii*, Moscow 1996, 11–12; E. Acton, "Novyi vzgliad na russkuiu revoliutsiiu", *OI*, 5/1997, 77–8.

34 G.A. Gerasimenko, *Narod i vlast': 1917*, Moscow 1995; D. Raleigh, *Revolution on the Volga: Saratov in 1917*, Ithaca NY; London 1986 (Russ. edn: *Polit. sud'by ross. gubernii: 1917 v Saratove*, Saratov 1995); D.O. Churakov, *Russkaia revoliutsiia i rabochee samoupravlenie: 1917*, Moscow 1998; N.N. Kabytova, *Vlast' i obshchestvo v ross. provintsii: 1917 g. v Povolzh'e*, Samara 1999.

35 Sal'nikova, *Istorich. istochnik*; Kudinova, *Otech. istoriografiia revoliutsii*; Malysheva, *Ross. Vremennoe pravitel'stvo* . . .; idem, *Vrem. Pravitel'stvo*.

4 The Civil War

1 V.P. Danilov and A. Berelowitch (eds), *Sovetskaia derevnia glazami VChK-NKVD, 1918–1939: OGPU-dok. i mat. v 4 tt.*, Moscow 1998, i. 49; cf. Yu.A. Poliakov, *Sov. strana posle okonchaniia grazhd. voiny* . . ., Moscow 1986.

2 N.F. Kuz'min, "K istorii razgroma belogvardeiskikh voisk Denikina", *VI*, 7/1956, 18–32; S.F. Naida, "Pochemu den' Sovetskoi armii . . . 23 fevralia?", *VIZh*, 5/1964, 114–17.

3 L.M. Spirin, "Partiia bol'shevikov v grazhd. voine", *Kommunist*, 14/1990, 95. A.N. Yakovlev was editor-in-chief of the new Party history, which has yet to be published in full.

4 *Proiskhozhdenie i nachal'nyi etap grazhd. voiny: 1918 g.*, pt. 1, Moscow 1994, 6, 58; Malia, *Soviet Tragedy*, 113.

5 The worst offenders in this respect were military historians. Cf. *Grazhd. voina i voennaia interventsiia v SSSR: entsiklopedia*, Moscow 1983. They saw the Whites as mere puppets of their "imperialist" backers.

6 V.I. Goldin, *Interventsiia i antibol'shevistskoe dvizhenie na Russkom Severe 1918–1920*, Moscow 1993. See also the interesting article by A. Bykov of Vologda, based on US as well as Russian archives, about the foreign diplomatic corps' stay in that city in 1918: *Izvestiia*, 18 July 1997.

7 "Grazhd. voina: novoe prochtenie starykh problem", *Istor. issled. v Rossii*, 219.

8 *Izvestiia TsK KPSS*, 6/1989, 175–8.

9 In 1989 V. Kozhinov and G. Nazarov put all the blame on "the Jew" Sverdlov, but this was just crude antisemitism. Today historians are inclined to hold the entire Soviet leadership responsible: A.I. Kozlov, *Vozrozhdenie kazachestva* . . ., Rostov-on-Don 1995, 132; V. Danilov and N.S. Tarkhova, Introduction to idem and T. Shanin (eds.), *Filipp Mironov: Tikhii Don v 1917–1921 gg.: dok. i mat.*, Moscow 1997, 12–14. Cf. the important article on "decossackization" by P. Holquist in *CMRS*, 38 (1997), 127–62.

10 V.V. Kabanov and L.A. Molchanov, in *OI*, 3/1999, 204.

11 G.V. Nabatov et al., *Politicheskaia Rossiia v gody grazhd. voiny: uchebnoe posobie*, Nizhnii Novgorod 1997; S.V. Ustinkin, in *OI*, 3/1998, 83–102.

12 These republications of emigré works are welcome, but sometimes things are taken a little too far. R. Gul's work on the "Ice Campaign" in the Kuban' in the first months of 1918 has gone through no less than five identical editions, all based, not on the author's original, but on a version offered to Soviet publishing houses in the 1920s. *Istor. issled. v Rossii*, 211.

13 P.N. Miliukov, *Rossiia na perelome*, 2 vols., Paris 1927; S.P. Mel'gunov, *Tragediia admirala Kolchaka* . . ., 3 pts., Belgrade 1930–1.
14 Ushakov, *Istoriia grazhd. voiny*; Emel'ianov, *Mel'gunov*; V.Zh. Tsvetkov, "Beloe dvizhenie v Rossii", *VI*, 7/2000, 56–73.
15 S. Fitzpatrick, in *Grazhdanskaia voina v Rossii: perekrestok mnenii*, Moscow 1994, 344.
16 P. Kenez, in *Rossiia XIX-XX vv.*, 183, 186, 191.
17 G.A. Trukan, foreword to: *Rossiia antibol'shevistskaia: iz belogvardeiskikh i emigrantskikh arkhivov*, Moscow 1995, 3; idem, "Verkhovnyi pravitel' Rossii", *OI*, 6/1999, 27–46; A.I. Kozlov, "Anton Ivanovich Denikin", *VI*, 10/1995; *Beloe dvizhenie na iuge Rossii* . . ., Moscow 1997; A.I. Ushakov and V.P. Fediuk, *Belyi iug* . . ., Moscow 1997.
18 T.F. Pavlova et al. (comps.), "*Milaia, obozhaemaia moia Anna Vasil'evna*", Moscow 1997; L.V. Kuras, "Belaia Rossiia: ataman G.M. Semenov", *Inform. biulleten' Guman. obshch.-nauchnogo tsentra*, Irkutsk, 5/1995.
19 This had amounted to 1 milliard roubles when it fell into Kolchak's hands in 1918. Semenov eventually obtained 44 m. roubles, of which he gave half to the Japanese; a quarter went on maintaining his own men and some was seized by the Chinese. TsA FSB, d. N-18765, t. 25, d. 5. Cf. V.G. Sirotkin, *Zoloto i nedvizhimost' Rossii za rubezhom* . . ., Moscow 1997, 120–53.
20 N. Pereira, *Inside Siberia: the Politics of Civil War*, Montreal 1996 (Russ. edn. Moscow 1996); P.N. Dmitriev and K.I. Kulikov, *Miatezh v Izhevsko-votkinskom raione*, Izhevsk 1992; Vereshchagin, "Paradoksy"; Bordiugov et al., *Beloe delo*, 266–70; Mikhailov, "Beloe delo", 400–1.
21 "Gosud. rezhimy perioda grazhd. voiny v Rossii", *Istor. sovetskoi Rossii*, 55.
22 E.G. Gimpel'son, *Formirovanie sov. polit. sistemy, 1917–1923 gg.*, Moscow 1995; S.A. Pavliuchenkov, *Voennyi kommunizm v Rossii: vlast'i massy*, Moscow 1997.
23 *Gorozhanin kak politik: revoliutsiia, voennyi kommunizm i NEP glazami petrogradtsev*, St Petersburg 1999; idem, *Krest'ianin kak politik: krest'ianstvo severo-zapada Rossii v 1918–1919 gg.* . . ., St Petersburg, 1999.
24 Silvana Malle calculates that in 1918–1919 the peasants paid twice as much to the state as all their taxes and dues in 1912: *Economic Organization of War Communism, 1918–1921*, London 1985, 500–1.
25 D.A. Kovalenko, *Oboronnaia promyshlennost' sov. Rossii v 1918–1920 gg.*, Moscow 1970, 252–3.
26 E.G. Gimpel'son, in *Ist. SSSR*, 3/1987, 63–4 and *OI*, 5/2000, 45; idem, *Sovetskie upravlentsy 1917–1920 gg.*, Moscow 1998; E. Ikeda, "Fenomen sovetskogo biurokratizma v gody grazhdanskoi voiny", in *Akademik Volobuev*, 362–3.
27 V.D. Bonch-Bruevich, *Vosp. o Lenine*, Moscow 1965, 226–8.
28 V.I. Lenin, *PSS*, xliii.64.
29 V.P. Danilov and T. Shanin (eds.), *Krest'ianskoe vosstanie v Tambovskoi gub. v 1919–21 gg.: "Antonovshchina": dok. i mat.*, Tambov 1994; V.I.

Shishkin (comp. & ed.), *Sibir'skaia Vandeia: vooruzh. soprotivlenie kom. rezhimu v 1920 g.*, Novosibirsk 1997.

30 *Sovetskaia derevnia* (see n. 1): this is a Franco-Russian joint project.

31 Today these insurgencies are no longer falsely labelled "kulak uprisings": see A.A. Kurenyshev, "Krest'ianstvo Rossii", 154.

32 R.W. Davies, "NEP i sovremennost'", *Kommunist*, 8/1990, 74–9; Orlov, "Sovremennaia otech. istoriografiia".

33 Some of the relevant works are: A.Ya. Livshin and I.B. Orlov (comps.), *Pis'ma vo vlast', 1917–1927: zaiavleniia, zhaloby, donosy . . .*, Moscow 1998; A.V. Kvashonkin et al. (comps.), *Bol'shevistskoe rukovodstvo: perepiska, 1912–1927: sb. dok.*, Moscow 1996; V.P. Naumov and A.A. Kosakovsky (comps.), *Kronshtadt 1921*, Moscow 1997; S.V. Zhuravlev et al. (eds.), *Golos naroda: pis'ma i otkliki riadovykh sov. grazhdan o sobytiiakh 1918–1932 gg.*, Moscow 1998; D.Kh. Ibrakhimova, *NEP i perestroika: massovoe soznanie sel'skogo naseleniia v usloviiakh perekhoda k rynku*, Moscow 1997.

34 Lenin, *PSS*, xliv. 428.

35 On the interwar period see esp. N.N. Pokrovsky and S.G. Petrov (eds), *Arkhivy Kremlia*, bk. 1: *Politbiuro i tserkov", v. 1922–1925*, Moscow Novosibirsk 1997; N.A. Krivova, *Vlast' i tserkov', 1922–1925 gg.: Politbiuro v bor'be za tserkovnye tsennosti . . .*, Moscow 1997; A.N. Kashevarov, *Gosudarstvo i tserkov' . . . 1917–1943 gg.*, St Petersburg, 1995; and articles by M.V. Sharovsky on the "Josephans" ("catacomb church") in *Minuvshee* 15, 1994, 441–63 (Eng. tr. in *Slavic Review*, 1995, 365–84); and O.Yu. Vasil'eva in *VI*, 8/1993 and 4/1994. This work complements recent Western studies by G. Freeze, D.J. Dunn, A. Luukkanen, G. Young, E.E. Roslof *et al.*

36 Two recent works are: *Rossiia v izgnanii: sud'by ross. emigrantov za rubezhom*, Moscow 1999; M.G. Vandalkovskaia, *Istor. nauka ross. emigratsii: "evraziiskii" soblazn*, Moscow 1997.

37 *The Cheka: Lenin's Political Police*, Oxford 1981.

38 TsA FSB RF, f. 1, op. 1–6.

39 "Then the Party workers depended on the NKVD organs to a greater extent than they did on us. To say the truth, it was not we who directed them but they who imposed their will on us." N.S. Khrushchev, *Vospominaniia: izbrannye fragmenty*, Moscow 1997, 51–2.

40 *Lubianka, 2: iz istorii otech. kontrrazvedki*, Moscow 1999, 164, 198.

41 N.V. Petrov, "Pervyi predsedatel' KGB gen. I. Serov", *OI*, 5/1997, 23–43; idem and K.V. Skorkin, *Kto rukovodil NKVD, 1934–1941: spravochnik*, Moscow 1999.

42 A.L. Litvin (ed.), *Levye SRy i VChK: sb. dok.*, Kazan' 1996; idem, *Genrikh Yagoda, narkom vnutrennykh del SSSR . . .: sb. dok.*, Kazan' 1997; R.G. Pikhoia (ed.), *Lubianka 1917–1960: spravochnik, dokumenty*, Moscow 1997; M.N. Petrov, *VChK-OGPU: pervoe desiatiletie (na materialakh sev.-zap. Rossii)*, Novgorod 1995; V.S. Izmozik, *Glaza i ushi rezhima: gosud. kontrol'za naseleniem sov. Rossii v 1918–1928 gg.*, St Petersburg 1995;

V.N. Khaustov, *Deiatel'nost' organov gosud. bezopasnosti . . . 1934–1941*, Moscow 1997.

43 R.H. Johnston, *New Mecca, New Babylon: Paris and the Russian Exiles, 1920–1945*, Kingston Ont.: (Montreal, Quebec 1988, 101, 141.

44 TsA FSB RF, f. 1, op. 2, d. 2, l. 118; *Otchet VChK za 4 goda*, Moscow 1921, 19.

45 TsA FSB RF, d. PF-9489, t. 1, ch. 2, l. 9.

5 The Age of Stalin

1 The most recent Western work, I. Kershaw and M. Lewin (eds), *Stalinism and Nazism : Dictatorships in Comparison*, Cambridge MA 1997, promises more than it delivers.

2 S. Fitzpatrick, *The Russian Revolution*, London 1995, and other works.

3 Volkogonov, *Stalin: Triumph and Tragedy*, London 1991 (Russ. edn in 2 pts., Moscow 1989), Tucker, *Stalin as Revolutionary, 1879–1929*, NY 1973 and *Stalin in Power: the Revolution from Above, 1928–1941*, NY; London 1990 (Russ. edn Moscow 1990, 1997).

4 Volkogonov, "Stalinizm: sushchnost', genezis, evoliutsiia", *VI*, 3/1990, 6; Tucker, "V tsentre vnimaniia – sov. istoriia", *Kommunist*, 9/1990, 82.

5 V. Grossman, *Zhizn' i sud'ba*, vol. 1, Moscow 1990, 264; for similar arguments see N.S. Simonov, "Termidor, briumer ili friuktidor? . . .", *OI*, 4/1993, 17; F.-X. Coquin, in *Rossiia v XX v.*, 344–51; G. Hosking, interview published in *OI*, 5/1997, 125.

6 *OI*, 5/1993, 215. The argument in favour of an ideological interpretation of Soviet history has recently been taken forward forcefully by M. Malia, *Russia under Western Eyes . . .*, Cambridge MA; London 1999.

7 Keep, "Stalinism in Post-Soviet Historical Writing", 1999, first published in *Neue Polit. Literatur*, 3/1995.

8 Reiman, "Zametki po probleme stalinizma", 228–9, 231.

9 Hösler, "Sowjetische und russische Interpretationen des Stalinismus", 67–8.

10 Pavlova, "Sovremennye zap. istoriki", 107–21; *idem*, "I snova ob istorikakh-'revizionistakh'", 125–6, 136–40.

11 V.A. Kozlov and S.V. Mironenko (eds), *'Osobaia papka' I.V. Stalina . . . 1944–1953 gg.: katalog dokumentov*, Moscow 1994; RTsKhIDNI, *Putevoditel' po fondam i kollektsiiam lichnogo proiskhozhdeniia*, vol. 2, Moscow 1996, 233–9 (the Stalin collection is no. 558 and has 16,174 units).

12 "I.V. Stalin o sebe . . .", *Izv. TsK KPSS* 9/1990; "Posetiteli kremlevskogo kabineta I.V. Stalina . . .", *IA*, 6/1994 *et seq*.

13 Here is one from the early 1930s: at a May Day parade an old man could be seen carrying a poster that read "Thanks to Stalin for Our Happy Childhood". A policeman stops him: "Have you gone out of your mind, old fellow? When you were a lad Stalin wasn't even born." "That's why I'm grateful", came the reply.

14 L.M. Spirin, "Kogda rodilsia Stalin . . .", *Izvestiia*, 25 June 1990.
15 *Idem*, "Zhivite 10,000 let . . .", *Nezavisimaia gazeta*, 13 August 1992.
16 *Loc. cit.*
17 Yu.G. Murin (comp.), V.N. Denisov (ed.), *Iosif Stalin v ob'iatiiakh sem'i: iz lichnogo arkhiva*, Moscow 1993. Maria Svanidze was the sister-in-law of Stalin's first wife, Yekaterina Svanidze, who died *ca.* 1909.
18 Tucker, *Stalin*, i. 217; *Argumenty i fakty*, 25 February 1989. The rumour at the time that Stalin actually shot his wife is still circulating: cf. *Komsom. pravda*, 14 April 1998.
19 Arkhiv KGB Rep. Tatarstan, file 1588, vol. 1, ff. 1, 154, 222, 238, 257: it cost the sum of 426 roubles and 5 kopecks. Cf. Litvin, "Poslednyi god Vasiliia Stalina", *Izvestiia*, 2 October 1993; "Interv'iu s K. Vasil'evoi", *Komsom. pravda*, 12 May 1999. For his rehabilitation: *Izvestiia*, 1 October 1999.
20 Ye. Dzhugashvili, "Epokha bor'by i pobed", *Mol. gvardiia*, 3/1991; S.G. Malenkov, *O moem ottse Georgii Malenkove*, Moscow 1992; S. Beria, *Moi otets – Lavrentyi Beria*, Moscow 1994; V. Alliluev, *Khronika odnoi sem'i*, Moscow 1995.
21 O. Moroz, "Poslednyi diagnoz", *Lit. gazeta*, 39/1988 (28 Sept.). Bekhterev died that year in suspicious circumstances.
22 *Byl li Stalin agentom Okhranki? Sb. statei, materialov i dokumentov*, Moscow 1999; E. Ellis Smith, *The Young Stalin . . .*, NY 1972; Tucker, *Stalin*, i. 108–14.
23 A. Ulam, "Gipnoz Stalina", *Izvestiia*, 29 May 1991; cf. his *Stalin: the Man and His Era*, NY 1973.
24 L. Gurints, "Iz zapisnykh kniazhek", *Zvezda*, 3/1988, 186.
25 L.D. Trotsky, *Stalin* (Russ. edn), ii. 250.
26 A. Litvin, *Dva sledstvennykh dela Yevgenii Ginzburg*, Kazan' 1994, 90.
27 V. Snegirev, "Boi na Lobnom meste", *Trud*, 18 June 1992; cf. P. Koroviakovsky, "Byli li pokusheniia na I. Stalina?", *Argumenty i fakty*, 10–16 February 1990; P. Cherkasov, "Strelial li v Stalin leitenant Danilov . . .?", *Izvestiia*, 5 Nov. 1995.
28 A. Zevelev, "'Otstavki' Stalina . . .", *Izvestiia*, 21 June 1989; Yu. Murin, "Eshche raz ob otstavkakh I. Stalina", *Rodina*, 7/1994, 72–3.
29 O.V. Khlevniuk, *Stalin i Ordzhonikidze: konflikty v Politbiuro v 30-e gg.*, Moscow 1993 (Eng. edn, tr. D.J. Nordlander, *In Stalin's Shadow: the Career of "Sergo" Ordzhonikidze*, NY; London 1995); M. Sultan-Galiev, *Izbr. trudy*, Kazan' 1998.
30 I. Kossakovsky, "Opponent Stalina", *Lit. gazeta*, 26 Dec. 1990. Frumkin was shot in August 1938 and rehabilitated in 1957.
31 "Kak ia stal 'poslednei zhertvoi'", *Pravda*, 29 September 1989.
32 N. Simonov, "Razmyshleniia o pometkakh Stalina na poliakh marksistskoi literatury", *Kommunist*, 18/1990; L. Spirin, "Glazami knig: lichnaia biblioteka Stalina", *Nezavisimaia gazeta*, 25 May 1993. We should recall that Stalin was the country's chief censor, as B.S. Ilizarov notes in *NNI*, 3/2000, 184.

33 "Interv'iu s A.T. Rybinym", *Mosk. komsomolets*, 9 Nov. 1991; "Interv'iu s A.N. Poskrebyshevym", *Vechernii klub*, 22 Dec. 1992.
34 A. Avtorkhanov, *Zagadka smerti Stalina (zagovor Beriia)*, Moscow 1992, 96–108; Khrushchev, *Vospominaniia*, Moscow 1997, 266–7.
35 A.L. Miasnikov, "Konchina", *Lit. gazeta*, 1 March 1989.
36 F. Konev, "Kak perezakhoranivali Stalina", *Argumenty i fakty*, 6–12 January 1990. Konev was a former commander of the Kremlin guard regiment.
37 "Protsess o chesti Stalina", *Novoe vremia*, 40/1988 (30 Sept.), 38–9.
38 *Sto sorok besed s Molotovym: iz dnevnika F. Chueva*, Moscow 1991, 390; cf. A. Golenkov, *I.V. Stalin*, Moscow 1994, 125.
39 "Interv'iu s R. Konkvestom", *Izvestiia*, 19 May 1990; cf. his collected essays, *Tyrants and Typewriters: Communiqués from the Struggle for Truth*, Lexington MA 1990.
40 V. Lel'chuk, "1934-i: beseda Stalinas Uellsom . . .", *Mosk. novosti*, 15 Oct. 1989.
41 A. Plutnik, "Moskva 1937 . . .", *Mosk. novosti*, 30 Oct. 1988.
42 D.A. Volkogonov, *Sem'vozhdei*, i. 260–1 (Eng. edn, tr. H. Shukman, *Autopsy for an Empire: the Seven Leaders who Built the Soviet Regime*, NY 1998). After Volkogonov's death in 1995 his archive was acquired by the Library of Congress, where it is accessible to scholars.
43 E. Maksimova, "Lichnyi fond Stalina . . .", *Izvestiia*, 30 Oct. 1999; A.A. Fursenko, "Poslednye gody Stalina", *Izvestiia*, 17 Dec. 1999; *idem*, "Konets ery Stalina", *Zvezda*, 12/1999, 184–5. For Western studies of recent archival practice, and researchers' difficulties, see Graziosi, "New Archival Sources", 13–64, and other contributions to this issue of *CMRS*.

6 The "Great" Terror

1 R. Conquest, *The Great Terror: A Reassessment*, London; NY 1990; *The Harvest of Sorrow: Soviet Collectivization and the Terror-Famine*, London 1988. A Russian-language edition of the first work was published in the West in 1972 but banned in the USSR; a two-volume translation appeared in Riga in 1991. Extracts from the second work were published in *VI*, 1–4/1990.
2 V.P. Danilov, "Diskussiia v zapadnoi presse o golode 1932–1933 gg. . . .", *VI*, 3/1988, 116–21; *idem*, "Otvet istoriku R. Konkvestu", *Mosk. novosti*, 14 May 1989. Cf. also N.A. Aralovets, "Poteri naseleniia sov. obshchestva v 1930–e gg. . . .", *OI*, 1/1995, 135–46; A. Graziosi, *The Great Soviet Peasant War: Bolsheviks and Peasants, 1917–1933*, Cambridge MA 1996; S.G. Wheatcroft, "Soviet Statistics of Nutrition and Mortality during Times of Famine, 1917–22, 1931–33", *CMRS*, 31 (1997), 514–58.
3 S. Maksudov (comp.), *Neuslyshannye golosa: dokumenty Smolenskogo arkhiva . . .*, Ann Arbor MI 1987; V.P. Danilov and N.A. Ivnitsky (eds),

Dokumenty svidetel'stvuiut: iz istorii derevni nakanune i v khode kollektivizatsii 1927–32 gg., Moscow 1989; R. Conquest, in *Slavic Review*, 53 (1994), 318–19; R.W. Davies *et al.*, "Stalin, Grain Stocks and the Famine of 1932–3", *ibid.* 54 (1995), 642–57; *Golod 1932–1933 gg.: sb. st.*, Moscow 1995; S. Merl, "Golod 1932–1933 g. – genozid ukraintsev . . .?", *OI*, 1/1995, 49–61; R.J. Pyrih *et al.* (comps.), F.M. Rudych *et al.* (eds), *Holod 1932–1933 rr. na Ukraine: ochyma istorykiv, movuiu dokumentiv*, Kiev 1990; *Tragediia sov. derevni: kollektivizatsiia i raskulachivanie: dok. i mat. v 5 tt.*, vol. 1, *mai 1927 – noiabr' 1929*, Moscow 1999; vol. 2, *noiabr' 1929 – dekabr' 1930*, Moscow 2000.

 4 I.E. Zelenin, "Revoliutsiia sverkhu . . .", *VI*, /1994, 34–5; V.P. Popov, "Pasportnaia sistema sov. krepostnichestva", *Novyi mir*, 6/1996, 185–203.

 5 G.M. Ivanova, *GULag v sisteme totalit. gosudarstva*, Moscow 1997, 31, 46; V.N. Zemskov, "Sud'ba kulatskoi ssylki", *OI*, 1/1994, 118; *idem*, "Zakliuchennye v 1930e gg. . . .", *OI*, 4/1997, 55, 58; M.B. Smirnov (comp.), N.G. Okhotin and A.B. Roginsky (eds), *Sistema isprav.-trudovykh lagerei v SSSR 1923–60: spravochnik*, Moscow 1998.

 6 *VI*, 10/1994.

 7 Zemskov calculates that between 1932 and 1940 no less than 629,042 inmates fled from places of settlement, of whom 235,120 were re-captured: *OI*, 1/1994, 128. Cf. also M.A. Benzin and T.M. Dimoni, "Sotsial'nyi protest kolkhoznogo krest'ianstva . . .", *OI*, 3/1999, 81–99; S. Fitzpatrick, *Stalin's Peasants: Resistance and Survival in the Russian Village after Collectivization*, Oxford; NY 1994, 230.

 8 *Argumenty i fakty*, 5/1990.

 9 *Istochnik* 1/1995, 117, 120.

10 Litvin, "Ross. istoriografiia Bol'shogo terrora", ii. 575.

11 *Izvestiia*, 12 Nov. 1999.

12 For the Western discussion see *inter alia*: V.N. Zemskov, J. Arch Getty, Gabor T. Rittersporn, "Victims of the Soviet Penal System in the Pre-War Years: A First Approach on the Basis of Archival Evidence", *Amer. Hist. Review*, 98 (1993), 1017–49 and subsequent correspondence; S. Rosefielde, "Stalinism in Post-Communist Perspective: New Evidence on Killings, Forced Labour and Economic Growth in the 1930s", *EAS*, 48 (1996), 959–87; S.G. Wheatcroft, "The Scale and Nature of German and Soviet Repression and Mass Killings", *ibid.*, 1319–53; *idem*, "Victims of Stalinism and the Soviet Secret Police . . .", *ibid.* 51 (1999), 315–45, with comments by J. Keep in *ibid.*, 1089–92, and *idem*, "Recent Writing on Stalin's Gulag" 91–112. For a review of Western literature to 1995: R. Stettner, *"Archipel Gulag": Stalins Zwangslager . . .*, Paderborn 1996.

13 V.V. Tsaplin, "Statistika zhertv stalinizma v 30–e gg.", *VI*, 4/1989, 181; *idem*, "Arkhivnye materialy o chisle zakliuchennykh v kontse 30-kh gg.", *VI*, 4–5/1991, 158, 161.

14 V.N. Zemskov, "Spetsposelentsy (po dokumentam NKVD-MVD SSSR)", *SOI*, 11/1990; *idem*, "Polit. repressii v SSSR (1917–1990)", *Rossiia XXI/*

1994, 1–2; V.P. Popov, "Gosud. terror v Sov. Rossii 1923–1953 gg. . . .", *OA*, 2/1992, 27.

15 Zemskov, "Zakliuchennye" (see fn. 5), 58–9. For a critique of Zemskov's figures see the letter by A.F. Stepanov, of Memorial, in *OI*, 1/2000, 197–200.

16 P.H. Solomon, *Soviet Criminal Justice under Stalin*, Cambridge; NY 1996, 232–9 (Russ. edn Moscow 1998, 226).

17 *Trud*, 4 June 1992.

18 Arhiv KGB RT, Protokoly zasedanii troiki. 1937 g., vols. 108–24.

19 *Ibid.*, 1938 g., vol. 69.

20 M. Panteleev, "Repressii v Kominterne 1937–8 gg.", *OI*, 6/1996, 161.

21 Yu.N. Zhukov, "Sledstvie i sudebnye protsessy po delu ob ubiistve Kirova", *VI*, 2/2000, 45. Of 220 cases examined by the OGPU in September 1935, 46.5 per cent concerned people charged with "counter-revolutionary propaganda" for expressing approval of the deaths of Kirov and V.V. Kuibyshev. *Istochnik*, 5/1999, 121.

22 N.A. Yefimov, "S.M. Kirov", *VI*, 11–12/1995, 49–67.

23 A.N. Yakovlev, "Bol'shevizm ne dolzhen . . .", *Otkrytaia politika*, 11–12/1996, 7–9.

24 Russian-language memoirs by dissidents include V. Bukovsky, *I vozvrashchaetsia veter . . .*, Moscow 1990; A. Marchenko, *Moi pokazaniia*, Moscow 1991; L. Sitko, "Dubrovlag pri Khrushcheve", *Novyi mir*, 10/1997; cf. F. Kondrat'ev, "Sovetskaia psikhiatriia: sekrety perevernutoi stranitsy istorii", *Ross. iustitsiia* 1/1994, 24–38.

25 *Bibliograf. ukazatel' izd. obshchestva "Memorial" 1988–1995*, Moscow 1995.

26 V.P. Danilov and S.A. Krasil'nikov (eds), *Spetspereselentsy v Zap. Sibiri*, Novosibirsk 1992–6 (the periods covered are: 1930 – spring 1931; spring 1931 – beginning of 1933; 1933–1938; we could not trace vol. 4); A.Yu. Zhukov *et al.* (comps.), *GULag v Karelii 1930–1941: sb. dok. i mat.*, Petrozavodsk 1992; "GULag v gody voiny", *Ist. arkhiv*, 3/1994, 60–86; cf. E. Bacon, *The Gulag at War . . .*, London 1994.

27 Ivanova, *GULag* (see n.5), 97; O.V. Khlevniuk, "Prinud. trud v eknomike SSSR 1929–1941 gg.", *Svob. mysl'*, 13/1992; S.G. Eberzhans and M.Ya. Vazhnov, "Proizvodstvennyi fenomen GULaga", *VI*, 6/1994; Zh. Medvedev, "Oni slishkom mnogo znali", *Poisk*, 17–23 May 1997, 7.

28 A.D. Sakharov, *Mir, progress, prava cheloveka*, London 1990, 78.

29 S.S. Vilensky (ed.), *Soprotivlenie v GULage: vospominaniia, pis'ma, dokumenty*, Moscow 1992; A.S. Kokurin, "Vosstanie v Steplage, iun'–iul' 1954", *OA*, 4/1994, 33–81; A. Graziosi, "The Great Strikes of 1953 in Soviet Labour Camps . . .", *CMRS*, 33 (1992), 419–46.

30 B. Starkov, "100 dnei lubianskogo marshala", *Istochnik*, 4/1993, 85, 90; O. Khlevniuk, "L.P. Beriia: predely istor. 'reabilitatsii'", *Istor. issled. v Rossii*, 149; A. Knight, *Beria: Stalin's First Lieutenant*, Princeton NJ 1993, 226.

31 Ordinance of Plenum of USSR Supreme Court of 4 February 1988, in

TsA FSB RF, fond N-13614, vol. 53, 152–61. It was then that the doctors (Prof. L.G. Levin, I.N. Kazakov) were rehabilitated; D.D. Pletnev, condemned for alleged participation in the murder of Gor'ky, Kuibyshev and Menzhinsky, had been rehabilitated a little earlier.

32 *Sbornik zakonodat. i normativnykh aktov o repressiiakh i reabilitatsii zhertv polit. repressii*, Moscow 1993, 196.

33 B. Piliatskin, "'Vrag naroda' Yezhov ostaetsia vragom naroda", *Izvestiia*, 4–5 June 1998; "Moi papa – narkom Yezhov", *Komsom. pravda*, 2 Sept. 1999.

34 *Komsom. pravda*, 5 May 1998; *Novye izvestiia*, 10 June 1998.

35 "Interv'iu s T. Khrennikom", *Novye izvestiia*, 6 June 1998; *Komsom. pravda*, 3 Nov. 1999.

36 *Komsom. pravda*, 6 Jan. 1998.

37 S. Grigoriants, "Ne mogu byt' v odnom riadu s ubiitsei", *Izvestiia*, 13 July 1994.

38 L. Razgon, "Obshchestvo zabyvaet, chto byl 37-i god", *ibid.*, 1 April 1998; *idem*, "I napivaius' kazhdyi god piatogo marta", *Novye izvestiia*, 1 April 1998.

39 *Obshchaia gazeta*, 23–29 April 1998. Frinovsky was a deputy head of the NKVD who explicitly sanctioned the torture of prisoners and bore much responsibility for preparing the fraudulent charges against Tukhachevsky and the other Red Army chiefs, as well as Bukharin and associates. In March 1939 he was himself arrested in the purge of Yezhov's men and shot in February 1940.

40 *Ibid.*, 11–17 Nov. 1999.

41 V.F. Nekrasov (comp., ed.), *Beriia: konets kar'ery*, Moscow 1991; *Inkvizitor: Stalinsky prokuror Vyshinsky*, Moscow 1992; A. Vaksberg, *Tsaritsa dokazatel'stv: Vyshinsky i ego zhertvy*, Moscow 1992; B. Starkov, "Narkom Ezhov", in J.A. Getty and Roberta Manning (ed.), *Stalinist Terror: New Perspectives*, Cambridge MA 1993, 21–39; A.L. Litvin *et al.* (eds), *Genrikh Yagoda: narodnyi komissar vnutrennykh del, general'nyi komissar gosud. bezopasnosti: sb. dok.*, Kazan' 1997; V.A. Ivanov, *Missiia Ordena: mekhanizm massovykh repressii v Sov. Rossii v kontse 1920-kh – 40-kh gg. (na materialakh Severo-zapada RSFSR)*, St Petersburg 1997; V.I. Berezhkov, *Piterskie prokuratory: rukovoditeli VChK-MGB 1918–1954*, St Petersburg 1998; Solomon, *op. cit.*

42 *Ogonek*, 26/1987, 6; "Dannye A.I. Todorskogo", in *Izv. TsK KPSS*, 4/1989, 42–3; O.F. Suvenirov, "Narkomat oborony i NKVD v predvoennye gody", *VI*, 6/1991, 26, 30; *idem*, "Tragediia pervykh komandirov", *OI*, 4/1996, 170–81; *idem*, *Tragediia RKKA 1937–8*, Moscow 1998, 313, 317.

43 Cited by Khrushchev in his 1956 "secret speech": Conquest, *Great Terror*, 122; Suvenirov, *Tragediia*, 80, 167–8, 195; "Posledniaia 'antipartiinaia' gruppa: stenogr. otchet iiun'skogo (1957 g.) plenuma TsK KPSS", *IA*, 3/1993, 86–8; *Izv. TsK KPSS*, 3/1989, 140.

44 L. Razgon, *Pered raskrytimi delami*, Moscow 1991, 17.

45 A.N. Mertsalov, L.A. Mertsalova, *G.K. Zhukov: novoe prochtenie ili staryi mif*, Moscow 1994, 48; Suvenirov, *op. cit.*, 114–16.

46 Suvenirov, "Za chest' i dostoinstvo voinov RKKA . . .", *Oni ne molchali*, Moscow 1993, 383; Conquest, *op. cit.*, 440.

47 E.G. Plimak and V.S. Antonov, "Taina 'zagovora Tukhachevskogo'", *OI*, 4/1998, 123–8; *idem*, "Replika po povodu diskussii . . .", *OI*, 6/1999, 182–4; Yu.N. Zhukov, "Tak byl li 'zagovor Tukhachevskogo'?", *OI*, 1/1999, 178–81; cf. M.A. Tumshis and A.A. Papchinsky, "Pravda i lozh" A. Orlova', *OI*, 6/1999, 179–81.

48 V. Suvorov, *Ochishchenie: Zachem Stalin obezglavil svoiu armiiu?*, Moscow 1998; M.I. Mel'tiukhov, "Repressii v Krasnoi armii: itogi noveishikh issledovanii", *OI*, 5/1997, 118.

49 *Reabilitatsiia: politicheskie protsessy 30-50-kh gg.*, Moscow 1991; O. Khlevniuk (ed.), *Stalinskoe politbiuro v 30-e gody: sb. dok*, Moscow 1995; *Pis'ma I.V. Stalina V.M. Molotovu 1925–36 gg.: sb. dok.*, Moscow 1995 (Eng. tr. L. Lih *et al.* (eds), *Stalin's Letters to Molotov, 1925–1936*, New Haven CT; London 1995); V.Z. Rogovin, *1937*, Moscow 1996; *idem*, *Partiia rasstreliannykh*, Moscow 1997; Khlevniuk, *Stalin i Ordzhonikidze: konflikty v Politbiuro v 30-e gg.*, Moscow 1993 (Eng. tr. D.J. Nordlander, *In Stalin's Shadow: the Career of "Sergo" Ordzhonikidze*, NY; London 1995); *idem*, *Politbiuro: mekhanizmy politicheskoi vlasti v 1930-e gg.*, Moscow 1996.

50 *Kremlevskii samosud: sekretnye dokumenty Politbiuro o pisatele A. Solzhenitsyne*, Moscow 1994.

51 N.Ya. Mandel'shtam, *Vospominaniia*, Moscow 1989; P. Grigorenko, *V podpol'e mozhno vstretit' tol'ko krys . . .*, Moscow 1997; cf. S.S. Averintsev, "Sud'ba i vest' O. Mandel'shtama", in Mandel'shtam, *Soch.*, i, Moscow 1990.

52 *Nepravednyi sud: poslednii stalinskii rasstrel: stenogramma sudebnogo protsessa nad chlenami evreiskogo antifashistskogo komiteta*, Moscow 1994; A. Borshchagovsky, *Obviniaetsia krov'*, Moscow 1994; V. Levashov, *Ubiistvo Mikhoelsa*, Moscow 1998.

53 Artizov, "Sud'by shkoly Pokrovskogo"; F.D. Anshin and V.M. Alpatov, "*Delo slavistov*": *30-e gg.*, Moscow 1994; S.E. Shnol', *Geroi i zlodei ross. nauki*, Moscow 1997.

54 A. Vaksberg, *Gibel'burevestnika: M. Gor'kii: poslednie 20 let*, Moscow 1999, 4, 379–80; A.V. Maslov, *Smert' ne postavila tochku: rassledovaniia sudebnogo medika*, Moscow 1999, 245–59.

55 *Literaturnyi front: istoriia polit. tsenzury 1932–46 gg.: sb. dok.*, Moscow 1994. Vasil'ev was arrested in 1932 for verse which began: "O muza segodnia vospoi Dzhugashvili sukina syna . . .": TsA FSB, d. N-35052, f. 103. G. Gorelik, "Za chto sidel L. Landau", *Izvestiia*, 9 Jan. 1992; "Interv'iu V. Shentalinskogo", *Segodnia*, 23 Oct. 1993; "O knige V. Shentalinskogo 'Voskresshee slovo' . . .", *Izvestiia*, 19 Nov. 1993; V. Chentalinsky, *La parole resuscitée: dans les archives littéraires au KGB*, tr. G. Ackerman and P. Lorrain, Paris 1992.

56 Cf. *Neva*, 7/1988, 136, 8/1988, 143; Conquest, *op. cit.*, 118.

57 V. Astrov, in *Lit. gaz.*, 29 March 1989 and *Izvestiia*, 27 Feb. 1993; S. Cohen, *Bukharin and the Bolshevik Revolution: A Political Biography*, NY 1975, 382 (Russ. edn Moscow 1988, 451).

58 *Komsom. pravda*, 2 Nov. 1999.

7 World War II

1 *1941. 22 iiunia*, Moscow 1965 (withdrawn from circulation); a second expanded edition appeared Moscow 1995. German tr., *Der Genickschuss: die Rote Armee am 22 Juni 1941...*, Vienna 1969.

2 *Istoriia Velikoi otech. voiny Sov. Soiuza, 1941–5*, 6 vols., Moscow 1960–5.

3 D.A. Volkogonov, *Etiudy o vremeni*, Moscow 1998, 39–40; for the discussion see *Nezavisimaia gazeta*, 18 June 1991.

4 Gallagher, *Soviet History of World War II*; Pavlenko, *Byla voina...*; Kulish, "Sovetskaia istoriografiia"; cf. S. Creuzberger, in *Neue Zürcher Zeitung*, 19–20 Sept. 1998.

5 *Izvestiia*, 23 Feb. 1995.

6 Poliakov, *Nashe nepredskazuemoe proshloe*, 171; B.Ts. Urlanis, "Liudskie poteri v voinakh", *VI*, 5/1965, 48.

7 *Izvestiia*, 25 June 1998; for slightly different figures *Istochnik*, 5/1994, 88; G.F. Krivosheev *et al.* (eds), *"Grif sekretnosti sniat: poteri voor. sil SSSR v voinakh, boevykh deistviiakh i voennykh konfliktakh*, Moscow 1993, 94–125.

8 V.G. Pervyshin, "Liudskie poteri v Vel. Otech. voine", *VI*, 7/2000, 121–2.

9 B. Gusev, "'Pokhoronnoe delo' v blokadnom Leningrade", *Izvestiia*, 23 Dec. 1994.

10 V.M. Koval'chuk, "Tragicheskie tsifry blokady (k voprosu ob ustanovlenii chisla zhertv blokirovannogo Leningrada)", Fursenko (ed.), *Rossiia v XIX–XX vv.*, 362, 365.

11 S. Kraiukhin, in *ibid.*, 19 June 1997.

12 N. Tolstoy, *Victims of Yalta*, London 1977 (Russ edn Moscow 1996); M.I. Semiriaga, "Sud'by sov. voennoplennykh", *VI*, 4/1995; V.B. Konasov and A.V. Tereshchuk, "K istorii sovetskikh i nemetskikh voennoplennykh 1941–3 gg.", *NNI*, 5/1996; *Ross. vesti*, 27 Jan. 1995; A.N. Yakovlev, "Sud'ba voennoplennykh i deportirovannykh grazhdan SSSR", *NNI*, 2/1996, 91–113, which contains the official report on this matter by the governmental commission for rehabilitation of victims of political repression. Cf. also Zemskov, "Repatriatsiia sov. grazhdan i ikh dal'neishaia sud'ba 1944–56 gg.", *SOI*, 5/1996, 3–12, 6/1996, 3–13.

13 A. Nekrich, "Doroga k voine", *Ogonek*, 27/1991, 6: J. Hoffman, "Podgotovka Sov. Soiuza k nastupatel'noi voine 1941 g.", *OI*, 4/1993, 29. For a similar Western view cf. W. Post, *Unternehmen Barbarossa...*, 2nd edn, Berlin 1996. For a good survey of the whole issue see now S. Voss, *Stalins Kriegsvorbereitungen 1941*.

14 E.N. Kul'kov, O.A. Rzheshevskaia *et al.* (eds), *Zimniaia voina 1939–40 gg.: politicheskaia istoriia*, 2 vols., Moscow 1998. To 22 June 1941 Germany got goods worth 672 md. marks, incl. 1.5 m. tons of grain, 100,000 tons of cotton, 2 m. tons of oil products, 1.5 m. tons of timber, 140,000 tons of manganese, and 26,000 tons of chrome. Cf. A.A. Shestiakov in *VI*, 4–5/1991, 164–70.

15 Sh. Rado, *Pod psevdonimom Dora: vosp. sovetskogo razvedchika*, Moscow 1973, 90; "Pochemu ne poverili d-ru Sorge?", *Argumenty i fakty*, 18/1989; L. Farago, *Voina umov: analiz shpionazha i razvedki*, Moscow 1956, 297–8; "Neuslyshannye signaly voiny: Dokladnye zapiski L.P. Berii . . . Stalinu . . .", *IA*, 2/1995; *1941 god: dokumenty*, Moscow 1998.

16 G.K. Zhukov, *Vosp. i razmyshleniia*, Moscow 1974, i. 258, cited by L.M. Mlechin, *Predsedateli KGB: rasskrechennye sud'by*, Moscow 1999, 417–18; V.K. Vinogradov *et al.* (comps.), L.N. Seliverstova *et al.* (eds), *Sekrety Gitlera na stole u Stalina: razvedka i kontrrazvedka o podgotovke germanskoi agressii protiv SSSR, mart – iun' 1941g.: sb. dok.*, Moscow 1995; cf. M.I. Mel'tiukhov, "Sov. razvedka i problema vnezapnogo napadeniia", *OI*, 3/1998, 3–20.

17 I.V. Boldin, *Stranitsy zhizni*, Moscow 1961; I. Kh. Bagramian, *Tak nachinalas' voina*, Kiev 1975; L.M. Spirin, "Stalin i voina", *VI KPSS*, 5/1990; *idem*, "Kak nachalas' voina", *Izvestiia*, 12 June 1991.

18 V. Suvorov, *Ledokol: Kto nachal II-uiu mirovuiu voinu?*, Moscow 1992; *idem*, *Den' M: kogda nachalas' II-aia mirovaia voina? . . .*, Moscow 1994.

19 D. Volkogonov, in *Izvestiia*, 16 Jan. 1993, M.I. Mel'tiukhov, "Spory vokrug 1941 g. . . .", *OI*, 3/1994; *idem*, "Sovremennaia istoriografiia i polemika vokrug knigi V. Suvorova 'Ledokol'", *Sov. istoriografiia*, Moscow 1996; *Gotovil li Stalin nastupatel'nuiu voinu . . .?: sb. mat.*, Moscow 1995; G. Gorodetsky, *Mif "Ledokola": nakanune voiny*, Moscow 1995; *idem*, *Rokovoi samoobman: Stalin i napadenie Germanii na Sov. Soiuz*, Moscow 1999; V.A. Nevezhin, "Strateg. zamysli Stalina . . .", *OI*, 5/1999.

20 R. Raack, *Stalin's Drive to the West, 1938–1945: the Origins of the Cold War*, Stanford CA 1995, 160; *Drugaia voina, 1939–1945*, Moscow 1996, 175–84.

21 *VIZh*, 6/1991, 32–40.

22 This speech has since been published in *IA*, 2/1995, 26–30.

23 V.A. Anfilov, *Nachalo Vel. Otech. voiny . . .*, Moscow 1962.

24 *VIZh*, 3/1995, 41.

25 Cf. V. Popov, "1941: taina porazheniia", *Novyi mir*, 8/1998, 172–87.

26 *Drugaia voina*, 27, 71; Yu. N. Afanas'ev, "Drugaia voina . . .", *Izvestiia*, 17 May 1995.

27 M.N. Suprun, *Lend-liz i severnye konvoi 1941–1945 gg.*, Moscow 1997; A. Paperno, *Lend-liz: Tikhii okean*, Moscow 1998; N.S. Lebedeva, *Katyn': prestuplenie protiv chelovechestva*, Moscow 1995; I.V. Bezborodova, "Inostrannye voennoplennye . . .", *OI*, 5/1997, 171.

28 *Vtoraia mirovaia voina: aktual'nye problemy . . .*, Moscow 1995, 311; *Svob. mysl'*, 14/1993, 91.

29 P.A. Pal'chikov, "Istoriia gen. Vlasova", *NNI*, 2/1993; I.I. Levin, *General Vlasov po tu i etu liniiu fronta: dokumenty, vospominaniia, pis'ma*, Murmansk, 1995; I.A. Giliazov, *Na drugoi storone: kollaboratsionisty iz povolzhsko–ural'skikh tatar v gody II-oi mirovoi voiny*, Kazan' 1998.
30 Poliakov, *Istor. nauka*, 194.

8 The Nationalities Problem

1 N.F. Bugai, "Deportatsiia narodov v SSSR – novoe napravlenie v otech. istoriografii: problemy izucheniia", *Rossiia v XX v.*, 506–13.
2 A. Nekrich, *The Punished Peoples: the Deportation and Fate of Soviet Minorities at the End of the Second World War*, NY 1978; A. Avtorkhanov, *Sovetskii tip kolonializma*, Vilnius 1990 (tr. from German edn 1988).
3 N.F. Bugai, "'Pogruzheny v eshelony i otpravleny k mestam poselenii . . .'": L. Beriia – I. Stalinu", *OI*, 1/1991, 4/1992; *idem* (ed.), *I. Stalin – L. Berii: "Ikh nado deportirovat' . . ."*, Moscow 1992; P.D. Bakeev *et al.* (comps.), K.N. Maksimov *et al.* (eds), *Ssylka kalmykov: kak eto bylo*, Elista, 1993; Bugai (ed.), *Repressirovannye narody Rossii: chechentsy i ingushy: dokumenty, fakty, kommentarii*, Moscow 1994; *Deportatsiia karachaevtsev: dokumenty rasskazyvaiut*, Cherkessk 1997; O.V. Volobuev, "Krymsko-tatarskii vopros po dokumentam TsK KPSS . . .", *OI* 1/1994; "Repressii protiv narodov: dokumenty GARF svidetel'stvuiut", *Narody Rossii: problemy deportatsii i reabilitatsii*, Maikop 1997.
4 S. Gaev *et al.*, *Khaibakh: sledstvie prodolzhaetsia*, Grozny 1994.
5 *Rossiia v XX v.*, 510; "Spravka otdela spetsposelenii NKVD o kolichestve spetsposelentsev na okt. 1946 g.", *OI*, 1/1992, 157; "Neizvestnaia initsiativa Khrushcheva", *OA*, 3/1992, 31.
6 N.F. Bugai and A.M. Gonov, *Kavkaz: narody v eshelonakh (20-e – 60-e gg.)*, Moscow 1998.
7 *Ibid.*, 119, 288, 302, 327; TsA FSB RF, Spravka: Operatsiia "Chaika" (o vyselenii karachaevtsev v 1943 g.), 1996.
8 M. Jégo and S. Shihah, "Les Difficultés d'être un historien caucasien en Russie", *Le Monde*, 28 February 2000.
9 L. Usmanov, *Nepokorennaia Chechnia*, Moscow 1997, 20.
10 S.Kh. Alishev, "Tatarofobiia v sov. literature", *Fenomen narodofobii: XX vek: mat. nauchnoi konferentsii*, Kazan' 1994; K. Aimermakher, G. Bordiugov (eds), *Natsional'nye istorii v sovetskom i postsovetskikh gosudarstvakh*, Moscow 1999, 122–3, 138–9, 286–7.
11 *Islam v tatarskom mire: istoriia i sovremennost'. Materialy mezhdunar. simpoziuma, Kazan', 29.IV – 1.V. 1996*, Kazan' 1997.
12 *Rodina*, 7/1994; 26; Yu. Kanigin, "Put'ariev", *Visnik NAN Ukraini*, 1–6/1995, rev. P. Tolochko, *ibid.* 3–4/1996, 90.
13 G. Yegorov, *Voskresenie shumerov*, Cheboksary 1993, rev. in *Komsom. pravda*, 2 Sept. 1999; S.R. Maliutin, *Problemy etnogeneza i etnicheskoi istorii chuvashei: Khunnskaia epokha*, Cheboksary 1996.

14 A. Kappeler, *Russland als Vielvölkerreich: Entstehung, Geschichte, Zerfall*, Munich 1993 (Russ. edn Moscow 1996, 7, 314–18 *passim*).
15 A. Kappeler, "'Rossiia – mnogonatsional'naia imperiia': nekotorye razmyshleniia vosem' let posle publikatsii knigi", *Ab imperio* 1/2000, 14, 21. Cf. P.I. Savelev (ed.), *Imperskii stroi Rossii v regional'nom izmerenii (XIX–nach. XX v.): sb. nauchnykh statei*, Moscow 1997; A.N. Sakharov and V.A. Mikhailov (eds), *Rossiia v XX v.: problemy natsional'nykh otnoshenii*, Moscow 1999; Sanders, *Historiography*.
16 D.A. Amanzholova, "Istoriografiia izucheniia nats. politiki", *Istor. issled. v Rossii*, 326; cf. A.P. Nenarokov, *K edinstvu ravnykh: kul'turnye faktory ob'edinitel'nogo dvizheniia sov. narodov 1917–24*, Moscow 1991; *Istoriia nats. polit. partii Rossii*, Moscow 1997.
17 *Tainy nats. politiki RKP: 4-e soveshchanie TsK RKPs otvetstvennymi rabotnikami . . . 9–12 iiunia 1923 g.: sten. otchet*, Moscow 1994, "Kak protivodeistvovali vykhodu Litvy iz SSSR", *IA*, 1/1992; "Tbilisi, aprel' 1989-go", *IA*, 3/1993; *Iz istorii ross. emigratsii: pis'ma A.Z. Validova i M. Chokaeva 1924–1932 gg.*, Moscow 1999.
18 M. Ferro, "Yevropotsentrizm v istorii . . .", *Metamorfozy Yevropy*, 16.
19 A.I. Solzhenitsyn, "'Russkii vopros' k kontsu XX v.", *Novyi mir*, 7/1994, 176; E.Yu. Zubkova and A.I. Kupriianov, "Vozvrashchenie k 'russkoi idee . . .", K. Aimermakher and G. Bordingov (eds.), *Natsional'nye istorii i partii v sov. i postsov. gosudarstvakh*, Moscow 1999, 299–328; *idem*, in *OI*, 5/1999, 4–28.
20 N.F. Bugai, "20-e – 50-e gg.: pereseleniia i deportatsii yevreiskogo naseleniia v SSSR", *OI*, 4/1993, 175–85; [N.F. Gamalei], "Po otnosheniiu k yevreiam tvoritsia chto-to neladnoe": pis'ma N.F. Gamaleii I.V. Stalinu, *VAPRF, Istochnik*, 3/1998, 119–23; G. Kostyrchenko, *V plenu u krasnogo faraona . . .*, Moscow 1994 (Eng. tr. by A. Riazantseva, *Out of the Red Shadows: Anti-Semitism in Stalin's Russia*, Amherst NY 1995); A. Vaksberg, *Stalin against the Jews*, tr. A.W. Bonis, USA 1995; L. Luks (ed.), *Der Spätstalinismus und die "jüdische Frage": zur antisemitischen Wendung des Kommunismus*, Cologne; Vienna 1999; Luks, "Zum stalinischen Antisemitismus . . .", *Jahrbuch des historischen Kommunismus*, 1997, 9–50.
21 V. Levashov, *Ubiistvo Mikhoelsa*, Moscow 1998; Yu. Aizenshtat, *O podgotovke Stalinym genotsida yevreev*, Jerusalem 1999, 74–5; O.V. Budnitsky (ed., comp.), *Yevrei i russkaia revoliutsiia: materialy i issledovaniia*, Moscow; Jerusalem 1999; "Iz istorii i mifologii revoliutsii: pochemu yevrei?", *OI*, 2/2000, 90, 121.
22 O. Platonov, *Ternovyi venets Rossii: istoriia russkogo naroda v XX v.*, vol. I, Moscow 1997, 517–19.
23 V.V. Kozhanov, *Rossiia: vek XX-yi, 1901–1939*, Moscow 1999, 320.
24 Aimermakher and Bordiugor (eds), *Natsional'nye istorii*, 318–19; *Lekhaim*, 11/1999, 23.
25 *Izvestiia*, 30 Oct., 30 Nov. 1999.
26 *Rodina*, 10/1999, 10.

9 Soviet Foreign Policy

1   *Istoriia vneshnei politiki SSSR*, 2 vols., Moscow 1986. Ponomarev was one of the Party's leading ideological functionaries; Gromyko (1909–89) joined the foreign service after the purges in 1939, became ambassador to the United States in 1943, deputized for Molotov after the war, and from 1957 to 1985 served as USSR Foreign minister. He left memoirs: *Pamiatnoe*, 2 vols. Moscow 1990–1 (tr. H. Shukman, *The Memoirs of Andrei Gromyko*, London 1989), but they are of less historical interest than those of his son, who gives details of Gorbachev's accession to power: A.A. Gromyko, *Andrei Gromyko: v labirantakh Kremliia: vosp. i razmyshleniia syna*, Moscow 1997.

2   E.I. Chapkevich, "Sov. istoriografiia . . . vneshnei politiki Rossii", *Rossia v XX v.*, 430–1.

3   R.G. Pikhoia, *Sovetskii Soiuz: istoriia vlasti, 1945– 1991*, Moscow 1998, 8, 10.

4   V.Ya. Sipols, *Tainy diplomaticheskie*, Moscow 1997, 100; L.A. Bezymensky, "Sov.-germanskie dogovory 1939 g.: novye dokumenty i starye problemy", *NNI*, 3/1998, 13.

5   *Izvestiia*, 28 Dec. 1989.

6   For details see D.G. Nadzharov, "Sov.-germanskii pakt 1939 g.: pereosmyslenie podkhodov k ego otsenke", *VI*, 1/1999, 160–1.

7   They were first published in V.I. Semiriaga (comp.), "Sekretnye dokumenty iz osobykh papok", *VI*, 1/1993, 3–22; cf. B. Bonwetsch and M. Junge, "Die Vertuschung des deutsch-sowjetischen Geheimabkommen von 1939 . . .", *Osteuropa*, 43 (1993), 132–8.

8   L.N. Nezhinsky, "Puti i pereput'ia vneshnei politiki Rossii v XX st.", *OI*, 6/1999, 6.

9   *Sovetskoe obshchestvo: vozniknovenie, razvitie, istor. final*, Moscow 1997, 292.

10 G.A. Bordiugov, "Gitler prikhodit k vlasti . . .", *OI*, 2/1999.

11 R. Raack, *Stalin's Drive to the West, 1938–1945: the Origins of the Cold War*, Stanford CA 1995, 160–1.

12 L. Bezymensky, "The Secret Protocols of 1939 as a Problem of Soviet Historiography", in G. Gorodetsky (ed.), *Soviet Foreign Policy*, London 1994, 75–85; V.A. Nevezhin, *Sindrom nastupatel'noi voiny: sovetskaia propaganda v preddverii "sviashchennykh boev" 1939–41*, Moscow 1997.

13 M.M. Narinsky, "I.V. Stalin i M. Torez, 1944–1947 gg.: novye materialy", *NNI*, 1/1996, 18–30; Li Van-Chon, "Stalinskaia teoriia 'dvukh lagerei' . . .", *Rossiia v XX v.*, 549–50.

14 N.V. Zagladin, *Istoriia uspekhov i neudach sov. diplomatii*, Moscow 1990; *Sovetskaia vneshniaia politika v gody "kholodnoi voiny" 1945–1985: novoe prochtenie*, Moscow 1995; *SSSR i kholodnaia voina*, Moscow 1995.

15 *Izvestiia*, 12 Feb. 1992.

16 *Ibid.*, 5 Nov. 1995.

17 *Ibid.*, 10 Dec. 1999.

18 Churchill's speech was not published in Russia until 1992: *Nezavisimaia gaz.*, 28 May.
19 V.S. Lel'chuk, "SSSR v usloviiakh kholodnoi voiny", *Doklady IRI RAN 1995–6*, Moscow 1997, 209, 215.
20 V. Mal'kov, "Khotel li Stalin razviazat' tret'iu mirovuiu voinu?", *Rossiia. XXI* 7–8/1997, 171, 173–4; cf. M.M. Narinsky, "Berlinskii krizis 1948–1949 gg.: novye dokumenty iz ross. arkhivov", *NNI*, 3/1995, 16–29.
21 E.-M. Stolberg, *Stalin und die chinesischen Kommunisten 1945–1953 . . .*, Stuttgart 1997, 237–41; *"Belye piatna" i bolevye tochki v istorii sov.-kitaiskikh otnoshenii*, vol. I, Moscow 1992; "'Okazat' pomoshch' koreiskim tovarishcham': perepiska vozhdei", *Istochnik*, 1/1996, 123–36; A.M. Ledovsky, "Peregovory I.V. Stalina s Mao Tzedunom v dek. 1949 – fev. 1950 g.: novye arkhivnye dokumenty", *NNI*, 1/1997, 27–47; P. Wingrove, "Mao in Moscow 1949–1950: Some New Archival Evidence", *Journal of Communist Studies and Transition Politics*, 11 (1995), 309–34.
22 B.G. Putilin and N.A. Shepova, *Na kraiu propasti: Karibskii krizis 1962 g.*, Moscow 1994; K. Lechuga, *V tsentre buri: F. Kastro, N.S. Khrushchev, Dzh.F. Kennedi i raketnyi krizis*, Moscow 1995.
23 "Na pritsele – Eizenkhauer", *Rodina*, 12/1999, 72–4.
24 Pikhoia, *Sov. Soiuz* (see n. 3), 388–9.
25 *Sov. obshchestvo* (see n. 9), vol. 2, 545.
26 L. Onikov, *KPSS: anatomiia raspada: vzgliad iznutri apparata TsK*, Moscow 1996, 93–4.
27 D.A. Volkogonov, *Sem' vozhdei*, Moscow 1995, bk. 2, 362–3, 373.
28 *Idem, Etiudy o vremeni*, Moscow 1998, 355–6; "Predskazanie polk. Para", *Rodina* 4/1999, 76.
29 L.N. Nezhinsky, "Puti i pereput'ia . . .", *OI*, 6/1999, 11–12; M.A. Khaldin, "Geopolit. gorizonty Rossii", *Sov. obshchestvo*, ii. 627–31.

10 Conclusion

1 "Otnoshenie k proshlomu – kliuch k budushchemu", *OI*, 6/1999, 85–8.
2 *Izvestiia*, 21 Dec. 1999.
3 *Komsom. pravda*, 21 Dec. 1999; *Izvestiia*, 24 Dec. 1999.
4 *VI ICCEES World Congress, Tampere, Finland, 29 July – 3 August 2000: Abstracts*, Helsinki, 337, 405.
5 S. Gribanov, *Zalozhniki vremeni*, Moscow 1993; F.I. Chuev, *Soldaty imperii: besedy, vosp., dokumenty*, Moscow 1998.
6 A.A. Arsutiunov, *Dos'e Lenina bez retushi: dokumenty, fakty, svidetel'stva*, Moscow 1999.
7 S. Courtois, N. Werth *et al.*, *Le Livre noir du communisme: crimes, terreur et repression*, Paris 1997 (Russ. edn with introd. by A.N. Yakovlev, Moscow 1999. Eng. edn: *The Black Book of Communism: Crimes, Terror, Repression*, tr. J. Murphy and M. Kramer, Cambridge MA 2000.)
8 V.G. Sirotkin, *Zoloto i nedvizhimost' Rossii za rubezhom: istoriko-publitsisticheskoe rassledovanie*, Moscow 1997.

9 *OI*, 4–5/2000 (round table, comp. S.S. Sekirinsky).

10 V.A. Malyshev, "Dnevnik narkoma", *Istochnik*, 5/1997, 136.

11 B.N. Mironov, *Sotsial'naia istoriia Rossii perioda imperii (XVIII – nach. XX v.): genezis lichnosti, demokraticheskoi sem'i, grazhdanskogo obshchestva i pravovogo gosudarstva*, 2 vols, St Petersburg 1999, vol. 1, 11.

12 S.L. Frank, "Etika nigilizma", in *Vekhi* (1909), repr. Moscow 1990, 209.

13 Kashtanov, *Russkaia diplomatika*, 143, 171; Afanas'ev, *Istorizm protiv eklektiki*.

14 Mironov, *Sotsial'naia istoriia*, vol. 1, 16–17.

15 S.F. Cohen, *Izuchenie Rossii bez Rossii: krakh amerikanskoi postsovetologii*, Moscow 1999, 34; A.N. Sakharov, "Konstitutsionnye proekty i tsivilizatsionnye sud'by Rossii", *OI*, 5/2000, 36.

16 *Ibid.*, 17.

Appendix B

1 *Izvestiia*, 11 Feb. 1992.

2 *Argumenty i fakty*, 37/1999, 11.

3 *Komsom. pravda*, 28 Nov. 1997.

Bibliography

This bibliography comprises works referred to in the Notes in short form, most of which are concerned with historiography in the narrower sense, plus some other pertinent works. Collective volumes are where possible entered under the name of the editor or compiler.

Abbreviations of journal titles (place of publication Moscow unless otherwise stated):

CMRS	*Cahiers du monde russe (et soviétique)*, Paris
EAS	*Europe–Asia Studies*, Glasgow
IA	*Istoricheskii arkhiv*
IS	*Istoriia SSSR*
JGOE	*Jahrbücher für Geschichte Osteuropas*, Munich
NNI	*Novaia i noveishaia istoriia*
OA	*Otechestvennye arkhivy*
OI	*Otechestvennaia istoriia*
RR	*Russian Review*, Columbus OH
SOI	*Sotsiologicheskie issledovaniia*
SR	*Slavic Review* (USA)
VI	*Voprosy istorii*
VIKPSS	*Voprosy istorii Kommunisticheskoi partii Sovetskogo Soiuza*
VIZh	*Voenno-istoricheskii zhurnal*

Afanas'ev, Yu.N. 1996 "Fenomen sovetskoi istoriografii", in idem (ed.), *Sov. istoriografii*, 7–41.
—— 1980. *Istorizm protiv eklektiki: frantsuzskaia istoricheskaia shkola "Annalov"v sovremennoi istoriografii*, Moscow.
—— (ed.) 1988. *Inogo ne dano: sud'ba perestroiki, vzgliadivaias' v proshloe, vozvrashchenie k budushchemu*, Moscow.
—— (ed.) 1996. *Sovetskaia istoriografiia*, Moscow (Rossiia. XX vek. Vol. II).
—— (ed.) 1997 *Sovetskoe obshchestvo: vozniknovenie, razvitie, istoricheskii final*. Vol. I: *Ot vooruzhennogo vosstaniia do vtoroi sverkhderzhavy mira*, Moscow (Rossiia. XX vek. Vol. IV (1).
Aimermakher, K. and Bordiugov, G. (eds) 1999. *Natsional'nye istorii v sovetskom i postsovetskikh gosudarstvakh*, Moscow.
Akademicheskoe delo 1929–1931 gg., fasc. 2: *Delo po obvineniiu akad. Ye. V. Tarle*: see Leonov.
Aleksandrov, V. 1998. *Put'v istoriiu, put'v istorii. Moia zhizn'*, Moscow.
Alekseeva, G.D. 1968. *Oktiabr'skaia revoliutsiia i istoricheskaia nauka v Rossii (1917–1923 gg.)*, Moscow.

—— 1997. "Oktiabr'skaia revoliutsiia i istoricheskaia nauka", in idem *et al.* (eds), *Istor, nauka*, 43–58.
——, Sakharov, A.N., and Sidorova, L.A. (eds) 1997. *Istoricheskaia nauka Rossii v XX veke*, Moscow.
Alekseeva (Alexeeva), L. 1985. *Soviet Dissent: Contemporary Movements for National, Religious and Human Rights*. Tr. C. Pearce and J. Glad. Middletown CT. (Russ. edn *Istoriia inakomysliia v SSSR: noveishii period*. Vilnius 1992.)
Alferov, Zh.I., Leonov, V.P. *et al.* (eds) 1993. *Akademichekoe delo 1929–1931 gg.* Fasc. I. *Delo po obvineniiu akademika S.F. Platonova*, St Petersburg 1993.
Akademischeskoe delo: see Alferov *et al.* (eds), Leonov.
Amal'rik, A. 1991. *Notes of a Revolutionary*. Introd. S. Jacoby. NY 1982. (Russ. edn *Zapiski dissidenta*, Moscow.)
Amanzholova, D.A. 1996. "Istoriografiia izucheniia natsional'noi politiki", in Bordiugov (ed.), *Istor. issled.*, 308–31.
American Association for the Advancement of Slavic Studies. 1995. "Final Report of the Joint Task Force on Archives, AAASS and American Historical Association, 1 April 1995", *SR*, 54: 407–26.
Amiantov, Yu.N. 1993–1994. "Die Bestände des . . . RTsKhIDNI", *International Newsletter* 1: 3–4, 8.
—— and Tikhonova, Z.N. (contribs.) 1996. "Stenogramma soveshchaniia po voprosam istorii SSSR v TsK VKP(b) v 1994 g.", *VI*, 2–6.
Anan'ich, B.V. and Paneiakh, V.M. 2000. "O peterburgskoi shkole i ee sud'be", *OI*, 5: 105–13.
—— 1995. "Prinuditel'noe 'soavtorstvo': k vykhodu v svet sb. dok. 'Akad. delo 1929–1931 gg', vyp. I", in *In memoriam. Istor. sbornik pamiati F.F. Perchenka*, Moscow; St Petersburg.
Anatomiia revoliutsi. 1917 god v Rossii; massy, partii, vlast'. 1994. St Petersburg.
Artizov, A.N. (contrib.) 1999. '"Gotova podchinit'sia liubomu resheniiu partii': dva pis'ma A.M. Pankratovoi 1937 g.", *OA*, 3: 64–8.
—— 1991. "Kritika M.N. Pokrovskogo i ego shkoly (k istorii voprosa)", *IS*, 1: 109–19.
—— 1998. "M.N. Pokrovsky: final kar'ery – uspekh ili porazhenie?", *OI*, 1: 77–96, 2: 124–42.
—— 1994. "Sud'by istor. shkoly M.N. Pokrovskogo (seredina 1930-kh gg.)", *VI*, 7: 34–48.
Baberowski, J. 1995 "Wandel und Terror: die Sowjetunion unter Stalin 1928–1941: ein Literaturbericht", *JGOE*, 43: 97–129.
Barber, J. 1981 *Soviet Historians in Crisis, 1928–1932*, London; Basingstoke Hants.
Baron, S.H. and Heer, N.W. (eds) 1977. *Windows on the Russian Past: Essays on Soviet Historiography since Stalin*, Columbus OH.
Barsukov, N.A. 1966. "XX s'ezd v restrospektive Khrushcheva", *OI*, 6: 169–77.

Beyrau, D. 1999. "Die korrekte Moral und die historische Profession: ein Kommentar", [on S. Courtois et al. *Le Livre noir...*], *JGOE*, 47: 254–62.

Bezborodov, A.B. 1996. "Istoriografiia istorii dissidentskogo dvizheniia v SSSR 50 – 80-kh gg.", in Afanas'ev (ed.), *Sov. istoriografiia*, 401–28.

Blinkova, M. 1998. *Vremia bylo takoe: ocherki, portrety*, Tel Aviv.

Blitstein, P.A. 1999. "Selected Bibliography of Recent Published Document Collections on Soviet History", *CMRS*, 40: 1–2, 307–26.

Bohn, T.M. 1998. *Russische Geschichtswissenschaft von 1880 bis 1905. Pavel N. Miljukov und die Moskauer Schule* (Beiträge zur Geschichte Osteuropas, vol. 25), Cologne; Weimar; Vienna.

Bolkhovitinov, N.N. 1990 "Kommentarii k stat'e R.U. Devisa 'Sovetskaia istoricheskaia nauka v nachale period perestroiki'", *Vestnik AN SSSR*, 8: 78–80.

―――― 1991. "Sovetskaia amerikanistika na pereput'e: starye dogmy i novye podkhody", *VI*, 7–8: 3–12.

Bonwetsch, B. 1987. "Die Bewältigung der Vergangenheit: Geschichts- und Gesellschaftswissenschaften in der 'Perestroika'", in Mommsen, M. and Schröder, H.-H. (eds), *Gorbatschows Revolution von oben*, Frankfurt, 74–88.

―――― 1988. "'Nur vorwärts und vorwärts'? Die 'Umgestaltung in der sowjetischen Geschichtswissenschaft'", *Osteuropa*, 38: 457–68.

Bordiugov, G.A. 1992. "Wie autonom ist die russische Geschichtswissenschaft? Alte Vorurteile und neue Ansätze", in Eimermacher, K. and Hartmann, A. (eds), *Der gegenwärtige russische Wissenschaftsbetrieb: Innenansichten*, Bochum.

―――― (ed.) 1996. *Istoricheskie issledovaniia v Rossii: tendentsii poslednikh let*. Moscow.

―――― 1998. Ushakov, A. and Churakov, V. (eds) 1998. *Beloe delo: ideologiia, osnovy, rezhimy vlasti: istoriograficheskie ocherki*, Moscow.

Brachev, V.S. 1995 *Russkii istorik S.F. Platonov*, 2 parts, St Petersburg.

Bugai, N.F. 1996. "Deportatsiia narodov v SSSR – novoe napravlenie v otechestvennoi istoriografii: problemy izucheniia", in Sakharov et al. (eds), *Rossiia v XX v.*, 506–13.

Buldakov, V.P. 1996. "Istoriograficheskie metamorfozy 'krasnogo Oktiabria'", in Bordiugov (ed.), *Istor. issled.*, 179–205.

―――― 1998. "Oktiabr' i XX vek: teorii i istochniki", in Tiutiukin et al. (eds), *Okt. revoliutsiia*, 11–36.

Burdzhalov, E.N. 1989. "O sostoianii sovetskoi istoricheskoi nauki i rabote zhurnala 'Voprosy istorii'. [Doklad] na vstreche s chitateliami 19–20 iiunia 1956 g. v Leningradskom otdelenii Instituta istorii AN SSSR", *VI*, 9: 91–96, 11: 113–38.

Byrnes, R.F. 1991. "Creating the Soviet Historical Profession, 1917–1934", *SR*, 50: 297–308.

―――― 1995. *V.O. Kliuchevsky, Historian of Russia*, Bloomington IN.

Chapkevich, E.I. 1994. *Poka iz ruk ne vypalo pero... (Zhizn'i deiatel'nost' akademika E.V. Tarle)*, Orel.

—— 1996. "Sovetskaia istoriografiia 20 – 50-kh gg. vneshnei politiki Rossii", in Sakharov *et al.* (eds), *Rossiia v XX v.*

Chernobaev, A.A. (comp., ed.) 1998. *Istoriki Rossii: kto est' kto v izuchenii otechestvennoi istorii: biobibliograficheskii slovar'*, Saratov.

—— 1997. *Istoriki Rossii o vremeni i sebe*, 2 fascs, Moscow.

—— 1992. *"Professor s pikoi", ili Tri zhizni istorika M.N. Pokrovskogo*, Moscow.

Chesnokov, V.I. 1989. *Pravitel'stvennaia politika i istoricheskaia nauka Rossii 60 – 70-kh gg. XIX v. Issledovatel'skie ocherki*, Voronezh.

Chistiakova, Ye V. 1987 *M.N. Tikhomirov*, Moscow.

Chubar'ian A.O. (ed.) 1993 *Metamorfozy Yevropy*, Moscow.

Confino, M. 1994. "Present Events and the Representation of the Past: Some Current Problems in Russian Historical Writing", *CMRS*, 35: 839–68.

Danilevsky, I.N. *et al.* (eds) 1998. *Istochnikovedenie*, 2 parts, Moscow.

Danilov, V.P. 1996. "Sovremennaia rossiiskaia istoriografiia: v chem vykhod iz krizisa?", in Sakharov *et al.* (eds), *Rossiia v XX v.*: 22–30.

Davidson, A.B. 2000. "Nash tsekh istorikov v memuarakh: v sviazi s vykhodom knigi akad. Yu. A. Poliakova", *NNI*, 2: 80–9.

Davies, R.W. 1989 *Soviet History in the Gorbachev Revolution*, London.

—— 1997. *Soviet History in the Yeltsin Era*, London.

—— 1990. "Sovetskaia istoricheskaia nauka v nachal'nyi period perestroiki", *Vestnik AN SSSR*, 8.

Dedkov, N.I. 1996 "'Kak ia dokumental'no ustanovil' ili 'Smeiu utverzhdat'. O Knige D.A. Volkogonova 'Lenin'", in Bordiugov (ed.), *Istor. issled.*: 115–38.

D'iakonov, I.M. 1995. *Kniga vospominanii*, St Petersburg.

Dmitriev, S.S. 1999, 2000. "Iz dnevnikov Sergeia Sergeevicha Dmitrieva", *OI*: 3–6 (1999), 1–5 (2000), 1 (2001).

Drabkin, Ya.S. and Komolova, N.P. (eds) 1996. *Totalitarizm v Yevrope XX v. Iz istorii ideologii, dvizhenii, rezhimov i ikh preodoleniia*, Moscow.

Drezer, M. 1997. "Krainosti istorii i krainosti istorikov", in Ushakov, A.I. (eds), *Krainosti*, 145–56.

Druzhinin, N.M. 1995, 1996, 1997. "Dnevnik N.M. Druzhinina", *VI*: 9–12 (1995), 1–4, 9–10 (1996), 1, 3–4, 6–8, 10 (1997).

Dumova, N.G. 1993. *Liberal v Rossii: tragediia nesovmestimosti. Istoricheskii portret P.N. Miliukova*, Moscow.

Dzhimbinov, S. 1990. "Epitafiia spekskhranu?", *Novyi mir*, 5: 243–52.

Emmons, T. 1990. "Kliuchevskii i ego ucheniki", *VI*, 10: 45–61.

Enteen, G.M. 1995. "Intellektual'nye predposylki utverzhdeniia stalinizma v sovetskoi istoriografii", *VI*, 5–6: 149–55.

—— 1978. *The Soviet Scholar-Bureaucrat: M.N. Pokrovsky and the Society of Marxist Historians*, London:

—— 1996. "Sovetskaia istoricheskaia nauka 1920–1930 gg. v osveshchenii angliiskoi i amerikanskoi istoriografii", in Sakharov (ed.), *Rossia XIX–XX vv.*: 117–37.

—— 1989. "Spor o M.N. Pokrovskom prodolzhaetsia", *VI*, 5.

—— 1994. "Vzgliad so storony: o sostoianii i pespektivakh rossiiskoi istoriografii", *VI*, 9: 190–1.

Ferro, M. 1993. "Yevropotsentrizm v istorii: rastsvet i upadok", in Chubar'ian (ed.), *Metamorfozy*.

Fitzpatrick, S. and Viola. L. (eds) 1990. *A Researcher's Guide to Sources on Soviet Social History in the 1930s*, Armonk NY; London.

Fokeev, V.A. 1970. "Iz istorii izucheniia i rasprostraneniia proizvedenii V.I. Lenina v pervye gody sovetskoi vlasti (1917–1923)", *Knigovedenie* 2.

Fursenko, A.A. 1999. "Konets ery Stalina", *Zvezda* 12: 173–88.

—— (ed.) 1998. *Rossiia v XIX–XX vv.: sbornik*, St Petersburg.

Gallagher, M.P. 1963. *The Soviet History of World War II. Myths, Memories and Realities*, NY; London.

Ganelin, R.Sh. 1998. "Stalin i sovetskaia istoriografiia predvoennykh let", *Novyi chasovoi*, 6–7: 100–17.

Gerasimenko, G. 1998. *Istoriia rossiiskoi istoricheskoi nauki (dooktiabr'skii period)*, Moscow.

Geyer, D. 1995. *Klio in Moskau und die sowjetische Geschichte*, Heidelberg.

Goldin, V. 2000. *Rossiia v grazhdanskoi voine: ocherki noveishei istoriografii (II-aia pol. 1980-kh – 1990-e gg.)*, Archangel.

Golubev, A.V. 1996. "Noveishaia istoriia Rossii v uchebnikakh 1995 g.", in Bordiugov (ed.), *Istor. issled.*: 56–65.

Gorodetsky, E.N. 1989. "Zhurnal 'Voprosy istorii' v seredine 50-kh gg.", *VI*, 9: 69–90.

Gorskaia, N.A. 1999. *Boris Dmitrievich Grekov*, Moscow.

Got'e, Yu.V. 1997. *Moi zametki*, Moscow.

—— 1988. *Time of Troubles: the Diary of Iuryi Vladimirovich Got'e, Moscow, July 8, 1917 to July 23, 1922*. Tr., ed. T. Emmons. Princeton, London.

Govorkov, A.A. 1976. *M.N. Pokrovsky o predmete istoricheskoi nauki*, Tomsk.

Grazhdanov, Yu.D. 1993. "Gosudarstvennye rezhimy perioda grazhdanskoi voiny", in *Istoriia sovetskoi Rossii: novye idei, suzhdeniia. Tezisy dokladov II-oi respublikanskoi nauchnoi konferentsii*, Tiumen'.

Graziosi, A. 1999. "The New Soviet Archival Sources: Hypotheses for a Critical Assessment", *CMRS*, 40: 1–2, 13–64.

Grimsted, P.K. 1993. "Archival Rossica", *CMRS* 34 (Abbreviated version: *OA*, 1: 20–53.)

—— 1997. *Archives of Russia five years after: "purveyors of sensation" or "shadows cast to the past"*. IISH Research Papers, Amsterdam.

—— 1997. "Increasing Reference Access to Post-1991 Russian Archives", *SR*, 56: 718–59.

Grossman, A.S. (comp.) 1989. "'Kruglyi stol' sovetskikh i amerikanskikh istorikov", *VI*, 4: 97–117.

Gurevich, A.Ya. 1991. "O krizise soveremennoi istoricheskoi nauki", *VI*, 2–3: 21–36.

Hildermeier, M. 2000. "Der Stalinismus im Urteil russischer Historiker", in Frei, N., Van Laak, D., Stolleis, M. (eds), *Geschichte vor Gericht: Historiker, Richter und die Suche nach Gerechtigkeit*, Munich.

Holloway, D. and Naimark, N. (eds) 1996. *Re-examining the Soviet Experience: Essays in Honor of Alexander Dallin*. Boulder CO.
Hösler, J. 1995. *Die sowjetische Geschichtswissenschaft 1953 bis 1991. Studien
zur Methodologie- und Organisationsgeschichte*, (Marburger Abhandlungen
zur Geschichte und Kultur Osteuropas, 34), Munich.
—— 1998. "Sowjetische und russische Interpretationen des Stalinismus",
in Plaggenborg, *Stalinismus*.
Husband, W.B. 1991. "Secondary School History Texts in the USSR: Re-
vising the Soviet Past, 1985–1989", *RR*, 50: 458–80.
Igritsky, Yu.I. 1993. "I snova o totalitarizme", *OI*, 1: 3–17.
Il'ina, I.V. (comp.) 1991. "Novye dokumenty o soveshchanii istorikov v
TsK VKP(b) (1944)", *VI*, 1: 188–205.
Illeritskaia, N.V. 1996. "Stanovlenie sovetskoi istoricheskoi traditsii: nauka,
ne obretshaia litsa", in Afanas'ev (ed.), *Sov. istoriografiia*.
Inogo ne dano: see Afanas'ev (ed.).
*International Newsletter of Historical Studies on Comintern, Communism and
Stalinism* 1995–. Aachen.
Iskenderov, A.A. 1996. "Istoricheskaia nauka na poroge XXI veka", *VI*,
4: 3–31.
"I snova ob istorikakh- 'revizionistakh'" 1999. Articles by Igritsky, Yu.I.,
Olegina, I.N., Shcherban', N.V., Sokolov, A.K., Malia, M., *OI*, 3: 121–41.
Istoricheskaia nauka Rossii v XX veke: see Alekseeva et al. (eds) *Istoricheskie
issledovanie v Rossii: tendentsii poslednikh let*: see Bordiugov et al. (eds).
Istorik i revoliutsiia: see Smirnov
Istoriki Rossii o vremeni i sebe: see Chernobaev (ed.).
Istoriki Rossii: poslevoennoe pokolenie: see Maksimova.
Istoriki Rossii XVIII–XX vv.: see Sakharov (ed.).
*Istoriografiia i istoriia sots.-ekonomicheskogo i obshchestvenno-polit. razvitiia
Rossii (II-aia pol. XIX i I-aia pol. XX v.)* 1997. Penza.
Ito, T. (ed.) 1989. *Facing Up to the Past: Soviet Historiography under Perestroika*,
Sapporo, Japan.
Ivanov, Yu.F. (intro.) 1988. "Pis'ma Anny Mikhailovny Pankratovoi", *VI*,
11: 54–79.
Ivanova, L.V. 1968. *U istokov sovetskoi istoricheskoi nauki: podgotovka kadrov
istorikov-marksistov v 1917–1929 gg.*, Moscow.
Junge, M. 1999. *Bucharins Rehabilitierung: historisches Gedächtnis in der
Sowjetunion, 1957–1991*, (Diss.), Berlin.
Kabanov, V.V. 1998. "Istoricheskie istochniki sovetskogo perioda", in
Danilevsky et al. (eds), *Istochnikovedenie*.
Kaganovich, B.S. 1995. *E.V. Tarle i peterburgskaia shkola istorikov*, St
Petersburg.
Kan, A. 1996. "Anna Pankratova and 'Voprosy istorii': An Innovatory
and Critical Historical Journal of the Soviet 1950s", *Storia della storiografia*,
129: 71–97.
Kashtanov, S.M. 1998. *Aktovaia arkheografiia*, Moscow.
—— 1980. *Russkaia diplomatika*, Moscow.

—— 2000. "A.A. Zimin", in *A.A. Zimin: biobibliograficheskii ukazatel'*, Moscow.

—— and Chernobaev, A.A. 1998. "A.A. Zimin", in Sakharov (ed.), *Istoriki Rossii*, fasc. 5, Moscow.

Keep, J.L.H. 1988. "Recent Soviet Historiography: A Reader's Guide", in idem, *Moscow's Problems of History: A Select Critical Bibliography of the Soviet Journal 'Voprosy istorii'*, 2nd edn., Ottawa.

—— 1997. "Recent Writing on Stalin's Gulag: An Overview", *Crime, History and Societies*, 1 Paris, 2: 91–112.

—— 1965/1995: "The Rehabilitation of M.N. Pokrovsky", in idem, *Power and the People: Essays on Russian History*, Boulder CO; NY.

—— 1977/1995. "Soviet Historians on 'Great October'", in ibid.

—— 1992. "Die sowjetische Geschichtswissenschaft der 'Perestroika': Anfänge einer Aufarbeitung der jüngsten Vergangenheit", *Schweizerische Zeitschrift für Geschichte*, 42: 100–16.

—— 1999. "Stalinism in Post-Soviet Historical Writing", in K. McDermott and J. Morison (eds), *Politics and Society under the Bolsheviks. Selected Papers from the Fifth World Congress of Central and East European Studies, Warsaw 1995*, Basingstoke; London.

Kenez, P. 1996. "Zapadnaia istoriografiia grazhdanskoi voiny v Rossii", in Sakharov (ed.), *Rossiia XIX–XX vv.*

Khorkhordina, T.I. 1994. "Arkhivy i totalitarizm (opyt sravnitel'no-istoricheskogo analiza", *OI*, 6: 145–59.

—— 1996. "Arkhivy v 'Zazerkal'e': arkhivovedcheskaia kul'tura totalitarnykh rezhimov", in Afanas'ev (ed.), *Sov. istoriografiia*.

—— 1994. *Istoriia Otechestva i arkhivy, 1917–1980-e gg.*, Moscow.

Khvylev, L.N. 1978. *Problemy metodologii istorii v. russkoi burzhuaznoi istoriografii kontsa XIX – nachala XX v.* Tomsk.

Kireeva, R.A. 1996. "Iz istorii sovetskoi istoricheskoi nauki kontsa 40-kh gg.: pervoe veto v nauchnoi zhizni A.A. Zimina", in Sakharov *et al.* (ed.), *Rossiia v XX v.*

Kliuchevsky, V.O. 1968. *Pis'ma. Dnevniki. Aforizmy i mysli ob istorii*, Moscow.

Knight, A. 1993. "The Fate of the KGB Archives", *SR*, 52: 582–6.

Kobrin, V.B. 1997. "Aleksandr Aleksandrovich Zimin", in Alekseeva (ed.), *Istor. nauka*.

—— 1992. *Komu ty opasen, istorik?* Moscow.

—— and Aver'ianov, K.A. 1989. *S.V. Veselovsky. Zhizn'. Deiatel'nost'. Lichnost'*, Moscow.

Kodin, E. 1998. *"Smolenskii arkhiv" i amerikanskaia sovetologiia*. Smolensk.

Koenker, D. and Bachman, R.D. (eds) 1991. *Revelations from the Russian Archives: Documents in English Translation*, Washington D.C.

Kondakov, I.A. 1997. *Otkrytyi arkhiv: spravochnik opublikovannykh dokumentov po istorii Rossii XX v. iz gosudarstvennykh i semeinykh arkhivov. Po otechestvennoi periodiki 1985–1995 gg*, Moscow.

—— and Chernobaev, A.A. (comps.) 1999. *Istoricheskii arkhiv 1919–1999. Ukazatel' dokumental'nykh publikatsii*. Moscow.

Kotelenets, E. 1999. *V.I. Lenin kak predmet istoricheskogo issledovaniia: noveishaia istoriografiia,* Moscow.

Koval'chenko, I.D. and Shiklo, A.E. 1982. "Krizis russkoi burzhuaznoi nauki v kontse XIX v. – nachale XX v.", *VI,* 1: 18–35.

Kozlov, V.P. 1999. *Rossiiskoe arkhivnoe delo. Arkhivno-istochnikovedcheskie issledovaniia.*

Krivosheev, Yu.V. and Dvornichenko, F.Yu. 1994. "Izgnanie nauki: rossiiskaia istoriografiia v 20-kh – nachale 30-kh gg. XX v.", *OI,* 3: 143–58.

"'Kruglyi stol': istoricheskaia nauka v usloviiakh perestroiki" 1988. *VI,*3: 3–57.

"'Kruglyi stol': Sovetskii Soiuz v 20-e gg-" 1988. *VI,* 9: 3–58.

"'Kruglyi stol': Sovetskii Soiuz v 30-e gg." 1988. *VI,* 12: 3–30.

"'Kruglyi stol sovetskikh ...'": see Grossman.

Kudinova, N.T. 1998. *Otechestvennaia istoriografiia revoliutsii 1917 g. v Rossii (1917–1995).* Avtoreferat dokt. diss., Moscow.

Kulish, V.M. 1996. "Sovetskaia istoriografiia Velikoi Otechestvennoi voiny", in Afanas'ev (ed.), *Sov. istoriografiia.*

Kurenyshev, A.A. 1999. "Krest'ianstvo Rossii v period voiny i revoliutsii 1917–1920 gg. (istoriograficheskie aspekty)", *VI,* 4–5.

Leiberov, I.P. 1999. "Kak my zashchishchali P.V. Volobueva (iz vospominanii)", in Smirnov et al. (eds), *Istorik i revoliutsiia.*

Lenin, V.I. 1959. *Polnoe sobranie sochinenii,* 5th edn, Moscow.

Leonov, V.P. (ed.) 1998. *Akademicheskoe delo 1919–1931 gg.: dok. i mat. sledstvennogo dela, sfabrikovannogo OGPU,* fasc. 2: *Delo po obvineniiu akad. Ye.V. Tarle,* 2 pts., St Petersburg.

Likhotkina, G.A. (contrib.) 1994. "Golosa 1966 g." [Discussion of Nekrich], *Neva,* 1: 304–14.

Lindner, R. 1999. "Nationalhistoriker im Stalinismus: zum Profil der akademischen Intelligenz in Weissrussland, 1921–1946", *JGOE,* 47: 187–209.

Litvak, K.B. 1991. "K voprosu o partiinykh perepisiakh i kul'turnom urovne kommunistov v 20-e gg.", *VI KPSS,* 2: 79–92.

Litvin, A.L. 1994 *Bez prava na mysl'. Istoriki v epokhu Bol'shogo terrora. Ocherki sudeb,* Kazan'.

—— 1995. "Epistoliarnoe nasledie A.A. Zimina", in *Rossiia v X – XVIII vv.: Problemy istorii i istochnikovedeniia,* part 1, Moscow.

—— 1997. "Rossiiskaia istoriografiia Bol'shogo terrora", in L.V. Stoliarova et al. (comps.), S.O. Shmidt (ed.), *U istochnika: sbornik statei v chest' chlenakorrespondenta Rossiiskoi Akademii nauk Sergeia Mikhailovicha Kashtanova,* 2 pts., Moscow.

—— 1993. *Zapret na zhizn',* Kazan'.

—— (ed.) 1997. *Genrikh Yagoda. Narkom vnutrennikh del SSSR, General'nyi komissar gosudarstvennoi bezopasnosti. Sbornik dokumentov,* Kazan'.

Loginov, A.P. 1996. "Krizis istoricheskoi nauki v usloviiakh obshchestvennogo krizisa: otechestvennaia istoriografiia vtoroi poloviny 80-kh – nachala 90-kh gg.", in Afanas'ev (ed.), *Sov. istoriografiia.*

Lukin, N.M. *et al.* (intro.) 1992. "1937 god. Institut krasnoi professury", *OI*, 2.

Makarov, N.A. and Petrov, A.Ye. 2000. "Istoriki Rossii i RGNF v 1995–1999 gg.", *OI*, 3, 133–.

Maksimova, L.V. (comp.) 2000. *Istoriki Rossii: poslevoennoe pokolenie*. Moscow.

Malia, M. 1997. "Iz-pod glyb, no chto? Ocherk istorii zapadnoi sovetologii", *OI*, 5: 93–108.

——— 1994. *The Soviet Tragedy: A History of Socialism in Russia, 1917–1991*, NY; Oxford.

Malysheva, S.Yu. 1999. *Rossiiskoe Vremennoe pravitel'stvo 1917 g. Otechestvennaia istoriografiia 20-kh – serediny 60-kh gg*, Kazan'.

——— 2000. *Vremennoe pravitel'stvo Rossii: sovremennaia otechestvennaia istoriografiia*, Kazan'.

Markwick, R.D., 1999. "Precursor to Perestroika: the 'Democratic' Partkom, Institute of History, Soviet Academy of Sciences, 1965–68", in Thatcher, I.D. (ed.), *Reform and Society in 20th-Century Russia: Selected Papers from the Fifth World Congress of Central and East European Studies, Warsaw 1995*, Basingstoke Hants.

——— 2000. "P.V. Volobuev i istoriki 'novogo napravleniia'", in *Akademik P.V. Volobuev: neopublikovannye raboty, vospominaniia, stat'i*. Moscow.

Mawdsley, E. 1998. "The Great Fatherland War: A Post-Soviet Perspective", in N. Lobkowicz *et al.* (eds), *Forum für osteuropäische Ideen- und Zeitgeschichte*.

Medushevsky, O.M. 1996. "Istochnikovedenie v Rossii XX v.: nauchnaia mysl' i sotsial'naia real'nost'", in Afanas'ev (ed.), *Sov. istoriografiia*.

Mel'tiukhov, M.I., "Sovremennaia diskussiia i polemika vokrug knigi V. Suvorova 'Ledokol'", in Afanas'ev (ed.), *Sov. istoriografiia*.

Miagkov, G.P. 2000. *Nauchnoe soobshchestvo v istor. nauke: opyt "russkoi istoricheskoi shkoly"*, Kazan'.

Mikhailov, I.V. 2000. "Beloe delo: zigzagi, tupiki i perspektivy istoriograficheskogo osmysleniia" in *Akademik Volobuev: neopublikovannye raboty, vospominaniia, stat'i*, Moscow.

Miliukov, P.N. 1967. *Political Memoirs, 1905–1917*, ed. by A.P. Mendel, tr. by C. Goldberg, Ann Arbor MI.

——— 1990. *Vospominaniia, 1859–1917*, 2 vols., NY 1955, Russ. edn, Moscow.

Mints, I.I. 1990. "Metamorfozy masonskoi legendy", *IS*, 4: 107–22.

Mogilevsky, S. 1997. *Prozhitoe i perezhitoe: vospominaniia*, London; Jerusalem.

Natsional'nye istorii: see Aimermakher and Bordiugov (eds)

Nechkina, M.V. 1930. "V.O. Kliuchevsky", in *Russkaia istoricheskaia literatura v klassovom osveshchenii*, vol. 2, Moscow.

——— 1974. *Vasilii Osipovich Kliuchevskii. Istoriia zhizni i tvorchestva*, Moscow.

Nekrich, A. 1979. *Otrekshis' ot strakha: vospominaniia istorika*, London.

"Novye dokumenty": see Il'ina.

Oktiabr'skaia revoliutsiia: see Tiutiukin *et al.* (eds)

Organizatsiia sovetskoi nauki v 1926–1932 gg.: sbornik dokumentov 1974. Leningrad.

Orlov, I.B. 1999. "Sovremennaia otechestvennaia istoriografiia NEPa: dostizheniia, problematika, perspektivy", *OI*, 1: 102–16.

Otkrytyi arkhiv 1999: spravochnik opublikovannykh dokumentov po istorii Rossii XX v. iz gosudarstvennykh i semeinykh arkhivov, 1985–1996. 2nd ed. 1999. (ed. unknown; cf. Kondakov), Moscow.

Paneiakh, V.M. 1997. "Boris Aleksandrovich Romanov", in Alekseeva *et al.* (eds), *Istor. nauka.*

―――― 1997. "B.A. Romanov i I.I. Smirnov", in L.V. Stoliarova *et al.* (comps.), S.O. Shmidt (ed.), *U istochnika: sbornik statei v chest' chlena-korresondenta RAN S.M. Kashtanova*, 2 pts., Moscow.

―――― 1993. "Boris Alekskandrovich Romanov: pis'ma druz'iam i kollegam", *OI*, 3: 125–54.

―――― 1993. "Uprazdnenie Leningradskogo otdeleniia Instituta istorii AN SSSR v 1953 g.", *VI*, 10: 19–27.

Pantsov, A.V. and Cherevishnikov, A.L. 1996. "Issledovatel' i istochnik. O knige D.A. Volkogonova 'Trotskii'", in Bordiugov (ed.), *Istor. issled.*

Pashuto, V.T. 1992. *Russkie istoriki emigranty v Yevrope*, Moscow.

Pavlenko, N.G. 1994. *Byla voina . . .: razmyshleniia voennogo istorika*, Moscow.

Pavlenko, N.I. 1991. "Istoricheskaia nauka v proshlom i nastoiashchem (nekotorye razmyshleniia vslukh)", in *IS*, 4: 81–99.

Pavlova, I.V. 1998. "Sovremennye zapadnye istoriki stalinskoi Rossii 30-kh gg.", *OI*, 5: 107–21.

Perchenok, F.F. 1991. "Akademiia nauk na 'velikom perelome'", in *Zven'ia. Istoricheskii al'manakh*, fasc. 1, Moscow.

Piotrovsky, B.B. 1995. *Stranitsy moei zhizni*, St Petersburg.

Piatdesiat let sovetskoi istoricheskoi nauki. Khronika nauchnoi zhizni, 1917–1967 1971. Moscow.

"Pis'ma . . . Pankratovoi": see Ivanov.

Plaggenborg, S. (ed.) 1998. *Stalinismus: Neue Forschungen und Konzepte*, Berlin.

Pokrovsky, N.N. 1999. "O printsipakh izdaniia dokumentov XX v.", *VI*, 6: 32–45.

Poletika, N.P. 1990. *Vidennoe i perezhitoe*, 2nd edn, Jerusalem.

Poliakov, Yu.A. 1997. "Arkhivy – zolotaia kladovaia istoricheskoi nauki", *Arkheograficheskii ezehegodnik za 1997 g.*, Moscow.

―――― 1999. *Istoricheskaia nauka: liudi i problemy*, Moscow.

―――― 1999. "MIFLI 1941 g.: vospominaniia o M.Ya. Gellere", *VI*, 7: 103–13.

―――― 1995. *Nashe nepredskazuemoe proshloe. Polemicheskie zametki*, Moscow.

―――― 1994. "Pokhorony Stalina: vzgliad istorika–ochevidtsa", *NNI*, 4–5.

―――― 1996. "Put' poznaniia istorii", *OI*, 6: 140–51.

Polikarpov, V.V. 1996. "'Novoe napravlenie' 50 – 70-kh gg.: posledniaia diskussiia sovetskikh istorikov", in Afanas'ev (ed.), *Sov. istoriografiia.*

Preobrazhensky, A.A. 1998. "A.A. Novosel'skii", in Sakharov (ed.), *Istoriki Rossii*, fasc. 5, Moscow.

Pronin, A. 2000. *Istoriografiia rossiiskoi emigratsii.* Yekaterinburg.

Pushkarev, S. 1999. *Vospominaniia istorika, 1905–1945*, Biblioteka rossievedeniia, fasc. 3, Moscow.

Rabinovich, M.B. 1996. *Vospominaniia dolgoi zhizni*, St Petersburg.

Raeff, M. 1990. *Russia Abroad: A Cultural History of the Russian Emigration, 1919–1939*, NY (Russ. edn Moscow, 1994).

"Réécriture, la, de l'histoire russe et les débats méthodologiques dans la Russie d'aujourd'hui", 1998. *CMRS*, 39 (4): 539–58.

Reiman, M. 1989. "Perestroika i izuchenie sovetskoi istorii", *VI*, 12: 145–58.

—— 1996. "Zametki po probleme stalinizma v istoriografii", in Sakharov (ed.), *Rossiia XIX–XX vv.*

Repressirovannaia nauka: see Yaroshevsky (ed.)

Rossiia v XIX–XX vv.: see Fursenko.

Rossiia v XX v.: see Sakharov (ed.)

Rozhkov, N.A. 1923–6. *Russkaia istoriia v sravnitel'no-istoricheskom osveshchenii (osnovy sotsial'noi dinamiki)*, 12 vols., Moscow.

Russia. 1994. Arkhiv noveishei istorii Rossii. Vol. I: *"Osobaia papka" I.V. Stalina. Iz materialov NKVD – MVD SSSR 1944–1957 gg. Katalog dokumentov*, edited by V.A. Kozlov and S.V. Mironenko, Moscow; Pittsburgh PA.

—— 1994–7. Gosudarstvennyi arkhiv Rossiiskoi Federatsii, *Putevoditel'*. Vol. I: *Fondy GARF po istorii Rossii XIX – nachala XX vv* 1994. Edited by G. Freeze and S.V. Mironenko, Moscow. Vol. II: *Fondy GARF po istorii RSFSR* 1996. Edited by S.V. Mironenko and J. Burds, Moscow. Vol. III: 1997. *Fondy Gos. arkhiva RF po istorii SSSR*. Edited by A.I. Barkovets and S.V. Mironenko. Moscow. Vol. VI.: *Perechen' fondov GARF i nauchno-spravochnyi apparat k dokumentam arkhiva* 1998. Edited by S.V. Mironenko, Moscow.

—— 1994. Rossiiskii Gosudarstvennyi Istoricheskii Arkhiv. *Fondy RGIA*. Edited by V.V. Lapin, St Petersburg.

—— 1993, 1996. Rossiiskoe Tsentr Khraneniia i Izucheniia Dokumentov Noveishei Istorii [RTsKHIDNI, later RGASPI]. *Kratkii putevoditel'. Fondy i kollektsii, sobrannye Tsentral'nym Partiinym Arkhivom*. Vol. I edited by J.A. Getty and V.P. Kozlov, Moscow 1993. Vol. II: *Putevoditel' po fondam i kollektsiiam lichnogo proiskhozhdeniia* Moscow 1996.

—— 1998. *Gosudarstvennoe khranilishche dokumentov byvshego arkhivnogo fonda KPSS*, edited by V.P. Kozlov *et al.* Moscow.

—— 1997. [Rosarkhiv.] *Arkhivy Rossii: Moskva i Sankt-Peterburg: spravochnik-obozrenie i bibliograficheskii ukazatel'*, edited by V.P. Kozlov and P.K. Grimsted, Moscow.

Rustemeyer, A. 1998. "Eine systematische Karriere: der Historiker Nikolai Novombergskij im Zarenreich und der Sowjetunion", *JGOE*, 46: 546–71.

Sakharov, A.N. 1996. "Diskussii v sovetskoi istoriografii: ubitaia dusha nauki", in Afanas'ev (ed.), *Sov. istoriografiia*.

—— 1991. "Revoliutsionnyi totalitarizm v nashei istorii", *Kommunist*, 5: 60–71.

—— 1991. "Sovetskaia istoriografiia v otsenke zapadnykh issledovatelei", *Vestnik AN SSSR*, 3: 20–4.

—— (ed.) 1995, 1998. *Istoriki Rossii XVIII–XX vv*. Fascs. 1–2, Moscow 1995. Fasc. 5, Moscow 1998.

—— (ed.) 1996. *Rossiia XIX–XX vv. Vzgliad zarubezhnykh istorikov*, Moscow.

—— *et al.* (eds) 1996. *Rossiia v XX veke*, Vol. I. *Sud'by istoricheskoi nauki*. Moscow.

Sal'nikova, A.A. 1997. *Istoricheskii istochnik v amerikanskoi sovetologii*, Kazan'.

—— 1999. *Sovremennoe zarubezhnoe istochnikovedenie: teoriia i metod. Uchebnoe posobie*, Kazan'.

Samsonov, A.M. 1988. *Znat' i pomnit'. Dialog istorika s chitatelem*, Moscow.

Sanders, T. (ed.) 1998. *Russian and Non-Russian Historiography. Historical Profession, Practice and Interpretation in Ancien Regime Russia*. Alternative title: *Historiography of Imperial Russia: the Profession and Writing of History in a Multinational State*, Armonk NY.

Sandle, M. 1995. "New Directions, New Approaches, Old Issues: Recent Writings on Soviet History", *Historical Journal*, 38: 231–48, Cambridge.

Sekirinsky, S. (contrib.) 1997. "Novoe pokolenie rossiiskikh istorikov v poiskakh svoego litsa", *OI*, 4: 104–24.

Semennikov, L.I. (ed.) 1999. *Istoriki razmyshliaiut: sbornik statei*. Moscow.

Sharapov, Yu.P. 1995. *Litsei v Sokol'nikakh*, Moscow.

Shatsillo, K.F. 1990. [Remarks in:] "Otechestvennaia istoriia v sovremennoi publitsistike: vstrecha za 'kruglym stolom'", *IS*, 1: 176–90.

Shcherban', N.V. 1998. "Nevostrebovannye traditsii: V.O. Kliuchevskii – pedagog", *OI*, 6: 65–80.

Shelokhaev, V.V. 1998. *Proshchanie s proshlym*, Moscow.

—— *et al.* (eds) 1998. *Problemy politicheskoi i ekonomicheskoi istorii Rossii. Sbornik statei k 60-letiiu prof. Valeriia Vasil'evicha Zhuravleva*. Moscow.

Shliaifman, N. 1997. "Istoriia i pamiat': problema sootnosheniia proshlogo i nastoiashchego na primere Mozhaiska", in Ushakov *et al.* (eds), *Krainosti*.

Shmidt, S.O. 1996. "S.F. Platonov i 'delo Platonova'", in Afanas'ev (ed.), *Sov. istoriografiia*.

Shteppa, K.F. 1962. *Russian Historians and the Soviet State*, New Brunswick NJ.

Sibirskie arkhivy i istoricheskaia nauka. 1997. Kemerovo.

Sidorov, N. (comp.) 1996. "'Nasha istoriia est' istoriia draka.' Nesostoiavshaiasia seriia knig o grazhdanskoi voine", *Istochnik*, 2: 67–82.

Sidorova, A.L. 1997. "A.M. Pankratova", in Alekseeva *et al.* (eds), *Istor. nauka.*

—— 1997. *Ottepel' v istoricheskoi nauke. Sovetskaia istoriografiia pervogo poslestalinskogo desiatiletiia*, Moscow.

—— 1997. "Ottepel' v istoricheskoi nauke: seredina 50-kh – seredina 60-kh gg.", in Alekseeva *et al.* (eds), *Istor. nauka.*

—— 1999. "Shkoly v istoricheskoi nauke Rossii", *OI*, 6: 200–3.

Smirnov, N.N. *et al.* (eds) 1999. *Istorik i revoliutsiia: sbornik statei k 70-letiiu so dnia rozhdeniia A.N. Znamenskogo*, St Petersburg.

Sokolov, A.K. (ed.) 1994. *Professionalizm istorika. Ideologicheskaia kon'iunktura sovetskoi istorii*, 2 vols, Moscow.

Sokolov, O.D. 1970. *M.N. Pokrovskii i sovetskaia istoricheskaia nauka*, Moscow.

Sokolov, V.Yu. 1990. *Istoriia i politika (k voprosu o soderzhanii i kharaktere diskussii sovetskikh istorikov 1920-kh – nachala 1930-kh gg.)*, Tomsk.

Solovei, V.D. 1990. "Institut krasnoi professury: podgotovka kadrov partii v 20-e – 30-e gg.", *VI KPSS*, 12.
––––– 1990. "Istoricheskaia nauka i politika v SSSR, 20-e – 30-e gg.", in *Istoricheskoe znachenie NEPa*. Moscow.
Sovetskaia istoriografiia: see Afanas'ev.
Sovetskoe obshchestvo: see Afanas'ev.
Starikov, N.V. 1996. "Epokha 'ottepeli' i etapy evoliutsii stalinizma: voprosy istoriografii", in Afanas'ev (ed.), *Sov. istoriografiia*.
Starostin, E.V. and Khorkhordina, T.I. 1991. "Dekret ob arkhivnom dele 1918 g.", *VI*, 7–8: 41–52.
Startsev, V.I. 1989. "Rossiiskie masony XX v.", *VI*, 6: 33–50.
"Stenogramma . . .": see Amiantov and Tikhonova.
Stockdale, M.K. 1996. *Paul Milikukov: the Quest for a Liberal Russia, 1880–1918*. Ithaca NY; London.
Studer, B. *et al.* 1996. "La situation des archives centrales dans l'ex-Union Soviétique", *Internat. Newsletter*, 3 (7–8): 13–23.
Svak, D. 1998. "O nekotorykh metodologicheskikh problemakh sinteza v 'Istoriiakh Rossii'", *OI*, 6: 90–3.
Tarle, Ye.V.: see Chapkevich; Leonov; Yesakov.
Tatarstan, Republic of. 1999. Tsentral'nyi gosudarstvennyi arkhiv istoriko–politicheskoi dokumentatsii Respubliki Tatarstan. *Putevoditel'*, Kazan'.
Telitsyn, V.L. 1997. "Interv'iu s akademikom Pavlom Vasil'evichem Volobuevym", *OI*, 6: 97–123.
Tillett, L. 1969. *The Great Friendship. Soviet Historians on the Non-Russian Nationalities*. Chapel Hill NC.
Tiutiukin, S.V. 1998. "Sovremennaia otechestvennaia istoriografiia RSDRP", *OI*, 6: 54–64.
––––– *et al.* (eds) 1998. *Oktiabr'skaia revoliutsiia. Ot novykh istochnikov k novomu osmysleniiu*, Moscow.
Tsamatuli, A.N. 1986. *Bor'ba napravlenii v russkoi istoriografii v period imperializma. Istoricheskie ocherki*, Leningrad.
––––– 1995. "Glava peterburgskoi istoricheskoi shkoly S.F. Platonov", in Sakharov (ed.), *Istoriki Rossii*.
Ueberschar, G.R. and Bezymensky, L.A. (eds) 1998. *Der deutsche Angriff auf die Sowjetunion 1941. Die Kontroverse um die Präventivkriegsthese*. Darmstadt.
Ushakov, A.I. 1993. *Istoriia grazhdanskoi voiny v literature russkogo zarubezh'ia*, Moscow.
––––– *et al.* (eds) 1997. *Krainosti istorii i krainosti istorikov. Sbornik statei k 60-letiiu professora Al'berta Pavlovicha Nenarokova*, Moscow.
Vandalkovskaia, M.G. 1997. *Istoricheskaia nauka rossiiskoi emigratsii: yevraziiskii soblazn'*, Moscow.
––––– 1997. "Militsa Vasil'evna Nechkina", in Alekseeva *et al.* (eds), *Istor. nauka*.
––––– 1996. "O traditsiiakh dorevoliutsionnoi nauki", in Sakharov (ed.), *Rossiia v XX v.*
––––– 1992. *P.N. Miliukov, A.A. Kizevetter: istoriia i politika*, Moscow.

Vereshchagin, A.S. 2000. "Paradoksy istoriografii Izhevsko-Votkinskogo vosstaniia", in *Akademik Volobuev.*

Veselovsky, S.B.: see Yurganov.

Volkogonov, D.A. 1998. *Etiudy o vremeni,* Moscow.

———— 1990. "Stalinizm: sushchnost', genezis, evoliutsiia", *VI,* 3: 3–17.

Volobuev, P.V. 2000. *Akademik P.V. Volobuev: neopublikovannye raboty, vospominaniia, stat'i,* Moscow.

Volobuev, P.V. 1997. "Ot prirody ia optimist", in Chernobaev (ed.), *Istoriki,* fasc. 2.

Voss. S. 1998. *Stalins Kriegsvorbereitungen 1941: erforscht, gedeutet und instrumentalisiert: eine Analyse postsowjetischer Geschichtsschreibung,* Hamburg.

Yakushev, S.V. 1990. "Iz istorii sozdaniia partiinykh arkhivov v SSSR", *VI KPSS,* 5: 50–65.

———— 1991. "Tsentral'nyi partiinyi arkhiv v 30-e gg.", *VI,* 4–5: 23–33.

Yaroshevsky, M.G. (ed.) 1991, 1994. *Repressirovannaia nauka,* Leningrad; St Petersburg.

Yarov, S. 1999. *Gorozhanin kak politik: revoliutsiia, voennyi kommunizm i NEP glazami petrogradtsev,* St Petersburg.

Yekelchyk, S. 1999. "How the 'Iron Minister' Kaganovich Failed to Discipline Ukrainian Historians: A Stalinist Ideological Campaign Reconsidered", *Nationalities Papers,* 27: 579–604.

Yesakov, V.D. 1999. "Tri pis'ma Ye.V. Tarle vozhdiam (1934–8 gg.", *OI,* 6: 106–11.

Yurganov, A.L. and Makarov, A.G. (intro.) 2000. "S.V. Veselovsky: dnevniki 1915–1923, 1944 gg.", *VI,* 2: 89–117, 3: 84–110, 6; 93–111.

Zaionchkovsky, P.A.: see Zakharova.

Zakharova, L.G. Kukushkin, Yu.S., Emmons, T. (eds) 1998. *P.A. Zaionchkovskii (1904–1983 gg.): stat'i, publikatsii i vosopominaniia o nem,* Moscow.

Zankevich, E.Kh. 1957. *K istorii sovetizatsii Rossiiskoi Akademii nauk,* Munich.

Zelenov, M.V. 1997. "Glavlit i istoricheskaia nauka v 20-kh – 30-kh gg.", *VI,* 3: 21–36.

———— 2000. "Spetskhran i istoricheskaia nauka v Sovetskoi Rossii v 1920–1930-e gg.", *OI,* 2: 129–41.

Zhuravlev, V.V. 2000. "God 1917 v kontekste istoricheskikh traditsii Rossii", in *Akademik Volobuev . . .*

———— 1997. "Ot smeny kon'iunkturnykh paradigm k paradigme preemstvennosti", in Sekirinsky (contrib.), "Novoe pokolenie", 105–9.

Zimin, A.A. 1998. "'My ne uvidim plody nashikh posevov. No oni budut . . .' (Iz vospominanii A.A. Zimina)", *OA,* 6: 57–85.

Index